NOWTOPIA

NOWTOPIA

How Pirate Programmers, Outlaw Bicyclists, and Vacant-Lot Gardeners Are Inventing the Future Today

by Chris Carlsson

2008

AK PRESS
EDINBURGH · OAKLAND · WEST VIRGINIA

NOWTOPIA

by Chris Carlsson

www.chriscarlsson.com

ISBN 978 1 904859 77 2

Library of Congress Number: 2007939194

Book Design & Layout: Chris Carlsson
Cover Design & Layout: Chris Carlsson
Front cover image by Eric Drooker
Back cover photo by Chris Carlsson

AK Press
674-A 23rd Street
Oakland, CA 94612
www.akpress.org
akpress@akpress.org
510.208.1700

AK Press U.K.
PO Box 12766
Edinburgh EH8 9YE
Scotland
www.akuk.com
ak@akedin.demon.co.uk
0131.555.5165

Printed in Canada on 100% recycled, acid-free paper by union labor.

TABLE OF CONTENTS

*This book is dedicated to people everywhere who are already
engaged in re-inventing our lives, in redesigning our relationship
with technologies and planetary ecology, and who are too busy
making the new world to have time for their stupid jobs.*

ACKNOWLEDGEMENTS

A book that covers so many collective and cooperative projects is
only possible through the participation and support of dozens
of folks. Though I'm responsible for all errors and omissions, I
want to honor and thank the many people who gave me their time and
help on *Nowtopia*. I hope this modest volume will help advance every
contributor's own projects in its own way.

First I have to thank the friends who spent many hours reading the
first draft of *Nowtopia* and giving me really helpful criticism: Tina Ger-
hart, Becky Sutton, and Liam O'Donohue were wonderfully constructive and meticulous in their attention. Charles Weigl and the AK collective gave me a detailed critique that was crucial in rewriting the book.
My daughter Francesca Manning beat me up on a number of occasions,
and has been a great copy editor during the final months of production.
Adriana Camarena, Giovanni Maruzzelli, Pete Holloran, Maritza Shafer,
Michael Med-o Whitson, Eddie Yuen, Mariana Leguia, Katie Renz, Greg
Rodgers, Kevin Van Meter, and Bernard Marszalek all made important
suggestions. My friends at Blue Mountain Center gave me another
wonderful month to write the first draft in September 2006, for which
I'm eternally grateful. Colleagues there, especially Andrew Boyd, Alyce
Santoro, and Camellia Phillips, were very encouraging and supportive,
and even helped me to title the book. Laura Fraser, Jon Christensen,
Jesse Drew, Brenda O'Sullivan, Iain Boal, Hugh D'Andrade, George
Caffentzis, Enda Brophy, Lisa Ruth Elliot, Josh Wilson, Allyson Stein-
berg, Antonio Alcala and Steve Wright all read parts of the book and
gave me helpful comments.

I thank all the people who sat down and let me interview them, or
wrote answers to questions I sent by email. At Burning Man in 2003 I
spoke to more than two dozen people but for the most part I didn't get
their names, only their "day jobs" and their ideas. Peter Davidson, Pete
Morse, Cacey Cullen, Suzahna Poliwka, and Julie Sparling were among
the interviewees there, but I thank the others just as much. For the gar-

dening chapter I spoke with Pam Peirce, Mark Leger, Nan Eastep, Justin Valone, and Jeffrey Miller; Nick Bertoni at the Tinker's Workshop in Berkeley was gregarious and warm; Erik Ohlsen was glad to talk about permaculture, community gardening, and global politics; biofuel activists Claudia Eyezaguirre, Sara Hope Smith, Jonathan Youtt, Ben Gillock, Bianca Sopoci-Belknap, Sarah Lewison, and Nicole Cousino; programmers/organizers Will Doherty, Guillermo Payet, Ed Phillips; bicyclists Robin Havens, Martin Luegers, Ted White, Jessie Bassbaum, Catherine Hartzell, Eric Welp, Ben Guzman, Bill DiPaola, Jay Broemmel, Jarico, Karl Anderson, and Rachel Spiewak. I also thank the many writers whose words I've quoted liberally in *Nowtopia*. Thanks too, to Jasmine and Atessa Chehrazi, who went to Chain Reaction in Washington D.C. to pose my questions; Jasmine transcribed the interview and sent me transcripts to work with.

INTRODUCTION
A NEW POLITICS OF WORK

Nowtopia is a book about a new politics of work. It profiles tinkerers, inventors, and improvisational spirits who bring an artistic approach to important tasks that are ignored or undervalued by market society. Rooted in practices that have been emerging over the past few decades, *Nowtopia*'s exploration of *work* locates an important thread of self-emancipatory class politics beyond the traditional arena of wage-labor.

More and more people, recognizing the degradation inherent in business relations, are creating networks of activity that refuse the measurement of money. Dispersed and virtual networks have grown thanks to the spread of the Internet and other telecommunications technologies. New kinds of "families" based on shared values, alternative living arrangements, and non-economic relationships are growing within the old society. Nowtopians are establishing or re-animating human communities, networks, and circuits from which new initiatives will continue to emerge well into the future. These new communities manifest the efforts of humans to transcend their lives as wage-slaves. Tentatively they embrace a culture that rejects the market, money, and business. Engaging with technology in creative and experimental ways, the Nowtopians we meet here are involved in a guerrilla war over the direction of society. In myriad behaviors, people are appropriating their time and technological know-how from the market and in small "invisible" ways, are making life better right now—but also setting the foundation, technically AND socially, for a genuine movement of liberation from market life. These practical acts can be best understood in terms of class and ultimately, a classless society.

As capitalism continues its inexorable push to corral every square inch of the globe into its logic of money and markets, while simultaneously seeking to colonize our very thoughts and control our desires and behaviors, new practices are emerging that are redefining politics and opening spaces of unpredictability. Instead of traditional political forms like unions or parties, people are coming together in practical projects. Rarely do these new configurations emerge from specific workplaces or neighborhoods. Just as rarely do the individual participants conceive of their projects exclusively in political terms, mostly because the idea of "politics" has been colonized by the bizarre advertising campaigns of ritualized electoral democracy. The day-to-day issues about how we live, what we do, how we define and meet our needs, tend to be understood as beyond or outside formal politics. However, as we shall see, all Nowtopian activities are profoundly political.

The same inventiveness and creative genius that gets wrongly attributed to Capital and business is being applied to planetary ecology. Acting locally in the face of unfolding global catastrophes (many avoidable were we to really try), friends and neighbors are redesigning many of the crucial technological foundations of modern life. These redesigns are worked out through garage and backyard R&D programs among friends using the detritus of modern life. Our contemporary Commons takes the shape of discarded bicycles and leftover deep fryer vegetable oil, of vacant lots and open bandwidth. "Really really free markets," anti-commodities, festivals, and free services are imaginative *products* of an anti-economy, provisionally under construction by freely cooperative and inventive people. They aren't waiting for an institutional change from on-high but are getting on with building the new world in the shell of the old.

Independent of ideology or religion, nearly every human grouping is deeply rooted in mutual aid and self-reliance; the reliability of such support is the building block of communal solidarity, from brutalized workers to the religious right to networks of eco-activists. In the context of a globe-straddling economy that systematically preys on human creativity, cooperation, and community, it is deeply subversive to preserve and extend these extra-economic connections. Joining together to meet basic needs reproduces communities and can lead to new networks of human conviviality. The bonds thus created, and the material experience of cooperation outside of economic regulation, become a breeding ground for strategic and tactical thinking and practice that confronts the everyday objectification to which capitalism reduces us all.

A lot of words have been written trying to describe the new social fractions that keep emerging from the complex and multi-layered hierarchies and conditions of modern life. Slackers, bohemians, Generation X, Y and Z, "no collar" workers, and many other terms try to capture the rootless, temporary, partial identities that have supplanted old ideas of the working class. These new fractional identities designate a wider sense of self with vaguely dissident politics but one that is still linked to employment, however tenuously. Radical workers' movements of the past two centuries have always been firmly rooted in the capitalist workplace. In fact, *workers* as such have been defined by their relationship to capitalist production. Today's radical impulses are being developed outside the constraints of wage-work, envisioned and enacted by people who are determined to escape the bounds of being "mere workers."

Traditional theories tend to dismiss such efforts as simply hobbies, or lifestyle choices, failing to see the deeper trajectory of exodus from capitalist society that such *work* defines.

We meet a wide range of people in this book who are grappling with the split between making a living and expressing their full humanity partly through freely chosen work. These people represent a different kind of "working class" response to the conditions of life at the beginning of the 21st century precisely because their response is taking place in their "free" time, outside of their wage-labor-defined jobs. Ben Guzman makes TV commercials in Los Angeles as a video editor to earn his money, but his real passion led him to co-found the Bike Kitchen, one of dozens of do-it-yourself bike repair shops that have emerged around the world during the past decade. Robin Havens is now teaching public high school, but started out providing free after-school bike repair classes in one of San Francisco's most troubled neighborhoods. She's been in the middle of the "outlaw bicycling" subculture for over a decade, self-publishing and putting into practice the anti-business do-it-yourself culture. Will Doherty is a drop-out from a large computer company who founded the Online Policy Group, an organization that freely provides computer resources for politically edgy groups. Guillermo Payet is a former dotcom entrepreneur who has dedicated his time and know-how to creating an open source software project to help local agriculture and the small farmers who do it to build an alternative food system (*localharvest.org*). Meanwhile, anonymous programmers around the world are engaged in complex collaborations that are leading to an unprecedented communications infrastructure that might someday be the backbone of a self-managed society.

What we see in the Nowtopian movement is not a fight for workers' emancipation *within* the capitalist division of labor (which is the best that could be hoped for the unions' strategy, *if* we give it the benefit of the doubt). Instead we see people responding to the overwork and emptiness of a bifurcated life that is imposed in the precarious marketplace. They seek emancipation *from* being merely workers. To a growing minority of people, the endless treadmill of consumerism and overwork is something they are *working* to escape. Thus, for many people time is more important than money. Access to goods has been the major incentive for compliance with the dictatorship of the economy. But in pockets here and there, the allure of hollow material wealth, and with it the discipline imposed by economic life, is breaking down.

In the yearning for a life beyond money, the annual Burning Man festival has drawn tens of thousands of revelers seeking authentic connections and artistic freedom to the northern Nevada desert. Part-time

secretaries, biochemists-turned-janitors, retired professors, social workers, handymen, mechanics, legal aides, and many more job holders escape to the desert to remake themselves and discover new relationships
in a commerce-free (ironically expensive) environment.

We also see dozens of people literally jumping on the biodiesel band-
wagon by making their own wagons (and fuel)—from the five women
who made the documentary *Fat of the Land* in the mid-1990s about their
cross-country road trip on waste veggie oil, to the hundreds of trips
made since by biofueled bus caravans. Claudia Eyzaguirre, a teacher, responded to 9-11 by co-founding the Berkeley Biodiesel Collective. The
tinkering and experimenting that went on in hidden corners during the
past few decades has been seized upon and expanded radically during
the past ten years of grassroots biofuels activism, leading to the much
publicized "arrival" of biofuels as promoted by the government and major multinationals. But the story is far from finished.

Urban horticulture is similarly emerging on the foundation of widespread gardening initiatives in cities across the continent. Immigrants
and the poor have reclaimed abandoned and deindustrialized zones
with traditional and inventive practices, coaxing food and life from
blasted landscapes, creating new human communities in the process.
Nan Eastep is part of the City Slicker Farms in West Oakland, producing
small crops in vacant lots to provide fresh produce in areas that have
been excluded from the new gourmet food movements. Mark Leger is a
long-time white-collar worker, but has built on his childhood memories
of California's Central Valley to help sustain and expand a burgeoning
community garden movement in Brooklyn, New York (in his free time).
Pam Peirce is a founder of the now-defunct San Francisco League of
Urban Gardeners (SLUG), and was previously an important figure in
the People's Food System that grew in the wake of the communalist tide
of the late 1960s and 1970s. She has participated in the nonprofit efforts
to institutionalize the grassroots food and gardening movements, in the
wake of which remain over 100 locally-controlled public gardens with
their associated communities and political processes.

In this book, I investigate what people are doing vis-à-vis work, specifically the self-directed work carried on outside of wage-labor. This work
can be best understood in terms of class and ultimately, a classless society. The two crucial components are *time* and the *technosphere*. People are
engaged in activities that go on outside of their jobs, in their so-called
"free" time. These practices, often very time-consuming and strenuous,
require sharing and mutual aid and constitute the beginnings of new
kinds of communities. This represents a "re-composition" of the working class, even though most of the participants wouldn't embrace such

a framework. Because these people are engaged in creative appropriation of technologies to purposes of their own design and choice, these
activities embody the (partial) transcendence of the wage-labor prison
by "workers" who have better things to do than their jobs. They are tinkerers and smiths working in the waste streams and open spaces of late
capitalism, conjuring new practices while redefining life's purpose.

I make no claim to being comprehensive, or that my relatively small
selection of interview subjects is necessarily the "real story"; other investigations based on different assumptions, questions and individuals could
produce rather different insights. But I argue that the people I talked
to reflect a deeper shift. I asked about the work people are doing un-
remunerated, usually collaboratively and in networks of intensive social
cooperation, with an eye towards how those practices either stay "free"
of market logic or get reincorporated into commodified, economically
defined behaviors. Usually there is an ongoing conflict, or at least tension, at the point of contact between these different ways of engaging in
work. It may seem surprising or paradoxical, but my investigation shows
that, when freed from the coercive constraints of wage-labor and arbitrary
hierarchy, people *work hard*.

The subjects of my inquiry are all engaged in local efforts, firmly rooted in their daily lives and physical locales. Such local examples
could be dismissed as meaningless anomalies in the context of an ever-
expanding, voracious world market whose logic continues to disrupt
and destroy human and natural life in favor of profit and plunder. But
as the geographer David Harvey has noted, examples of "militant par-
ticularism" like we find in *Nowtopia* start local but can spread across society with surprising speed. The new apparatus of global production
helps speed up the extension of market society of course, but inevitably
it is also speeding the spread of social opposition, the sharing of experiments and alternatives. Our moment in history is at least as exhilarating
as it is daunting.

Efforts to break away, to create islands of utopia (be it socialism in
one state, or co-ops, collectives, and other smaller-scale social alternatives), have always flourished on the margins of capitalist society, but
never to the extent that a radically different way of living has been able
to supplant market society's daily life. The pull of business, of buying
and selling, of surviving economically, all exert enormous pressure on
the initiatives described in *Nowtopia*, too. Nowtopians, and anyone determined to free themselves from the constraints of economically defined
life, face the same historic limits that have beset all previous efforts to
escape. Can the emerging patterns of creativity and technological inventiveness and new communities go beyond the co-optation and re-in-

CHAPTER 1
SEEDS OF THE NEW COMMONS

Refusal certainly is the beginning of a liberatory politics, but it is only a beginning. . . We need to create a new social body, a project that goes well beyond refusal. Our lines of flight, our exodus must be constituent and create a real alternative. Beyond the simple refusal, or as part of that refusal, we need also to construct a new mode of life and above all a new community.
—*Michael Hardt and Antonio Negri*, Empire[1]

Just as one does not judge an individual by what he thinks about himself, so one cannot judge such a period of transformation by its consciousness, but, on the contrary, this consciousness must be explained from the contradictions of material life, from the conflict existing between the social forces of production and the relations of production...

At a certain stage of development, the material productive forces of society come into conflict with the existing relations of production... From [helping] development of the productive forces these relations turn into their fetters. Then begins an era of social revolution.
—*Karl Marx*[2]

Upon meeting, people still commonly ask each other "What do you do?" The answer is usually about what we get paid to do, our jobs. This is a holdover from earlier times when jobs were long-lasting, important commitments by individual workers and their employers. But it is also an indication that we still unconsciously evaluate each other in terms of our place in the division of labor. Presumably, our "choice" of jobs is the social manifestation of our personal worth and our life's meaning. Our jobs inform assumptions about where we live, what we are able to buy, what we "earn," what our tastes are, and so on.

American society is religiously meritocratic. Americans believe that individuals choose their fates and that objective circumstances can always be overcome by hard work and self-sacrifice. Very few people want to let this go, even when the evidence around them, in their families and among their friends and acquaintances, flies in the face of such a rosy fluidity.

Against the deeply rooted individualism of American life, the idea of a working class is a difficult one. Class is quickly dismissed because it tends to flatten specific lives and conditions into shared generalities. Many Americans who come into contact with class analysis (of which there are relatively few) feel objectified rather than emancipated. Meanwhile, the day-to-day objectification that people in America suffer at the hands of the market economy tends to go unnoticed. Refusing class identities, people create other ways of knowing themselves and resent attempts to objectively categorize them in terms of class (except for the generally embraced idea that everyone is in the "middle class").

In order to speak about class in this "egalitarian" society, one must first describe how it applies to real human lives and ultimately, how it offers a useful explanatory framework. And there is no simple, one-size-fits-all definition of class. Whole disciplines in the humanities have been dedicated to framing class as questions of income, relative wealth, cultural expressions, consumption patterns, and much more.[3] In spite of this academic industriousness, few Americans want to think about their own lives in terms of class and the constraints a class society imposes on their personal liberty. In place of class, variations on "identity politics" have provided alternative narratives to explain the stratification of society. This has led to a rich literature and a deepening inquiry into specific ethnic and gender experiences, but has also tended to focus political attention on the static reality of being, rather than on the creative and unpredictable reality of doing. In other words, who you are racially or sexually has more weight in how you are understood socially than what you do all day at work or in your free time, or crucially, what you might do in the future.

My interest in class is partly rooted in my personal history, a tangled tale of growing up in 20th century American inner cities. I have a Danish mother who immigrated from a comfortable upbringing in Copenhagen and a father who escaped a poor New England childhood to become a life-long white-collar worker in the insurance industry (ultimately reaching a vice-presidency before his retirement in the mid-1990s; my childhood was spent in low-income neighborhoods in Brooklyn, Chicago, and Oakland during which my mother also worked part-time retail jobs to make ends meet). The first work I ever did for money was carrying golf bags for the wealthiest people in the Bay Area with coworkers who were largely alcoholics from skid row in downtown Oakland (to my 15-year-old eyes, my coworkers' intelligence far outstripped the idiocy of the wealthy we worked for). Meanwhile I was one of the few white kids in the predominantly black public schools I attended in the East Bay where I grew up. We were surrounded by the turmoil of the Black Panthers, the anti-Vietnam war movement, early feminism and environmentalism, the oil shock of the early 1970s, and Watergate.

Entering college in January 1975 I was a typical left-leaning student. I helped the United Farmworkers by standing in supermarket parking lots promoting their grape boycott. In the summer and fall before I started college I worked in brand new malls in the suburbs of Philadelphia for Waldenbooks, followed by jobs for Books Inc. in Santa Rosa while I attended college. Fights over wearing a tie, reading at work, and the compulsion to "look busy" were too reminiscent of years of learned boredom at school doing repetitive exercises. My "bad attitude"[4] pit me against every workplace that ever hired me. At the end of 1978 I was fired from Books Inc. for trying to start a union (the local Retail Clerks union had been completely unresponsive to my entreaties!).

During the next six months I canvassed for an environmental group around the Bay Area, while volunteering with the J.P. Stevens textile boycott. The dysfunctionally cautious approach of the legalistic textile union was a lesson in futility. Meanwhile, the environmental canvassing experience was putting me on doorsteps in every neighborhood of the region, asking people about their work, and finding out how disconnected they were from the decisions or results of their own activity. All of these overlapping experiences helped shape my early politics, and by 1981 I had joined some friends to co-found *Processed World* magazine. In its pages we hoped to describe our daily experiences at corporate jobs in downtown San Francisco, but also to articulate the points of leverage we might find collectively as workers at the point of circulation in the headquarters of global capitalism.

My own class consciousness arose out of this strange late 20th century stew. I reached adulthood in a society bent on obscuring and denying class, but most of my life had strongly reinforced my sense that I live in a world not of my own making—and not under the control of anyone I knew. I don't conceive of classes changing with every ten thousand dollars of more (or less) income. I share the skepticism of many people towards anyone who wants to draw edges too clearly around a given class schematic. Nevertheless, as a way of analyzing power relations in society, I find class indispensable. In analyzing work as the broad category of human life, class is a crucial component. Somehow the system under which we live keeps expanding, keeps using the energy and goodwill we bring to our work lives to make a world quite different than one any of us would choose freely. How is it that so many of us go to work with the best of intentions and yet find our efforts contributing to a world that is brutalizing so many?

The vast majority of us have to sell ourselves to a paid job in order to survive and it is precisely at that point of sale that we relinquish control over our lives. Once sold (hired) we must do as we are told and if we don't, we are likely to be fired and cut off from the income on which we depend. This is partly ameliorated by self-employment and co-operative arrangements, but we still lack control over the deeper questions surrounding the aggregate division of labor in society, how and why resources are dedicated to some activities and not others. The day-to-day loss of power embedded in the wage-relation is the starting point of class division. But it has become more confusing and opaque with the expansion of the social factory, a system of capitalist reproduction in which almost anything we do can be a source of someone else's profits and a reinforcement of our own alienation and powerlessness.

In a society that perpetually celebrates itself as democratic, public discussion about our greatest public secret, work, is rarely heard. There isn't any public control over the fundamental decisions that shape our lives, whether it be *what* work is done, *how* work is done, who we will work with, or more broadly, the nature of scientific research, the types of technologies we might choose or refuse (depending on a public airing of the consequences of various choices), and so on. It is in this deep separation that class arises, the separation of most of us from the world we (re)produce with our shared labor.

This understanding of class has the additional effect of undercutting the age-old personalization of class antagonism, since in fact there are very few people who have any real power over the issues I listed above. As some of my informants have argued, class is embedded in a system of social life, and the capitalists who make the big decisions about development, technology, science, etc. are very small in number. Many of their "decisions" are determined by their own imprisonment in technologies and investments that precede their brief occupation of the seat of power. The opponent we face is much more often a faceless undemocratic economic system than a cigar-smoking industrialist (though of course there are still such people too). Class denotes a position in the division of labor, or the separation of responsibility from execution. Once employed, very few people really get to make meaningful choices, even if they're well paid and socially valued.

This book explores class in America, not from a traditional leftist perspective of exhorting people to wake up to their "true status"—be it class status or specific identitarian affinity—but as a way of understanding this historic period, where we've been and where we might be heading. More than four centuries ago, the first stirrings of modern capitalism began with the seizure and privatization of common lands in Europe, and the relentless European occupation of the Americas. The feudal order slowly disintegrated, and along with it many of the customary behaviors and knowledges that underpinned the rhythms of life. In today's madly sped-up world, new technologies have become the medium for a return of many of those forgotten ways of doing and knowing. Newly forming political agents, rooted in myriad overlapping identities and histories, are reimagining the world. They are beginning to create one that is very different from the world we endure under the whiplash of capitalism. Amidst the insanity there are seeds of a new world growing, emergent pieces of a new common wealth, based on ecologically redesigned technologies that revitalize human communities and the connection between human life and natural processes.

The social identities that helped shape society and gave individuals meaningful connections over the past two centuries are steadily weakening. A sense of self itself is historically determined, and shifts over time too. Thinking about class requires at least two frames: first, the objective truth of social divisions. Second, the interior, subjective experience of identity and place in society. In the late 20th century many people rejected their assigned roles, whether women refusing to accept the limits imposed on their lives, or racial groups revolting against racist assumptions about their abilities, or workers who began to find fulfillment beyond their jobs. The subjective sense of class lost its hold, replaced by an egalitarian sensibility that assumes equal rights and equal opportunities even if real life often disappointed such presumptions. In this erosion of class subjectivity, fewer people came to see themselves as reducible to any of the common categories we lump together as "identity." They are not mere "workers," nor can their lives be adequately described primarily in terms of gender or race. Instead, hybrid identities connect across multiple intersecting and overlapping networks. No single aspect of their lives, least of all what they do for money, adequately describes their full complexity as people.

Karl Polanyi wrote *The Great Transformation* during WWII, in which he analyzed the rise of market society in the early 1800s and its success at subordinating all other values to its instrumental and pecuniary rationality.[5] Rather than sharing Marx's enthusiasm for the revolutionary effect of capitalist development, Polanyi instead recognized an important source of resistance in pre-industrial cultures that revolt against the imposition of market society. He describes the unsuccessful efforts of farmers and the landed gentry to preserve customary rights and expectations in the face of the harsh and unforgiving logic of so-called free markets (his book is a great history of the indispensable role of the state in the establishment and maintenance of "free markets"). Rather than endorsing capitalist development (and its devastating destruction of human and natural life) as "progress," Polanyi gave us an alternate framework that corresponds more accurately with many historic and contemporary struggles. To make good use of class as an analytical framework in the 21st century we have to employ it creatively and find fresh ways of rethinking old concepts in light of changing conditions.

Since the 1960s, certain Marxist theorists have been pursuing just such a path. They developed a frame of reference that goes by different labels, from "autonomist" to "Operaista ["workerist"]." These theorists have popularized terms for understanding aspects of society, e.g. the "social worker," "general intellect," "post-Fordism," "immaterial labor," etc. There are a number of key contributors and primary publications in this genre, but there is no one-stop pocket guide to this theoretical approach.[6] On the contrary, among this small fraction of political thinkers there is widespread disagreement and debate; the very terms of discussion shift and mutate while under scrutiny, making the theoretical foundation a bit muddy and uncertain. In spite of this slipperiness, the analytical tools developing in this tendency are illuminating, and anyway, uncertainty in this chaotic historic time seems appropriate for an open-minded and flexible inquiry.

What we are living through is just the latest in a cycle that Marxist theorists of the autonomist school have framed with the concept of "class composition."[7] Parting with a more mechanistic Marxism that focuses on the internal contradictions of the capitalist economy, the theory of class composition posits the necessity of examining what people ("workers") are actually doing in their daily lives. Instead of framing history as the march of capitalism towards ever greater concentration, higher production, technological improvement, etc., the autonomists look at how working-class practices (conscious or not) such as workplace resistance, political organization, withdrawal from exploitative relations—anything that erodes or threatens the aggregate rate of profitability—are the real motor force of historical change.

A research method developed within this milieu is called in Italian "inchiesta" or investigation, which sets out to carefully examine what workers are actually doing and experiencing in their workplaces and their daily lives. The early work in 1970s' Italy involved examining the shifting experiences within large factories introduced by the arrival of a new workforce from the rural south of Italy. Later they turned their inquiry to the structure of small enterprise work, the rise of precarious self-employment via contract labor, and the role of women and immigrants in the restructuring of production. More recently this technique was employed by some Germans who investigated the conditions of call center workers in Germany.[8]

These efforts provide a methodological and theoretical starting point to identify potentialities that are difficult to see amidst this era's collapsing ecosystems and fraying social contracts. The collapse of the Left over the past few decades has opened space for new thinking, new arguments, and a new relationship with prior theoretical work; this historical juncture demands it. It's time to closely examine how people are redefining work and how it contradicts capitalist society. Without fresh eyes we can only see what we've looked for; today's task is to open our eyes anew to what workers are actually doing.

I use class in broad terms, as a way of shedding light on a common experience that undergirds our often very different and very specific lives. Michael Hardt and Toni Negri characterized this new understanding of class with the term "multitude." Criticized by some for supposedly trying to replace a traditional concept of working class as an agent of political and historical change with their label 'multitude,' I think the concept is better understood as a preliminary effort to describe a new experience of social reproduction. The term tries to bridge the gap between our specific life experiences and our productive participation in common dynamics based on shared contexts and meanings. Each of us has a unique life based on our particular location in time, space, and social hierarchies; but each of us, too, is a producer of a common life, participating in common roles in the global capitalist economy, contributing to shared social knowledge.

Hardt and Negri put it this way: "The becoming common of labor, on the one hand, and the production of the common, on the other, are not isolated to software engineers in Seattle and Hyderabad but also characterize health workers in Mexico and Mozambique, agriculturists in Indonesia and Brazil, scientists in China and Russia, and industrial workers in Nigeria and Korea. And yet the new centrality of the common does not in any way diminish the singularity of the various situated subjectivities. This coincidence of the common and singularities is what defines the concept of the multitude."[9] The Nowtopian experience is fundamentally similar to this description, simultaneously individual and specific, while inherently also about producing a shared life.

The fall of the Soviet Union and old-style statist leftism is a healthy—and in any case historical—precedent to this new period of social conflict. But the fall of so-called "really existing socialism" (which was just a version of state capitalism) provided a convenient mechanism to flush away all ideas about class too. It is only now, fifteen years later, that the idea of class in America is starting to regain respectability. (Of course, it has been widely reported in the "alternative" lefty press that we've been enduring a class war all these years that only the ruling class has been waging.)

An old saw of the Marxist left, never followed by any leftists who actually took state power, was that the emancipation of the working class was the task of the working class itself. Furthermore, the emancipation of the working class would take the form of the abolition of all classes, along with the vestiges of capitalist society—wage-labor, money, and private property (a social institution, as opposed to "personal property"—your clothes and other personal possessions). These may sound like tired old formulations but in the first decade of the 21st century, they are once again haunting the globe. In this book we'll meet Nowtopians who are refusing the limits of wage-work to begin producing an emancipated, ecologically grounded future. *Nowtopia* identifies a new basis for a shared experience of class, specifically, the increasingly common exodus from wage-labor on one side, and the embrace of meaningful, freely-chosen, and "free" work on the other.

CHAPTER 2
CLASS DISMISSED!

U.S. politics tends to gravitate towards claims of what's good or bad for the "middle class," a group that ostensibly includes everyone but the bag ladies and street homeless on one side and the jetsetting super-rich on the other. The most confusing piece of this puzzle in the past decades has been the gradual disappearance of the working class, replaced in some politicians' speeches by references to "working families," or in the rhetoric of leftist organizers as "working people," but defrocked of its status as a class. Many people in blue- and white-collar jobs think of themselves as middle class, a self-affirming status confirmed by having a relatively new car, buying the right products, living in the suburbs or expensive urban neighborhoods.

Trying to anticipate someone's politics based on their occupation, economic stratum, or race is impossible. Today a factory worker can be—and often is—a knee-jerk, pro-tax-cuts, pro-war, right-winger. Conversely, those derisively dismissed as "middle-class" or "professional," due to salary or educational level (and thus perceived as "privileged"), are perfectly capable of opposing the degradation of life imposed by capitalism and its propagandists, beneficiaries, and enforcers.

In 2004 and 2005 articles about class in America began to reappear in the mainstream press. *The New York Times, The Economist,* and *The Los Angeles Times,* all weighed in with multi-part series about class. None of these treatments could be called Marxist, and none were remotely systemic in their analysis. *The New York Times* even offered an interactive tool on their website, whereby through a series of selections from multiple choice lists in six categories, you could determine your own class status. This fed a pop-psychological approach to class, reinforcing an ahistorical view that sees class as a temporary status defined by home ownership, income level, education, and various other categories. Instead of framing class as a question of social power, these analyses saw class as a sociological phenomenon and use the term to describe a wide variety of strata as classes (upper-middle, lower-middle, etc.).

The term "class" has lost a great deal of meaning in the U.S. Does this collapse of meaning correspond to a disappearance of referents? Are we living in a classless society? Of course not. But the conceptual tools required to understand and make sense of this society have been radically degraded. The missing arrow in our quiver is the one that pierces class society, that explains the systemic dynamics that produce a small group of extremely wealthy at one pole, and an ever greater number of impoverished at the other. Between the extremes of untold wealth and absolute immiseration most of us live quiet lives, coping as best we can with the cards we're dealt.[1]

In the U.S., where even the poorest 10% are wealthier than two-thirds of the world's population, decades of Cold War, consumerist propaganda, and a balkanized academic curriculum have atomized the population into market niches and an endless series of personal crises.[2] The influence of psychology grew enormously during the latter half of the 20th century, strongly reinforcing a sense of self that was celebrated by consumer society as the final arbiter of meaning and value. People were encouraged to express their individuality by owning distinctive products, from cars and clothes to furniture and books, a process that helped turn "the masses" into self-expressing individuals committed to their uniqueness rather than their shared realities. Further, the focus on consumption demoted awareness of production, shifting the locus of personal political behavior from the previously class-based notion of the work done, to the individualized notion of what shopping choices a person made. During the past few decades political movements associated with work and workers' rights have notably diminished while the politics of consumption has moved to center stage (consumers' decisions are the main focus for campaigns against sweatshop labor, pesticides, gas-guzzling cars, and much more).

In spite of this increased individuation, *together* all these individuals still comprise a great social majority. Few have anything to sell but labor and consequently live from payday to payday, dependent on wages and salaries for survival. But as individualized consumers, the experience of being part of a broad class of people sharing a fundamental relationship to power and wealth in this society became less tangible. Politicians like Ronald Reagan and Margaret Thatcher tapped into this expansive individualism with their anti-government rhetoric, as well as their frontal assaults on the historic power of trade unions.[3]

Class emerges as a unifying experience at specific historical periods, usually corresponding to shifts in economic structures. The emergence of a class-conscious working class in the U.S. during the 1930s grew out of early Fordist mass production and the severe hardships of the Depression. Previous periods of class-consciousness arose during earlier periods of industrialization in the mid-19th century and early 20th century, often stimulated by cyclical efforts to establish the 8-hour day, e.g. in the 1860s, 1880s, and 1900s. Radical sociologist Beverly Silver has usefully framed the rise and fall of labor movements with the work of both Karl Marx and Karl Polanyi.

The insight that labor and labor movements are continually made and remade provides an important antidote against the common tendency to be overly rigid in specifying who the working class is (be it nineteenth-century craftworkers or the twentieth-century mass production workers). Thus, rather than seeing an "historically superseded" movement or a "residual endangered species," our eyes are open to the early signs of new working class formation as well as "backlash" resistance from those working classes that are being "unmade." A key task becomes the identification of emerging responses from below to both the creative and destructive sides of capitalist development.[4]

THE RISE AND DEMISE OF A BLUE-COLLAR WORKING CLASS

The United States has a long and violent history of class war. Labor histories tell the story of early unionization, brutal assaults, and murders by hired thugs and sometimes local police and national guard, and the dogged efforts of newly industrialized workers to establish their rights to independent organization. The ebb and flow of 19th century workers' organization, from the Knights of Labor to the early craft unions that made up the American Federation of Labor, have many heroic and often tragic chapters.

But often glossed over in these accounts is the stark fact that when industrialization began in the middle 1800s, the U.S. was a society still saddled with human slavery. The newly employed working class began organizing itself but was already cursed with the deep disunity inculcated by slavery and racism. Exploited workers from Ireland and southern Europe found a step up out of the underclass by asserting their "whiteness," a process that continues in our own time, as some groups assimilate into middle America while others are systematically excluded (see the curious juxtaposition of Asian assimilation and Latino and Black exclusion).[5] Black slavery in the south and east found its near mirror in the treatment of Chinese immigrants in the Gold Rush west. The union label, a source of pride and solidarity among organized labor for more than a century, was started when white cigar workers wrapped their cigars with a label prominently displaying "made by WHITE MEN" to distinguish them from those made by immigrant Chinese workers. Anti-capitalist working class movements in the 1870s were also vehemently anti-Chinese immigration, a stance echoed in the western black press of the era.[6]

The racial divisions implanted in the industrial working class are paralleled by the division between men and women, wherein men's work in factories was given an elevated importance vis-à-vis the equally essential reproductive work carried on by women (unpaid within the family unit, and badly paid in laundries, schools, hospitals, and elsewhere) right up to the present. The lack of basic suffrage and other rights for women further reinforced the apparent advantages, prerogatives, and self-importance of while male workers.

Meanwhile, the other great human tragedy of 19th century America was reaching its crescendo: Indian genocide. Culminating a centuries-long process of conquest and extermination, the post-Civil War United States directed its ever more formidable industrial killing capacities against the remaining independent cultures of North American tribes. Already severely decimated by disease, duplicity, and decades of war and forced migration, tribes such as the Lakota Sioux, the Nez Perce, the Mescalero Apaches, the Comanches, the Shoshone, and many more, were pursued by the U.S. military, attacked and massacred with impunity, and ultimately forced onto the abysmal reservation system. The white soldiers and settlers who were all part of the broad working class had little compunction about participating in this genocide. (It would be another century before the nearly exterminated cultures and sensibilities that had occupied North America for millennia would start to recover at all, and would become an inspiration for the new tribalists of the late 20th century.)

The American Civil War led to the formal emancipation of slaves but within a decade, Reconstruction had been derailed by white supremacists, and a de facto apartheid society was re-established in the South, with Jim Crow segregation laws and customs extending across the country. In spite of this deplorable working class defeat, skilled workers—the first labor aristocracy—began to exert their collective power in mass strikes that erupted in 1877 and 1894, book-ending an era that saw the emergence of a powerful movement for the 8-hour day. May Day, the original workers holiday, started in Chicago in the 1880s as part of the 8-hour campaign, after the infamous Haymarket Massacre.

Bullets and bombs fueled the violent class conflict that shaped America and the political forces that fought to control it right up to the 1917 entry of the U.S. into WWI. Violence quelled the Homestead Steel strike in 1892, coal miners were subject to relentless attack by Pinkertons and police over decades, the infamous Ludlow (Colorado) massacre of 1914 left 20 dead coal miners and their families at the hands of the local National Guard after a 14-month strike. In San Francisco in May 1907, a gun battle erupted between striking streetcar workers and the scabs driving the streetcars, leaving two dead and dozens injured. In 1916 a bomb exploded in downtown San Francisco during a Chamber of Commerce-sponsored

"Preparedness Day" March, a crime attributed to anti-war labor radicals but never solved. The forty years from 1877 to 1917 were among the most violent in U.S. history, with Indian massacres, thousands of lynchings, and endless industrial conflict peppering the entire period.

The Russian Revolution and failed German Revolution at the end of WWI galvanized the U.S. owning class into a campaign of severe repression. After wage controls and no-strike agreements expired at the end of the war, labor across the country demanded raises and improved conditions. On the west coast, a general strike erupted in Seattle in February 1919 which ended after a few days but became a justification for police repression. Later that year a waterfront strike in San Francisco was broken by hired thugs who sent hundreds of striking dockers to the hospital. The Palmer Raids were staged across the U.S. in 1919–1920, as the federal government rounded up and deported ten thousand radical workers and agitators, mostly immigrants, including such anarchist luminaries as Emma Goldman and Alexander Berkman.

After the ferocious repression, organized labor was in full retreat and the 1920s were a quiescent period in terms of class war. The owners had their way, and also benefited from the new media that started the long process of molding the new individualism. In that time it was radio, and with its rise came the beginning of advertising and consumer culture. The 1920s also saw the frenzied expansion of the stock market, promising small investors that they too could get rich quick by picking the right stocks. The markets surged and paper riches were at everyman's fingertips until the October 1929 crash that led to the Great Depression. The decade characterized by the open-shop, low-wage "American Plan" came crashing down with all the fantasies and propaganda of an endlessly easy path to riches through the American Way of Life.

In the 1930s the Depression renewed the battles across the country. Sitdown strikes, urban warfare, and even general strikes in Minneapolis and San Francisco carried working class power to new heights. Several years into the Depression, with unemployment at unprecedented heights and capitalism's appeal at a new low, Franklin Roosevelt was elected president with promises of a New Deal, and his government put in place the basic elements of the welfare state that saved capitalism from itself. Social security and unemployment insurance, and crucially, the establishment of a legal right for workers to organize independently into trade unions, helped forge a new social contract that averted more radical approaches and gave the state a newly prominent role in regulating the vicissitudes of savage capitalism. The humiliation and rage that was radicalizing working class communities was channeled into support for the state and the new industrial trade unions (for example, the

United Autoworkers, the United Steelworkers, United Electrical Workers, International Longshoremen's and Warehousemen's Union, and many others). These new industrial unions became crucial institutional foundations for the prosperity and booming economy that followed the U.S. victory in World War II, in no small part by their acceptance of the limits of trade unionism in the corporatist, imperial state that emerged from the newly permanent war economy.

World War II scrambled the working class communities that had thrown up these new powerful unions, but as at the end of the first World War, returning soldiers and demilitarized workers expected radical improvements in their lives for all the sacrifices made during wartime. Over two million workers went on strike in 1946, which once again pushed the owning class into a rigorous counterattack. Institutionally the power of unions was greatly narrowed by the passage of the Taft-Hartley Act in 1948. Ideologically the hysterical anti-communism that helped launch the Cold War was especially useful domestically to rid workers' and social organizations of leftists and radicals of all sorts, not just avowed communists. The Taft-Hartley Act itself had required unions to expel known communists, in addition to foregoing tactical solidarity in the forms of sympathy strikes and mass picketing. By 1955 when the old American Federation of Labor craft unions (AFL) formally merged with the new industrial unions of the Congress of Industrial Organizations (CIO), the so-called "red unions" like the west coast longshoremen (ILWU) and the United Electrical Workers were excluded.[7]

The paranoia and fear associated with the Cold War and communism drove apolitical workers further away from ideas of collective responses to shared predicaments. The carrot of the GI Bill, with its low-cost mortgages and support for higher education (disproportionately made available to white soldiers), helped underpin the ideological assertion that America was the best place to live (and the "mixed economy" was the proper way to structure society). Vast government subsidies to the private automobile industry helped build the interstate highway system, which altered the physical environment of most cities, promoting the now infamous suburban sprawl that did so much to (literally) cement atomization. While returning GIs began buying homes and moving to the suburbs, people dependent on wage-work started to see themselves not as part of a working class, but as part of a broad middle class. Upward mobility and college educations promised "professional careers" to ever more people. Average workers supported their offspring for longer and longer, so they could go to college and "move up."

During the Depression of the 1930s a strong working class culture flourished, sponsored in part by federal work programs for artists and other cultural workers. Plays, books, tour guides, public murals, and much more were produced in great profusion, tacitly or overtly honoring work and workers. After WWII, cold war hysteria was directed against communists and left-wingers in trade unions, stigmatizing any cultural expression that openly honored being a worker. A new culture celebrating technology and convenience was born in the mass production factories retooled from war production. Progress became a bludgeon used to push aside workers who fought to retain control over labor processes and workplace technologies. Domestic life was redesigned around a host of new household machines that promised to bring new levels of hygiene and safety, comfort and convenience to the everyday life of Americans. Housewives, who had only a decade earlier been working in wartime production, were now expected to administer (without pay) the increasingly technologized domestic sphere, while husbands brought home a family wage.

The concurrent rise of television during the 1950s introduced a new dimension to social reproduction, described by the Situationists in the 1960s as the "Society of the Spectacle."[8] Not reducible to a clichéd notion of mass media, the Spectacular society is one in which lived experience seems less real than the received, edited representations of life through various channels. Time is flattened into an endless *now*, as history itself disappears, leaving behind only a stream of nostalgic episodes and the souvenirs that accompany them. Spectacular society itself is the lone self-referential expression of reality; anything that contradicts its self-satisfied premises is ignored and soon forgotten.

Spectacular society was made possible when newspapers and radio were augmented by television, the most powerful propaganda system yet devised. The commercial messages pouring out of television from its inception gradually reshaped the way people came to understand their lives. Daily experiences at work and school became personal and particular, and insofar as the received "truth" represented on television did not match, the blame for dissatisfaction with life was shifted from shared, collective predicaments to personal failure. If TV said this was the best of all possible worlds, and you didn't think your life was so hot, well, there must be something wrong with you rather than a systemic problem, since everyone *else* was apparently happy and prospering.

The individualistic world-view promoted by Spectacular society reinforced a working class politics that had already accepted subordination to capital much earlier. Working class politics in the U.S., going back to the late 1930s and the rise of the CIO unions, renounced a leading or initiating role in society. No independent effort to determine what work should be done or by whom, how it should be organized, or to what end (nor how society as a whole might shape its own role in democratically organizing our material lives) was encouraged or developed by an independent labor movement. Labor politics were limited to negotiating the price of labor in specific capitalist businesses, or at best across industries. Old socialist demands for shorter working hours were submerged into industry-by-industry negotiations over vacation time, higher wages, and pensions. National health care was framed as creeping socialism, and instead, employers set up insurance plans company by company, an historic concession rapidly unraveling in the 21st century.

The demise of an alternative working class power was sealed by organized labor's submission to capitalism's leadership. Decades of U.S. economic prosperity following WWII and the integration of organized labor into the Cold War military-industrial-consumerism "deal" further depoliticized the working class. Mid-20th century working class communities slowly disintegrated through urban redevelopment and white flight to the suburbs (union racism being a contributing force). Organized labor was framed politically as a "special interest" by self-serving corporate lobbyists. The union movement shaped the reforms that produced 40-hour work weeks and much-loved weekends, but by the mid-'60s found its social foundations uprooted by suburbanization and the overwhelming cultural imperative to consume. Collective pride (and political agency) based on occupation was corroded by the gradual but nearly complete reconceptualization of workers as *consumers*. The mighty engine of marketing helped turn people's attention away from what they *did* and toward what they *owned* as the basic mechanism of self-definition. Over time personal pride became more associated with the status value of one's possessions than from one's work or contribution to society.

The allure of a technologically defined life of leisure, as promoted incessantly on TV and in the movies, clashed with the numbing stupidity of many jobs. Whether in regimented, tightly controlled factory shopfloors, or in the gray-suited, white-collar conformity of office life, workers increasingly called in sick, quit, stole time and goods, giving rise to a newly assertive insubordination. The cultural upheavals of the late 1960s further helped fuel an unprecedented refusal of work in the U.S. Slowdowns, sick-outs, wildcat strikes, and mass political protests all contributed to a collapse of the post-WWII "deal" and the profits that sustained it.

The successful Vietnamese resistance to U.S. forces from 1968–72 combined with mass protests and widespread rank-and-file mutiny in the military further undermined the system's ability to rule. The breakdown in capitalist profitability led President Nixon to abrogate the gold standard in 1971 and free the dollar to float against emerging global competitors, hoping to bolster sagging profits with currency manipulations, a model that continues to underpin U.S. global economic strategy to this day. Sudden oil price increases in 1973–74 were deftly manipulated to enrich desperate corporate treasuries while reimposing insecurity and fear on the recently insubordinate working class in America.

CLASS UNMADE

Proceeding from the economic crisis of that time, life has been restructured. After several decades of rampant destruction of long-term residential neighborhoods, workplaces, and industries, most of the old ways that people came together have broken down. There is ample evidence showing that social networks that reached their peak in approximately the mid-1960s have since that time collapsed.[9] Not coincidentally the late 1960s was also the time when worldwide capitalist competition re-emerged in earnest. Along with these macro-level changes, the daily lives of American workers came under new pressure as the first oil shocks and the ensuing recession and inflation began eroding living standards and reimposing insecurity. The Sixties' New Left had mounted forceful challenges to war, racism, sexism, homophobia, and a whole panoply of modern maladies. The emptiness and banality of the affluent society itself was rejected by much of the counterculture; the more politicized wing addressed the ongoing divide between rich and poor. While those dramas unfolded, the affluence that was considered almost a right by so many Americans (whether they personally enjoyed it or not) was quickly slipping away.

Shared identities and life experiences based on long-term work patterns, generations-old neighborhoods, and a certain sense of stability largely fractured. "Globalization" is the buzzword of our time, describing in a word the redesign of work, computerization, relocation of production within and without national borders, rolling back of unions and the welfare state, privatization of public goods, rapid and extreme concentration of wealth and power, and the reduced reliability of jobs and careers. Another way of stating it is that since the ebbing of profits in the early-1970s, capital has carried out a worldwide counterattack. The "just-in-time" pace of work pioneered by Japanese automakers (some call it "Toyota-ism") sped up production while decentralizing workers' power among dozens of geographically dispersed subcontracting firms (who often fought off unionization too).[10] The redesign and redevelopment of cities (inner city decay and abandonment followed by rampant speculation and gentrification), the huge increase of incarceration, massive waves of human migration within nations and across borders, all have contributed to a growing individual isolation. Where once there were stable communities, neighborhoods, and familiar faces at workplaces, where one might work for a lifetime, now people move from place to place and job to job, blown by the winds of unrelenting insecurity and the threat of being left behind.

Trade unionism as practiced in the United States failed to challenge the direction of technology or the larger division of labor, leaving workers to be whipped to and fro by the vicissitudes of globalization. The strike weapon lost much of its force in the face of deindustrialization and offshoring of production. Unions discovered they could not preserve job security, and then, that bargaining was increasingly on the terms of the owners who used the new mobility of capital as a blunt weapon against organized workers. Desperate to survive on any terms in the post-Fordist economy, unions conceded wages, pensions, medical coverage (just about everything they originally traded workplace power for), just to remain institutionally alive.

Leftist organizers have held on with increasing desperation to old paradigmatic understandings. Futile efforts to unionize the vast non-union workforce have been tried repeatedly. Organizers encouraging workers to join unions promote identification with the work, building a stable, rooted future by fighting for improved wages and benefits, better safety conditions, a more corporatist structure of quasi-self-management and consultative labor relations. Organizing campaigns appeal to workers' fear of falling, to dignity and pride, or make demands for fairness, but all such campaigns depend foremost on the objects of such a campaign being identified as *workers*. Ultimately union campaigns depend on and are *defined by* the reduction of the individual to his or her occupation.

Historic changes make this paradigm a tougher and tougher sell, witness the falling rates of unionization and corresponding soaring rates of casualization—part-time and temporary employment. Alongside this deep structural change in the employment marketplace, which parallels the export of manufacturing jobs to lower-wage areas both in and outside of the U.S., is a breakdown of the concept of occupation. Traditional job categories are continually overrun by technological change and restructuring. Commitments to stable employment between individual employers and employees are widely acknowledged as obsolete in the so-called New Economy. In this era steady employment has tangibly diminished but people often work multiple jobs and increased hours to maintain their standards of living.

For anyone at a job in the U.S., at almost any level of income, the future is uncertain. Specific jobs and firms vanish quickly. Organizing on the job, trying to stabilize an historic moment in an ever-evolving division of labor, tends to accelerate automation and job relocation. Ineffective programs to "retrain" displaced workers have come and gone, while the burden has shifted to individuals to continuously upgrade skills and submit to "life-long" learning—not for their own edification but just to keep pace with the rapidly changing demands of capital.

Throughout this process, work itself has been degraded. Even where jobs remain steady over some years, work is controlled by the intense pace of machines and/or the expectations of one's "teammates"/co-workers. There is little room as an individual worker for autonomy, a human pace, values and needs unmeasured by company profits or remuneration. Concurrent with the dispersion of production across regions, nations, and the planet, new technologies have been deployed to sap work of human skill. The high-tech economy that trumpets its need for skilled workers actually depends on vast amounts of highly regimented, simplified, repetitive work that requires very little skill (many jobs can be learned in an hour or two, making workers easily replaceable). Industrial robots are applied to some of these jobs, but the expansion of mind-numbing, physically crippling factory work to supply the global networks of production and consumption shows no signs of diminishing.

Meanwhile, the economy in the U.S. shifted more and more to a "service" basis. But what was this work? Banking and finance, advertising and media, tourism, software, restaurants, retail sales, and real estate, became prosperous centers of capitalist investment and employment. All of these occupations require real people to do mental and physical tasks, but the products of all this labor is essentially "immaterial," that is, it produces no physical product. Instead it produces experiences, memories, ideas, and concepts, often depending on the sharing of emotions as the defining quality of "good work." At a rudimentary level we see the smiling sales clerk whose "good attitude" is the key to her job. More abstractly we also find in this category of work financial advisers, therapists, interior designers, disc jockeys, tour guides, and security guards. These new occupations offer long-term employment to only a select few, while some redesign their own and other industries' divisions of labor. The entry and exit by countless small businesses made these fields even more unstable in terms of steady employment. This insecure and flexible economy largely escaped the logic of trade unionism, which depends on fixed contractual agreements between large employers and "bargaining units" of steady workers.

The breakdown of stable workplaces, communities, and families (the "decomposition" of the working class) resulted from the furious, unforgiving pace of contemporary capitalism. Conveniently for the needs of capital, it is precisely within those lost social networks that otherwise buried histories and counter-narratives were kept alive and passed along. As the traditional communities of workplace and neighborhood have been ripped asunder by plant closings, urban redevelopment, and the new transience, the historical memories of communities that had organized and resisted unfettered exploitation in the past have nearly been lost too. Popular movements, with memories of their own political power based on collective action, have diminished as workplace and neighborhood foundations have been kicked out from beneath them. Constituents have moved to new places, jobs have been exported to other regions or other countries, new people have arrived with different experiences, cultures, languages, memories, and expectations.

This process of social and economic dis-integration is as old as capitalism itself. But its destructive power is not omnipotent. Social currents that exploded decades ago didn't just disappear but went underground, not as organized movements but as a whole range of cultural experiments and practices. The dissenting political voices that were so loud in the 1960s and 1970s fell silent, or so we might think if the Spectacle is our only source of information (as it seeks to be). Important continuities from four decades ago are foundations for radical alternatives today. This continuity is perhaps most visible in the burgeoning food politics of our era. As described in "Vacant-Lot Gardeners" (Chapter 5), the rejection of corporate agribusiness with its chemical-soaked, processed foods starts at the height of 1960s political revolts, notably at Berkeley's People's Park. The exploding organic food market of the past decade is being fueled by political currents that have been percolating beneath the radar in the United States ever since.

A smaller example, though perhaps of real importance, is the current of left radicalism that descends from the 19th century anarchists, through the left communists who were purged by the Bolsheviks in the Soviet Union and murdered by the social democrats in Germany, reappearing during the Spanish Civil War only to vanish into small periodicals and tiny political groups for decades. The Root & Branch group in Boston briefly brought one such current into the New Left (Paul Mattick Sr., a respected Marxist theoretician, had been a part of the German Revolution before emigrating to the U.S. in the mid-1920s; his son was a key member of the Root & Branch collective), while divergent threads from anarchism to the Situationists to radical ecologists to autonomist Marxists in the anti-nuclear movement all kept the flames and ideas alive across decades in spite of repression by both opposed wings of the Cold War. *Processed World* magazine was another outpost of these ideas, as was the underground zine called *Temp Slave*. In both of these latter publications, new sensibilities about work and workers found their voice during the 1980s and early 1990s.[11] Anti-authoritarian values gained many adherents during the past few decades, in spite of incessant propaganda extolling "free markets" and global business.

Everyday life never matches up with the imaginary, edited, and sanitized world we see on TV. Fear of crime is rampant, helped by TV's wide reporting of urban crimes ("if it bleeds, it leads"), but crime fear is based on a false sense of omnipresent mayhem. Most people never experience it directly, but the learned fear of strangers and street life has further isolated many. Skepticism and outright mistrust are nourished by a steady diet of executive war crimes, routinely massive corporate fraud, and a visibly decaying—perhaps dying—physical environment (for which there's always an amazing technological fix coming soon). The glaring contradictions are slamming people who live at the precarious edge. But supposedly "comfortable" middle-class people face the same disconnect between life as *represented* versus life as lived. Many lefty students in the 1960s and 1970s are now middle-aged professionals (and ex-professionals and pseudo-professionals) working to escape the corporate world.

THE REVOLT AGAINST PROFESSIONALISM

> Professionalism—in particular the notion that experts should confine themselves to their "legitimate professional concerns" and not "politicize" their work—helps keep individual professionals in line by encouraging them to view their narrow technical orientation as a virtue, a sign of objectivity rather than of subordination."
> —*Jeff Schmidt*[12]

One of the defining characteristics of "middle class" workers has been their fierce attachment to "professionalism," in part to reassure themselves that they are not mere workers. The concept has been diluted in recent years after being applied to countless working class jobs, from autoworkers being called "associates" to fast-food clerks who are admonished to behave "professionally" while dressed in ridiculous uniforms working for minimum wage. Professionalism is an idea often used as a blunt weapon in the workplace. Denouncing a worker (whether above, below, or alongside the denouncer) for "unprofessional" behavior is often a powerful way to curb "unwelcome" speech or behavior.

Professional status usually requires graduate college degrees and extensive training in a specific work culture, e.g. medicine, law, corporate management, science, or academia. Professional training is as much about excluding as training, using "objective" standards to weed out those who won't fit the existing self-perpetuating elite culture. For every new scientist or lawyer there are several people who drop out along the way. Sometimes people complete the training and receive accreditation only to abandon the career path at the culminating moment. Professional training intentionally produces more drop-outs than it does professionals.

Even supposedly successful pros walk away from their chosen careers often enough. Professionalism is no vaccine against disillusionment with the limits of paid work. Instead of finding meaning and purpose in the overwork imposed by corporate life—or in hospitals, or even respected universities—a lot of professionally trained folks are opting for a more direct engagement with purposeful work. Jeff Schmidt's dissection of professionalism illuminates the powerlessness that characterizes crucial aspects of the careerist experience: "Professionals control the technical means but not the social goals of their creative work. The professional's lack of control over the political content of his or her creative work is the hidden root of much career dissatisfaction… Professionals are licensed to think on the job, but they are obedient thinkers."[13] Schmidt further argues that by leaving unchallenged the employer's control of the political content of his work, the professional "surrenders his social existence, his control over the mark he makes on the world.[14] This is a core aspect of the deep dissatisfaction experienced by many so-called successful professionals. Reclaiming their dignity and full humanity often leads such professionals to disengage, to walk away from apparently successful lives.

The emergence of "assertive desertion" and various types of dropping out is not new. But it is striking that so many of the adherents of new social formations are people who have been weeded out by the imposed degradation of advanced education and employment; or they have "self-weeded," relieving themselves of the pressure to conform to a hostile ideological culture. Many bicycling activists, free software developers, biofuels advocates, etc. are either themselves well-educated, or are the children of the professional stratum. But "professionalism" has lost its hold. Increasingly, people are walking away from the supposed benefits of the professional life, often precisely because of the narrowness imposed by the professional credo.

Buried within the social approval of "professionalism" is an implicit endorsement of the ideology of expertise. Average people are assumed ignorant unless bearing a certificate of expertise granted by an educational or other profession-sanctioning institution. For many people this selective system renders their innate talents and knowledge gathered outside of accredited institutions socially invisible. What's more, it channels what ought properly to be social and political decisions up the social hierarchy into safely-controlled corporate or university boardrooms.

Challenging technological choices on social grounds is invalidated unless the challengers can do it with esoteric "tech talk" and show credentials that give them "license" to address the technology on specifically technical grounds. But the whole frame of reference is already skewed against the challengers because the discussion has eliminated social evaluation in favor of narrow technical debate. Lack of a credential has been used repeatedly to delegitimize anyone who opposes technological choices on social grounds, such as placing waste incinerators or sewage plants in low-income neighborhoods occupied by people of color.

Nevertheless, dissident professionals and self-educated non-institutional experts have altered the landscape of science and technology over the past few decades. Famously, the nuclear power industry was halted by the mid-1980s in the U.S. after a burgeoning protest movement that employed all tactics, from expert counter-testimony to grassroots organizing and direct action.[15] The expanding movement for environmental justice is another example of citizen-based "science activism" that directly challenges the ideology of professional expertise. Where it has been successful, it has insisted on transparency of scientific data on, e.g. toxic releases, an openness that makes it possible for laymen to begin evaluating the consequences of heretofore "private" decisions by business-employed, biased experts. From the origins of the environmental movement following Rachel Carson's 1962 exposé *Silent Spring* to the early 1970s' movements that led to federal legislation like the Clean Air Act, the Clean Water Act, and the Endangered Species Act, thousands of non-experts have forced hidden technological decisions into the public eye. An interesting example of ongoing grassroots, citizen-based science activism is the *Volunteer Monitor* and its hundreds of local groups carrying out water-quality monitoring with homemade devices, simple observations, and open record keeping.[16]

The dominance of AMA-style doctors, industrial medicine, and pharmaceuticals, while greater than ever in economic terms, has been steadily losing credibility and adherents to dozens of alternative therapeutic approaches. Key to undermining the legitimacy of formal medicine has been first the rise of a women's health care self-help movement (especially for reproductive rights) in the 1960s, and then the furious challenge mounted by AIDS activists in the 1980s over the priorities and approaches of research and development in the face of the HIV epidemic (both movements still very much alive in the 2000s).[17] Self-help online medical advice short-circuits dependence on pricey services. Herbalists, often self-taught and associated with community gardens, are filling an important intermediate role between untreated illness and the unaffordable and often ill-advised high-tech treatment promoted by professional medicine.[18] Public and pay-what-you-can clinics help decommodify medicine, but they are a small fraction of the U.S. health industry.

Another category of "professionalism," journalism, has lost its former elevated status due to the rapidly shifting media landscape caused by the web. Independent news sites like the indymedia network and the new global reach of online journalism from previously inaccessible sources (e.g. *Asia Times* from Hong Kong, *La Jornada* from Mexico, *Al-Jazeera* from Qatar, etc.) has eroded the authoritative voice of leading U.S. newspapers. Repeated self-censorship and publishing of government disinformation has further discredited the once respected *NY Times, Washington Post,* et al. Mainstream journalists repeatedly and publicly have sacrificed credibility for job security. Reporters with integrity have been driven from the field, charged with "unprofessional" conduct if they write stories contradicting the powers-that-be. Meanwhile the professional punditocracy is reeling under the onslaught of tens of thousands of highly literate, thoughtful blogs, which are following a trail blazed in the 1980s and 1990s by underground zines that preceded the web and have continued alongside it in great profusion. The formerly unquestioned expertise of professional journalists has collapsed. Frequent stenographic reporting carried out by the "most professional" journalists on the "most respected" papers, magazines, and broadcast media has left the brawling no-holds-barred niches of opinion and investigative reporting wide open to all comers.

The rejection of professionalism goes hand-in-hand with the emergence of grassroots do-it-yourself communities, often sustained by the donated labor of former or coulda-been professionals who turned away in search of a more rewarding life. The rat-race was aptly named decades ago—it's a crazy, home-wrecking, hollow, and thanklessly sacrificial life. Many people opt out to reclaim their basic human dignity. Meanwhile, pressure mounts from below. Capitalist agendas face ever more sophisticated opposition, sometimes bolstered by rebellious, ex-professional insiders. Grassroots movements increasingly confront so-called experts who make decisions on supposedly technical grounds that are actually profoundly social.

MYTH OF THE MIDDLE CLASS

> Behind the label of the independent "self-employed" worker, what we actually find is an intellectual proletarian, but who is recognized as such only by the employers who exploit him or her.
>
> —*Maurizio Lazzarato*[19]

To put it bluntly, the myth of the middle class is that it is not a part of the working class. These so-called middle-class lives are really the current state of the U.S. working class, broadly understood, because the middle class is simply the better paid fraction of the working class, a modern-day version of a "labor aristocracy." "Middle class" has been a brilliant marketing concept. People identify with a prosperous lifestyle that seems fundamentally egalitarian, a world where politics is an occasional annoying interruption to a real life which revolves around the next purchase or experience.

Tract homes stretching for miles, uniform green lawns and driveways in front of each, two- or three-car garages overflowing with the abundant junk of "middle class" lives. Within a few miles are endless seas of garish neon signs seeking to lure the ever-more obese shoppers into their undistinguished, cookie-cutter box stores full of more temporarily entertaining but ultimately useless junk. The corn-syrup soaked processed foods that are transferring so much of the earth's abundance to the sagging frames of American workers taste much like the plastic abundance that saturates the lived environment. This is the middle class American Dream, the same dream that tantalizes the planet's starving millions with fantasies of comfort and satiation. It is also a life that has depended on cheap and abundant oil. Beset with countless internal contradictions and external pressures, it will not continue much longer.

"Middle class" is a social mis-identity that has played a big role in neutering social conflict and stabilizing American society. Middle class people are neither owners nor working class, and yet almost everyone in the middle class has a job. The strangest aspect of the ongoing idea of a middle class is that it is so hard to pin down. Who is in it? Who isn't? Why? Where is the boundary between middle class and rich? Between middle class and working class? (For that matter, where is the boundary between working class and poor?) Can one be middle class by self-designation? Are there objective qualities that can be measured? Can one think oneself middle class and be wrong? Plenty of people in union jobs think of themselves as middle class due to home ownership, health insurance, and a "middle" income. Some argue that owning versus rent-

ing one's home is a key distinction, but that glosses over the many affluent renters with much more wealth than many poor homeowners.

The idea of the middle class is an historically specific notion. Whatever definition one settles on, the existence of a middle class corresponds to a period of history in which a significant number of people
in a particular area were not desperate and poor but at the same time
did not own the factories, stores, and offices (dare we say "the means of
production"?) of the society in which they worked. Some are "independent" professionals like doctors or lawyers, architects or programmers.
Others are middle managers and bureaucrats of various types. Plenty
more are self-employed, owning small shops, service businesses, or even
doing various types of (usually white-collar) contract labor.

Many writers have sought to analyze the middle class. A diverse literature examines the contradictory position affluent professionals and
intellectuals occupy between traditional understandings of the working
class on one side and those who really own and control the economy on
the other. One strain of thought sees it as a permanent buffer between
society's owners and workers. The far-flung networks of global business
employ a few million as managers and coordinators, and those people
are generally well-rewarded for their work; often their individual status
allows them to provide special educational and social benefits to their
offspring. This has led some to argue that there is a "coordinator class"
that enjoys special status and benefits from its role in managing and
reproducing capitalism, and has even been able to pass on its status and
benefits through heredity.[20]

One of the best-known analysts of the middle class is Barbara Ehrenreich. In the 1970s she started out in the New Left with her then-hus-
band John writing about the "professional-managerial class,"[21] followed
a decade later with *Fear of Falling: The Inner Life of the Middle Class.*[22] A
recent book of hers looks at the plight of the middle sector (*Bait and
Switch: The (Futile) Pursuit of the American Dream*[23]). Ehrenreich is an acute
observer of the late 20th century dynamics of American life. Her progressive instincts led her first to codify a new class stratum, then ten years
later to examine the mystifications and realities surrounding the whole
idea of a middle class.

Finally, a quarter century after her quasi-Marxist claims for a new
professional-managerial class, she discovers with almost naïve amaze-
ment that the actual range of options for so-called middle class professionals is astonishingly narrow. In the wake of her best-selling *Nickel and
Dimed*[24] about the plight of low-wage, multi-job workers in hotels and
restaurants, she set out to get a job as a $60,000/year public relations
specialist in corporate America. She spent most of a year networking,

getting made over, trained, coached, and cajoled, but all for naught. Her efforts led only to two unsalaried sales jobs where commissions would only follow investment of time and money—and successful sales work. Along the way she meets dozens of panicky and depressed people whose sense of entitlement to the "good jobs" of corporate America is steadily eroding in the face of the everyday rejections and dead-ends that most of them experience. Ehrenreich is of course a successful author, and her experience of this soul-killing, humiliating job hunt became grist for her best-selling mill, luckily for her (less luckily for those she interviewed). For many former managers, a harsh world of low-wage employment has become the best they can hope for after falling outside the gated enclaves of upper-echelon corporate America.

The new leftish attempts to analyze professionals and managers as a class have largely been dropped in the wake of the ruthless rationalization imposed by globalization. These kinds of theories are heard less in the early 21st century than they were in the 1970s, in no small part due to the rapid shrinking of the middle management layer during the recent decades of globalization. Moreover, professionals in most fields have seen their autonomy and relative comfort whittled away through the old dynamics of capitalist consolidation.

Doctors and lawyers have become employees of multinational firms. Programmers and other technical workers have been subjected to workplace rationalization, increasing the monitoring of their work and ostensibly, their productivity. Freshly minted Ph.D.'s have seen tenure tracks disappear just as they entered the market and many have been reduced to glorified temp employment as short-term lecturers. Old jokes about Ph.D.'s driving taxis are more true today than ever, but with students carrying greater debt than ever before. The tremendous increase of personal debt imposed on college students is a structural way that (previously more free) graduates are now coerced into taking any work they can get in order to pay their debts. Mirroring much of the financialization of the world during the past few decades, new relations of debt peonage dominate the lives of "middle class" Americans as much as they do whole countries in the global south. Comparable to company stores in coal towns in the 19th century, student debt forces potentially free and creative thinkers to work at jobs over which they have no control or say.

Many of the people occupying "middle class" occupations haven't yet lost their social status as middle class. But it's clear that the difference between their lives and those of people working in factories or offices as blue- or white-collar workers is shrinking all the time. The former professionals were in important respects just very well-paid workers, enjoying a period of history (approximately three or four decades) in which their skills were in short supply and hard to replace with technology or reorganization or by moving the work elsewhere. As a type of historically specific labor aristocracy, the "middle class" workers of America are better understood as classic proletarians, as sociologist Beverly Silver explains:

> ...the "proletariat" consists of those who must sell their labor power in order to survive. The proletarian condition encompasses a range of concrete situations, from those who possess scarce skills that are in demand (and hence have relatively strong marketplace bargaining power) to those who are unemployed. It includes those who are employed by private entrepreneurs and those who are employed by the state, for the latter are ultimately no more insulated from the pressures of being treated as a commodity than, say, workers in the internal labor market of a large firm. In both cases, when push comes to shove, the demands of profitability (and their links with tax receipts) can wipe away in short order whatever insulation from the labor market had existed.
>
> —*Beverly J. Silver*[25]

Silver's analysis of the proletarian condition is a useful reframing of the middle class, since the vast majority of middle class people are simply workers whose skills have been relatively scarce, giving them real bargaining power as individuals. The new period of offshoring and outsourcing is bringing the well-educated and technically skilled of the world into direct competition with each other, with predictable results. Prevailing wages in India and China for computer programming, architectural drafting, and other professional skills are a fraction of the going rate in the U.S. or Europe. That alone would explain the shrinking security that middle class professionals have come to take for granted. Concomitantly, it is no longer so easy to move laterally from job to job. Instead, steady work is beginning to resemble musical chairs, and the great fear of professional workers is to be between jobs when the music stops. As Ehrenreich discovered, once you're out of the corporate workworld, it's very difficult to get back in, and the longer the gap between jobs grows, the more unlikely it is that you will ever be re-hired.

But the new global workplace of closely coordinated, just-in-time production cycles brings these globe-spanning workers into direct cooperation as well as competition, and that has the effect of radically altering the condition of work itself. A graphic designer in New York may work on a project that is getting its programming done in Dublin, Bangalore, and Sunnyvale, its printing in Singapore, while the actual final production and assembly of a commodity to go on retail shelves is done in China, shipped through the "hands" of highly paid longshore workers at computerized cranes in shipyards, who put containers onto trucks or intermodal trains, which in turn are driven by non-union self-employed truckers to warehouses where they are offloaded by minimum-wage (at best) migrant workers who only recently arrived. In order to hold a professional job in that system, the individual has to manage enormous time pressure.

The forty-hour workweek is a relic of the Fordist past. These days, a successful professional is expected to work upwards of 70 hours a week and to defer indefinitely time off for vacation. Worse, a lot of that working time is unpaid. British journalist Madeleine Bunting describes a common corporate strategy in this era: "Don't employ more people, just devise an organizational culture which will ensure that people will give you their free time for free." And given that nearly 46 percent of men and 32 percent of women do so in the UK, clearly it's *working*.[26] But just measuring the official work done fails to get the full picture. The British Mental Health Association has discovered that people spend an additional eleven hours a week working with cellphones, laptops, or puzzling out work problems in the bath.[27] The story in the U.S. is certainly comparable, if not worse.

"Middle class" workers are bearing the brunt of an absolute extension of the workday, like their lower-wage working class counterparts (the latter see their workdays extended by the necessity of working at two or even three jobs to make ends meet).[28] They are also undergoing a relative intensification of work. It's not just long hours. One hundred years of time-and-motion studies have now been applied to all forms of work, including the professionals'. The implantation of computers into most jobs is a technological means of speeding up and intensifying the work pace. A widely accepted 24/7 economy, combined with the enormous increase in self-employment and contract labor, has largely erased distinctions between work time and personal, private time. Focusing on results, employers and clients do not care when or how the work gets done, just that it does, and by the deadline. Quite often the goals of a project are simply impossible to achieve in the given time, unless the work hours are radically intensified and extended.

Under today's tightly managed schedules, the separation between personal lives and job demands has narrowed, and for all too many, vanished entirely, to the point that people live to work. This is the daily life that underlies the term "social factory"—a life in which work time blurs into all the hours one is not at sleep. The few hours that remain outside immediate productive activity are all geared towards recharging and recovering in order to plunge back in to another round of 60-hour weeks without breaks, eating at desks, limiting all social interaction to the needs of the job. Escape from this rat wheel for any length of time, and re-entry may be foreclosed. This tightly regulated, high-pressure, insecure work life is the reality underlying the empty labels "middle class" and "professional." The inhumane pace, the pointlessness of so much work, the ecological blindness and waste, and the absence of control over the purpose and content of one's work, all contribute to the erosion of status and morale. But the workers facing these dynamics predominantly seek individual solutions, paths of personal escape, sometimes to new jobs, or more commonly, to their "real" work in their "free" time.

CHAPTER 3:
"WHAT YOU SEE ME DOING, ISN'T WHAT I DO"[1]

> The central figure of our society... is the figure of the
> insecure worker, who at times "works" and at times does
> not "work," practices many different trades without any
> of them actually being a trade, has no identifiable profes-
> sion, or, rather, whose profession is to have no profes-
> sion, and cannot therefore identify with his/her work,
> but regards his/her 'true' activity the one he/she devotes
> himself to in the gaps between his/her paid work.
>
> —*Andre Gorz*[2]

It is difficult or impossible to make a living from many of the things
that people really want to do (e.g. art, dance, music, history, philosophy), and so there has been a steady increase of people living a
bifurcated life. On one side is the crushing necessity of making money,
on the other is the creative urge to find fulfilling work, whether or not
it is paid. Frequently this bifurcation results in "time-theft," the common practice of doing one's own activities while at work. "Time-theft"
can be as mundane as pretending to work while chatting with a friend
on the phone, or as assertive as using facilities and resources at work to
produce for oneself—appropriating building materials and consumer
items, writing novels, or designing one's own website.

Capital is a relationship of social power that warps human relations to
its perverse logic, but it faces persistent resistance. Seeking to overcome
blockages to profitability and continued capital accumulation, capitalists
redesign labor processes, integrate new machinery, move factories overseas or across the country, and use state power to enforce their interests
legally and militarily. People resist these forces in their normal daily lives
by carving out spaces of autonomy in which they act concertedly outside
(and often against) capital's attempts to commodify their activities. Capital inexorably seeks to colonize all such spaces and relationships and re-
integrate them into the market logic of buying and selling.

Since capital's counterattack began in the mid-1970s, the working
class has been systematically altered, or "decomposed." Movements
across the planet by the late 1960s had pushed for not only shortened
working hours and increased pay, but crucially, had begun contesting
the very definitions of life and work and the reasons why we live the way

we do. The oil shock of 1973–74 was the first loud response of a world capitalist elite afraid of losing its power and determined to rein in an unruly working class.[3] Historic wage highs were reached in the early 1970s in the U.S. and elsewhere. Since that time, working hours have been radically intensified and in the 1990s absolutely lengthened, while wages in real dollars have remained constant or diminished. In spite of an economy four times larger than it was in 1980 (as measured by the terribly inaccurate and misleading Gross Domestic Product, or GDP[4]) in the early 21st century we are working more hours per year and working much harder to sustain life that has not improved! Most people are just glad to have work and income in a world where "falling" is perceived as a real possibility, where one doesn't have to look beyond the next street corner to see how abject life can be if you don't stay in the good graces of ever-more demanding employers.

Abdication to the initiative of capital has led to the mind-numbing expansion of useless work, while social needs are neglected and creative capacities left dormant. People are richly rewarded to create advertising, to invent new "financial instruments," to design "anti-personnel" bombs, to analyze how to increase credit card use (debt), etc. The same society won't spend meaningful resources on early childhood education and starves public schools of the most basic resources. Vast public subsidies pour into agribusiness and oil company coffers while urban gardens are bulldozed to make way for box stores and warehouses, and organic farmers have to sell their unsubsidized products at higher prices.

Basic needs are going unmet for millions. Worse still, urgent efforts at long-term and medium-term planning to adapt to the increasingly visible collapse of natural systems are rejected out of ideological blindness. But individual human ingenuity is flowing in spite of government and corporate obstacles. People who work for solutions to the social and ecological crises of our time supercede the role of simple laborers in order to plan and carry out incredible amounts of necessary (if frequently unpaid) work.

WHY "CLASS COMPOSITION"?

> Many of those in what I have called the autonomist tradition have [noted] that the point of revolution is to end the identity of working class, or as Marx says in the *Grundrisse*, the existence of people as "mere worker."
> —*Harry Cleaver*[5]

> In place of a narrow conception of the working class
> (as the waged industrial proletariat) which ignored or
> sought to subordinate other oppressed segments of soci-
> ety, we have had for several decades a complex theory of
> class composition explicitly designed to grasp, without
> reduction, the divisions and power relationships within
> and among the diverse populations on which capital
> seeks to maintain its dominion of work throughout the
> social factory—understood as including not only the
> traditional factory but also life outside of it which capi-
> tal has sought to shape for the reproduction of labor
> power.... This theory explores how various sectors of
> the working class, through the circulation of their strug-
> gles, "recompose" the relations among them to increase
> their ability to rupture the dialectic of capital and to
> achieve their own ends. In response, over time and ac-
> cording to the dynamics of that recomposition, capital
> is forced to seek a restructuring "decomposition" of the
> class—which may involve the repression and/or the in-
> ternalization of self-activity—to restore its control.
>
> —*Harry Cleaver*[6]

Rooted in early industrialization and a teleological materialism that assumed progress towards communism was inevitable, traditional Marxist historiography grossly oversimplified real history into a series of linear steps and straightforward transitions, with more advanced stages inexorably supplanting more backward ones. Nowadays we know better. History is wildly contingent and unpredictable. Many alternate paths leave from the current moment, as they have from every previous moment too. Bitter struggles, military accidents, secret conspiracies, and the best-laid open plans, not to mention the vagaries of weather, nature, disease, and human culture have all pushed and pulled to bring us to this moment.

"Class composition" frames the ebb and flow of social movements that erupt and subside in relation to the dynamics of economic expansion and contraction, but it is not narrowly determined by that relationship. The complexity of daily life can lead at times to atomization, political fragmentation, or depoliticization, and at other times create common sensibilities or unified political responses. In order to overturn fatalism and unleash our potential to live consciously and collaboratively, it is fruitful to study the social conditions under which life is reproduced, and how those relationships and institutions that shape our lives are understood.

Some radicals have challenged or reinvigorated the pat definitions that have come down from earlier political movements. One of the freshest new analysts is John Holloway, who breaks with the nearly religious adherence to a glorified concept of the working class. He has written, "Capitalism is the ever renewed generation of class, the ever renewed class-ification of people."

> We do not struggle *as* working class, we struggle *against* being working class, against being classified... There is nothing good about being members of the working class, about being ordered, commanded, separated from our product and our process of production. Struggle arises not from the fact that we are working class but from the fact that we-are-and-are-not working class, that we exist against-and-beyond being working class, that they try to order and command us but we do not want to be ordered and commanded, that they try to separate us from our product and our producing and our humanity and our selves and we do not want to be separated from all that. In this sense, working-class identity is not something "good" to be treasured, but something "bad," something to be fought against, something that is fought against, something that is constantly at issue.

> The working class cannot emancipate itself in so far as it is working class. It is only in so far as we *are not* working class that the question of emancipation can even be posed... The working class does not stand outside capital: on the contrary it is capital that defines it (us) as working class. Labor stands opposed to capital, but it is an internal opposition. It is only as far as labor is something *more than* labor, the worker *more than* a seller of labor power, that the issue of revolution can even be posed.[7]

Precisely because so many people find their work lives inadequate, incomplete, degrading, pointless, stupid, and oppressive, they form identities, communities, and meaning outside of paid work—in spaces where they *are not* working class. It is in these activities that people who are reduced on the job to "mere workers" become fully human, fully engaged with their capacities to create, to shape, to invent, to cooperate without compulsion, to bring consciously to life relations, objects, and activities of their own choice. The semi-conscious war between these life-affirming, self-emancipating behaviors and the coercive domination of money, property, and survival amidst contrived scarcity is the core investigation of this book.

The decomposition of the working class imposed by three decades of global crisis and restructuring has isolated most people and broken the transmission belts of class and community memory, at least in North

America. Such a severe fragmentation stands in the way of the human need for community, solidarity, and cooperation. For the most part the glue that holds human society together seems to be commerce, but countless invisible daily interactions precede commerce, without which the economy could not exist. From a moment of conversation, to watching a child, to helping someone lift an object or make a choice, daily life is the pre-existing raw material that capital seeks to exploit.

The steady "mining" of daily life—of the capacities and increasingly the knowledge of people who sell their labor—feeds the expansion of new kinds of products. People, left to their own devices, learn, think, mature, and invent, etc. This makes them more productive workers, who can give greater skills and knowledge to capital when employed as wage-labor. This underscores one paradox lying at the heart of the technological advancement: When human labor is supplanted by machines, humans are free to work less and pursue their own interests, but the activities individuals pursue often bolster their usefulness to capital when they're employed. Moreover, capital seeps into every nook and cranny of life and creates new work as fast as it reduces the human labor needed in previous systems. In her book *Network Culture* Tiziana Terranova describes how this restructured capitalism has annexed more and more of our "free time":

> ... the paradox of immaterial labor in the age of general intellect, is that the production of value increasingly takes place in what was supposed to be "liberated time" and in "free action," in as much as at least in late capitalist societies, this liberated, intensive time is the force that drives innovation in the information economy.... in a sense, we might say that productivity starts before one even goes to work and cannot be measured according to traditional criteria.[8]

Instead of a steady reduction of working time, capital brings a vast intensification and expansion of work, such that we are now enduring one of the greatest "speed-ups" in human history (alongside one of the sharpest accelerations of wealth polarization). Modern capitalism spends enormous resources selling its products as replacements for human interaction, portraying commodities as superior alternatives. But technological mediation is unsustainable—not just in ecological terms (though it is that too) but crucially, in social terms. Human beings want to congregate, socialize, party, discuss and debate, share and cooperate. It may be the most powerful drive we have.

As businesses spend ever more money advertising endless rivers of New Stuff, increasing numbers of people are turning away. Still at the margins of modern life for now, many individuals and communities are making new ways to live together based on engagement with a range of ecologically informed technologies. These initiatives don't just promise to reinvent our relationships with transportation, food, energy, art, and culture, but underpin a deeper challenge to how we frame knowledge and truth. Out of these emergent convivial communities, which are largely grounded in unpaid practical work, a gradual reversal of the extreme atomization of modern life is beginning.

Terranova's argument, while brilliant and on the mark, can be taken too literally. Capital does co-opt, but not everything that we do in our free time is (or could possibly be) immediately co-opted by capital. In the context of a global ecological crisis, a crisis of the commons that is already centuries old, and the increasingly urgent necessity of shifting how we choose what work is done and how to do it, a new kind of class consciousness is taking shape. This new class consciousness escapes the boundaries that have been erected around the concept over the last two centuries.

BEYOND SUBORDINATION

> ...the foundation of complete, successful revolution that crafts new worlds lies in the infinity of atomistic and molecular rebellions through which people rupture the sinews of the capital-labor relation and create alternative relations—however temporary and limited those ruptures and those alternatives may be.
>
> —*Harry Cleaver*[9]

Capital shapes society and individual lives through the omnipresent Spectacle. An incessant stream of images and declarations create the impression that there is one form of life and everyone is contentedly living it, or urgently trying to achieve it. Alternatives are tolerated insofar as they reinforce the primary dynamics of spectacular society, where business dominates unchallenged and the public tacitly accepts wage-labor, where shopping is treated as the sole arena for individual freedom, where the mute consumption of representations of life replaces active living. But the system is riddled with fissures. The falseness of Spectacular representation steadily produces dissenters. Dissent may erupt into direct insubordination, but the common exodus from capitalism's hollow "choices" often amounts to *non*-subordination. Social movements create alternate systems of "self-valorization" (creating the meaning and purpose of one's own life). But these new modes of self-valorization, which fall outside the categories of jobs, shopping, and consumption, are buried beneath the reigning Spectacle and thus relatively invisible.

People may work on their homes, their cars, etc., (activities that remain within the logic of individual consumers) but when they fight for open space, create community gardens, challenge the design of cities and the auto-centric policies of planners, they are *producing* new kinds of life—which are then vulnerable to further co-optation and reintegration. It is an endless dialectic of partial escape, partial co-optation, and the production of new initiatives that strain to break the cycle.

Many initiatives outside the market reflect awareness of the false "externalities" created by capitalist logic. Cheap food in the supermarket depends on massive subsidized energy inputs (for example, the tax breaks for oil companies and trucking firms, or the billions of dollars spent on wars to maintain dominance over oil producing regions), as well as long-term exhaustion of arable soil, aquifers, and huge dead-zones where nitrogen-rich agricultural runoff leads to oceanic species collapse. Automobiles depend on those same hidden costs that subsidize the global oil/petrochemical industries, as well as public expenditures on roads and bridges, and incalculable medical costs from collisions, pollution, stress, and so on. Community gardening, alternative fuels, and bicycling, on the other hand, all represent technological revolts that integrate a positive ecological vision with practical local behaviors. The theory and practice of permaculture advances this logic much further (more on this in the next chapter). Taken together, this constellation of practices is an elaborate, decentralized, uncoordinated, collective research and development effort exploring a potentially post-capitalist, post-petroleum future.

We know exponentially more about planetary ecology than ever before, from micro to macro, from global climate to species interdependency. But the powers-that-be and the broad majority of the population continue to entertain false assumptions and defend daily behaviors that are demonstrably destroying Earth as a viable habitat for humans (and a rapidly expanding list of other species). A much warmer climate-challenged world might be a reality much sooner than scientists currently predict. When that sets in, basic industries like agribusiness, oil, chemicals, automobiles, asphalt (and many more), will probably contract suddenly, often into total collapse. In their place will emerge local, site-specific, derivative, ecologically sane alternatives under (some kind of new democratic) community design and control, based on the social and technological experiments going on already. Some of it will trickle down from labs and businesses that manage to shift their attention (in harmony with demands of social upheavals) to address existing and impending needs that are not defined by corporate profitability. But most of the solid alternatives will reside in the heads and the hands of the tinkerers who wouldn't wait for approval, and are already creating viable prototypes in the present. The clever inventors of human- and ecology-focused *technique* seek to adapt basic infrastructure to reproducible, long-lasting, biologically sound devices and processes.

DIY

> The Do It Yourself [DIY] ethic seeks to overthrow the idea that we will be provided for. We will provide for ourselves, through educating each other, through collective decision making. It fits into this larger concept of an ideal society.   ·
>
> *—Ben Gillock*[10]

> As with most subcultural phenomena co-opted by the mainstream, the term "DIY" has been exploited to the point of mediocrity by advertising agencies and corporate profiteers. Walk into any corporate chain hardware store and you'll be bombarded by a DIY that has become a hollow, menacing mockery of the fervent DIY ethos that fuels much of the subcultural underground.
>
> *—Kyle Bravo*[11]

> Like [DIY] zinesters, hobbyists are fleeing their alienated work experiences by creating their own product and sharing that experience with others… the fact that millions of "normal" Americans share the basics of a practice that distinguishes work done for money from work done for love, holds out the promise that such critiques of alienated labor are not the sole possession of underground malcontents.
>
> *—Steven Duncombe*[12]

Do-It-Yourself tinkering is rooted in ecological principles as well as an urgent desire for high-quality human connections based on conviviality and pleasure. The latter desire shapes emergent communities in which people make new relationships, developing trust through sharing skills and endeavors. This is the early glimmer of a recomposing working class after three decades of dispersion, defeat, and disillusionment—based not on wage-work but on freely chosen, self-directed collaborations.

DIY begins with curiosity and a willingness to experiment. Part of its ruling ethos is to solve problems without relying on pre-packaged commodities, corporations, or large sums of money. It is founded on a creative search for sustainable solutions that can replace our crippling dependencies on the alienating social relations of mainstream society. DIY is rooted in an instinctual mistrust of scientific expertise as promoted by elite institutions and their employees, but DIY tinkering *itself* is firmly rooted in science, nature, and ecology. DIY challenges the direction of science and technology from below. Instead of passively awaiting results from corporate and university laboratories that might actually be useful (which happens only accidentally, because there is no social mechanism to define or direct "useful" research) the protagonists of an autonomous technoculture are inventing practical technologies and developing and sharing everyday skills.

The work done in this grassroots realm can be read at least two ways. At its best it embodies a revolutionary exodus from the capitalist division of labor and its attendant hierarchies of elite expertise and inaccessible technologies. At worst, it becomes institutionalized as a business or non-profit organization that is better understood as a type of "farm team" for capitalism, where necessary reforms begin to percolate and develop. This frequently happens when a movement survives long enough—it becomes co-opted back into the larger dynamics of the world economy.

Autonomous grassroots technological initiatives give rise to new social constellations and self-directed practices, even if they eventually become businesses. Implicit in these efforts is the capacity to abruptly change direction, to shape the world consciously instead of reproducing it as it is. In DIY, the capacity to radically change things is already peeking out from the interstices of "normal" life, carried in the idea of general intellect (this is further developed in the next chapter).

Finally, DIY communities are developing a locally-based, self-reliant engagement with practical science and everyday technologies that redefines purposeful engagement with work. This demonstrates an emerging, self-organizing working-class recomposition based on exodus, sometimes emerging from so-called advantageous or privileged positions, sometimes from so-called disadvantageous or oppressed positions. DIY tinkerers directly satisfy socially determined needs and desires without their work or its results being reduced to products for sale.

The do-it-yourself idea has been around for most of the 20th century, but it only became a social signifier for alternative subcultures starting in the late 1960s. The cultural rejection of "straight culture," that started among the Beats of a generation earlier, stimulated a new interest in self-sufficiency and independence from an oppressive mainstream society. The 1968 appearance of the first *Whole Earth Catalog*, subtitled "access to tools," helped a generation of drop-outs share skills and technological know-how to renovate decrepit inner city buildings, start organic gardens and farms, and rediscover "obsolete" techniques. The *Whole Earth Catalog* reviewed classes, books, and journals, and circulated information about where to find tools for carpentry, masonry, gardening, welding, etc. The *WEC* was part of the great wave of experimental, often communal efforts that conceived of themselves as revolutionary movements to reinvent life. These revolutionary pretensions wore off quickly as the alternative marketplace of goods and services exploded, responding to a broader shift in capitalism away from uniform mass production and toward smaller batches of superficially different products for expanding niche markets.

Ben Guzman of Los Angeles's Bike Kitchen and Martin Leugers of San Francisco's Chopper Riding Urban Dwellers both refer to "punk rock" ethics to describe their sense of revolt and outsider sensibility. In fact, the entire late 20th century 'zine phenomenon can be traced to the wild explosion of punk rock in the 1977–80 era.[13] In Minneapolis, DIY stalwart Matte Resist, a bike mechanic/advocate and a 'zine publisher, also connects DIY to a "punk" sensibility:

> As long as I've been involved in this "punk" culture, I've been inundated with the idea of DO IT YOURSELF. And it makes sense that fixing your own bike will save you money, but I couldn't really see how these little things made that big of a difference. One of the things that frustrated me was that it is difficult to 'do it yourself' when you don't know how and there is no one to teach you... The more we network, the more we can really step away from consumer culture. I figure that the more I can do for myself, the more I can do for someone else too. I can fix bikes, someone else can garden, or plumb or build stuff... I keep reading more about these communities that are becoming more self-sufficient, and don't have to rely upon grocery and department store chains, and that's where I really see the benefit in DIY.
>
> —*Matte Resist*[14]

Back in the late 1970s and early 1980s, punk music exploded as a rejection of the co-optation of rock'n'roll by music corporations who were selling "glam" rock or disco as the latest fad. Out of nowhere, but soon out of everywhere, kids from New York, San Francisco, Los Angeles, and the gritty urban neighborhoods of deindustrialized England were discovering the raw thrill of doing it themselves. Anti-fashion and raw, untrained three-chord rock burst forth, sending popular culture into thousands of fragments, most of them doggedly DIY.

The rebellious energy that fueled the first punk upheaval was explicitly anti-capitalist. It burst onto the scene during the dull post-Vietnam and post-Nixon era of Jimmy Carter and the Eagles. Connecting to dissenting movements as far back as the early 20th century Dadaists, on through the surrealists, the beats, and the early hippies, first-wave punks rejected staid middle-class norms: the drudgery of 9-to-5 jobs, the pointlessness of daily lives and daily lies. But in all their fury of rejection, the punks were enormously creative. As Jello Biafra told V. Vale in the seminal San Francisco punk paper *Search & Destroy*, "the most important thing punk did was bring back the independent record and the coinciding birth of the independent homemade 'fanzine.'"[15] The fanzine, in turn, expanded its terrain well beyond the confines of punk rock, as we can see, for example in the bicycling subculture (see Chapter 6). The zines brought with them a broader sense of what "punk rock" meant. Steven Duncombe explains, "As staunch contrarians, zinesters construct who they are and what they do in opposition to the rest of society. Their identity is a negative one. This negative identity is in many ways a legacy of punk rock. To a great degree, punk itself was created in opposition: *against* the commercial music of the mid-1970s, *against* the peace-and-love vibes of the hippie scene that by that time seemed a sham."[16] A generation later, the punk DIY culture persists, attracting new adherents to subcultures that pride themselves on self-sufficiency and ingenuity.

The energy punks brought to the music industry fueled a major expansion of the marketplace into a series of new niches and styles. Capital quickly exploited the fragmentation and adapted to the niche markets that emerged, in an example of the dialectic that continues to haunt all cultural rebellions in modern capitalist society. Rebellious energy often gets channeled into new forms of business, and ultimately serves to reproduce the same dynamics of commodification that led to the staleness and insipidity that inspired the revolt in the first place. As Stephen Duncombe eloquently put it, "Contemporary capitalism *needs* cultural innovation in order to open new markets, keep from stagnating, invest old merchandise with new meanings, and so on. Far from being a challenge to The Man, innovations in culture are the fuel of a consumer economy."[17] DIY punks, anxious to assert their independence and self-sufficiency, would find it difficult to survive without the resources they derive from mainstream society's waste. Cultural entrepreneurs discovered long ago that the innovations of youth culture were best discovered among the street kids who don't spend much money, but do continually reinvent style, fashion, and taste, providing raw material for next season's wares in upscale boutiques.

The American economy eagerly welcomed the countercultural expansion of the market, inventing products tailored to a still-dependent, consumerist DIY practice. How-to books and magazines proliferated, and were augmented by instructional videotapes when VCRs were widely adopted in the early 1980s. Hardware and lumber chains became one-stop shopping centers for the weekend do-it-yourselfers. The co-optation extended to gas stations when self-service pumps replaced attendants who washed windows and checked oil while the gas flowed. By the end of the century banks embraced DIY, installing ATMs everywhere to encourage customers to do for free what bank tellers were employed to do.

The cultural shift to doing-it-yourself allowed businesses to transfer significant operational costs to their customers, who now automatically perform their own service work for free as a matter of course. But the shift also corresponds to a shift in politics. Reagan came to power in the U.S. in 1980, promising to "get the government off of people's backs." In England Margaret Thatcher led the Conservative Party to power around the same time. Writing about the UK's DIY culture in 1998, George McKay observed: "the turn to a politics of Do It Your*self*, of self-empowerment, can be seen as a corollary of the Thatcherite notion of the privileging of the individual ('there is no such things as society')."[18] A deeper enshrining of the self has been growing in the U.S. since the 1950s. Subcultures like the beats and hippies actively promoted the elevation of individualism and self-expression through fashion (or anti-fashion), though this fact was obscured by their vaguely oppositional politics.

Fred Turner's brilliant history, *From Counterculture to Cyberculture*, shows how an early split in the 1960s movements between the formally political New Left and the back-to-the-land "new communalists" reinforced for the latter a rejection of politics and the public realm in favor of private, "elite" social networks.[19] The New Communalists, after undergoing a complex evolution that saw the collapse of their communes and the beginning of the personal computer business in the 1980s, fully embraced the corporate cybernetic business, and even the military worlds against which so many of their values had emerged post-WWII. Their "counterculture" values migrated into the "New Economy" libertarian and millennialist rhetoric of the 1990s.

Nick Bertoni, a former employee of the Exploratorium, founded the Tinkers' Workshop in Berkeley in the mid-1990s.[20] The premise of the workshop was radically open and egalitarian: it provided well-equipped space for free do-it-yourself public use. Bertoni explains, "My philosophy was to give it to people, and then they would give back. If you exercise that muscle a few times they get the idea."[21] Over time Bertoni and volunteers collected an enormous warehouse of discarded or surplus equipment and parts. The Tinkers' Workshop invites anyone to come in and use the tools and materials to fix their own possessions or to construct something new and take it home. Classes are sometimes held but a great deal of the work that transpires there is very specific and practical. Among their facilities are a tool and machine room full of power tools, heavy equipment, a library full of how-to resources, an electronics shop, a sewing and art room, and a collection of public address systems freely donated to political events. As Bertoni put it, "We often pull stuff out of the waste stream, repair it, or cobble stuff together to make a working machine." He went on to explain part of the motivation for his place:

> We're losing our ability to do things, we don't know how to affect the world, we don't understand the world physically... Education in the physical realm, there's very little of it done in schools anymore. There are no shops or art classes. We're shrinking [our ability to] understand tangibly how to affect the world, and have some kind of way to judge ideas. I think you really have to understand the physical world before you can make political decisions.[22]

While fervent individualism underpins most of the radical political expression of the last quarter century (the same era in which traditional working classes were decomposed by deindustrialization and global restructuring) the punk rock DIY ethic imprinted itself on successive generations of rebellious youth who extended the ethic well beyond its origins in the music scene. DIY culture has looped back to embrace cooperative and collective practices, albeit well removed from the politics of the Old or New Left that nurtured those forms in past generations. Still, we can find echoes and shadows of earlier political practices in DIY subcultures. Richard J.F. Day describes the politics embedded in DIY:

> DIY practices include *dropping out* of existing institutions; *subversion* of existing institutions, through parody; *impeding existing* institutions, via property destruction, "direct action case work," blockades, and so on; *prefiguring alternatives* to existing institutions... and finally, *construction of alternatives* to existing forms that render redundant, and thereby take power from, the neoliberal project.[23]

Politically motivated DIY culture publicly rejects the insipid (albeit compelling to many) fantasies of the market. For some people engaged in the underground bicycle culture or the sustainable biofuels movement, it is a point of pride to make do with the materials and tools at hand. Recycling and re-using is an important value in itself. Buying new components, or even tools, is often scorned. Most people, however, eschew such purist standards and occupy a more fluid location between subcultural participation and market capitalism, improvising solutions without rigid guidelines.

If these social initiatives are nothing more than changing shopping habits, the capitalist way of life is reinforced, not undermined (though choosing to *re-use* already implies a different relationship to late capitalist culture's focus on throw-aways and new purchases). DIY tinkering and inventing goes further when it begins to *produce* a different way of life. From reinhabiting cities with new transit choices to growing one's own food in community gardens (challenging private property by making *common* the garden lands), to grassroots technological movements in fuels, software, and medicine, people are taking initiatives outside of wage-labor and business to make the world we want to live in *now*.

Bertoni's Tinkers' Workshop sponsors DIY and skill sharing workshops that attract a large and diverse population in West Berkeley, among it a cohort of young, passionate anarchists. As Bertoni says:

> We attract a lot of neo-anarchist and DIY types. They're survivalist, smart, constructive, courageous, wild, young, and they have a lot of energy and time to do things. They're full of zeal and they really plug and plow hard for a bit and then they go off somewhere. They gotta go to Costa Rica or go dumpster-dive (you know I was dumpster-diving 40 years ago! But don't tell them that! It ruins their party). They see valuable skills here that they want to learn.
>
> [We have people helping us transition to a new facility who are] kind of dropouts, people who came away disillusioned from the science and engineering worlds and have other ideas and want a place in a community.[24]

And DIY practice has still deeper implications. By refusing to be mere workers, carrying on creative and self-directed work outside of the subordination of wage-labor, individuals embody two distinctly radical goals. First, their human complexity is fully engaged in creative, hands-on work. Secondly, they are producing a material world that exceeds the bounds of capital's limitations, simultaneously making manifest their individual freedom while proving an old Marxist assertion that the measure of wealth is no longer labor time but "disposable time," that time in which we can develop our talents as we choose. Instead of being exploited as surplus labor, the tinkerers are appropriating their own time and know-how to ends of their own choosing; in a real sense they are already redefining and redirecting social wealth away from capital and towards socially defined needs.

Richard Day sees these initiatives as the beginning of a different kind of future:

> [These are] new ways of conceptualizing the subject of political action, as well as the collectivities in which s/he participates, which s/he in fact *creates and maintains* through her/his activity. Here I am speaking not of the

"citizen" of the state/civil society nexus, nor of the revolutionary/ libertarian nomad, but of the smith, the autonomous subject of the coming communities."[25]

Of course many of the people who work in these emerging project-oriented communities put in some weeks or months or even years and then move on. The intimate and trusted relationships at the core of these groups depend on egalitarian practices and reliably fulfilled expectations of mutual aid and respect. DIY-based projects are usually ad hoc and temporary, but when they last, the long-term sustainability becomes a problem: Beyond the typical lack of time and resources, "successful" movements face institutionalized integration into capitalist society (rent, taxes, utilities, sometimes wages) which saps the original liberatory motivations. Still, the common values and material experiences gained during the life of these projects reinforce each contributor's imagination, self-esteem, and stamina, and provide indispensable lessons in self-organization. DIY experiences become key foundations for ongoing, sustainable commitments to radical change.

CHAPTER 4
CONTESTING THE EVOLUTION OF SCIENCE

This world is reaching a breaking point. After three centuries of capitalist expansion, the entire planet is facing unprecedented crises of urbanization, resource depletion, poverty, climate change, and the breakdown of political systems. Still, capitalist ideologues continue to claim that these problems will be solved by "staying the course" and relying on market competition. Meanwhile, a new epistemology for the 21st century is emerging from the anonymous contributions of millions of people across the globe, many of whom have nurtured traditional relationships to nature that are now being "rediscovered" for their harmonious and productive relationship to local ecologies.

Precisely because contemporary capitalism depends on technologically sophisticated workers who are joined together in dense networks of communication and cooperation, the notion of "general intellect" contains a kernel of radical possibility: a dramatic seizure and repurposing of socialized work. In other words, if we ourselves make the world every day through the infinite tasks we individually carry out *together*, why couldn't we stop making this impossibly crazy, degrading, and brutalizing world, and instead make *together* a world of *our own choosing*?

Nick Dyer-Witheford lays out the basic conflict in his excellent analysis of contemporary labor politics, *CyberMarx*:

> At its present very high level of technoscientific development, corporate power finds itself dependent on levels of cooperative activity, unimpeded communication, and free circulation of knowledge that, far from being easily integrated into its hierarchies, exist in persistent tension with its command.[1]

> The question of whether capital will successfully segment post-Fordist labor power, or if, on the contrary, rebellious subjects will break down these barriers to establish new alliances, lies at the core of what I call "the contest for general intellect." In this contest the contemporary proletariat fights to actualize "general intellect," not according to the privatizing, appropriative logic of capital, but in ways that are deeply democratic and collective, and hence truly "general."[2]

Taking Marx's point that "general intellect" is embodied in the scientific and technical apparatus of society, it follows that the realm of science and technology is a central location for the present battle between collective, human values and those of capital. A David-and-Goliath epic plays out between the large institutions with their strict profit motives who frequently dictate the pursuits and uses of science, and practical alternatives emerging outside of the academy or business, notably among permaculturists and other technological innovators. For example, the steady increase of pharmaceutical drugs overpriced for some and inaccessible for others, is met with a corresponding growth (or return to) herbal and other non-proprietary alternatives. Highly centralized energy "solutions" are answered by micronodal, decentralized alternatives. Media behemoths are whipsawed by new forms of media proliferating on the margins of mass culture. And so on.

Cognitive processes like scientific thought, technological imagination, and an ability to work at a planning level generally, are all more important than ever as productive forces in modern life. They have been massively co-opted to the needs of business, but also applied to problems defined outside the logic of the market. David Holmgren describes how permaculture designers apply their insights and theories to practical problems of labor and energy use:

> Permaculture designers use careful observation and thoughtful interaction to reduce the need for both repetitive manual labor and for non-renewable energy and high technology. Thus, traditional agriculture was labor intensive, industrial agriculture is energy intensive, and permaculture-designed systems are information and design intensive... Computers are the most obvious feature of the information economy, but changes in the way we think, especially the emergence of design thinking, are more fundamental to the information economy than the hardware and software we use. Permaculture itself is part of this thinking revolution.[3]

Holmgren points out rightly that technology changes design and productive processes, but also, more deeply, these resistant and affirmative new technologies and practices begin to reshape our ideas and assumptions, slowly producing experiences quite different than those defined by profit and capital. These contemporary behaviors, from permaculture and gardening to bicycling and programming, could be the material bases for new ways of thinking, presaging a deep shift in basic epistemology.

GENERAL INTELLECT

The concept of "general intellect" was first described by Karl Marx, but has been updated in the past decade and a half. Marx was attempting to show how the logic of capitalism would undermine itself by replacing the human labor on which profit and surplus value depended with machinery. He wrote that the creation of wealth in capitalist society depended more on "the general state of science and on the progress of technology, or the application of this science to production" than on direct labor time.[4] He understood how the fundamental role of individual human labor in social reproduction would be diminished. Workers and their skills would be gradually replaced by the general social knowledge embedded in industrial machinery. Insofar as the vast apparatus of industrialized society continued to function it would be evidence that life was under the control of an abstract "general intellect"; according to Marx.

> Nature builds no machines, no locomotives, railways, electric telegraphs, self-acting mules etc. ... They are *organs of the human brain, created by human hand*; the power of knowledge, objectified. The development of fixed capital indicates to what degree general social knowledge has become a *direct force of production*, and to what degree, hence, the conditions of the process of social life itself have come under the control of the general intellect and have been transformed in accordance with it.[5]

Recent theoreticians have postulated the idea of "mass intellectuality" to refer to the ways that people successfully function within this complex, technologized world. Going beyond Marx's notion that the general intellect was fixed in the physical machinery—or perhaps applying a more rigorous, updated Marxian analysis—theoreticians such as Paolo Virno and Maurizio Lazzarato have broadened general intellect to include the living labor producing the conceptual world that keeps the economy humming. Cooperative networks stretching across oceans, communicative links upon which modern business depends, and cultural commodities all underpin and ensure the reproduction of modern life. The complex global economy is seen in this view as a vast social factory in which everyone contributes whether they're paid or not, and surplus wealth is appropriated as profits by the most powerful and ruthless blocs of capital, backed by coercive global institutions and ultimately, brute force (a distinctly material phenomenon).

> The "general intellect" includes formal and informal knowledge, imagination, ethical tendencies, mentalities and "language games." Thoughts and discourses function

in themselves as productive "machines" in contemporary labor and do not need to take on a mechanical body or an electronic soul.... [A]ll the more generic attitudes of the mind gain primary status as productive resources; these are the faculty of language, the disposition to learn, memory, the power of abstraction and relation and the tendency towards self-reflexivity. General intellect needs to be understood literally as intellect in general: the faculty and power to think, rather than the works produced by thought—a book, an algebra formula, etc.

—*Paolo Virno*[6]

Among dissenting scientists and technologists the power to think is reshaping itself in directions beyond the narrow confines of capital. Permaculture has grabbed the imagination of many technical and ecological rebels, and as an extra-institutional discipline, there is room for many people to creatively engage with it practically and theoretically.

READING THE BOOK OF NATURE: THE NEW (OLD) SCIENCE OF PERMACULTURE

The landscape is the textbook.
    —*David Holmgren, co-founder of Permaculture, 2002*

Dürer and the other artisans [in the 1500s] laid the foundations for a new epistemology, a new *scientia* based on nature.
    —*Pamela H. Smith,* The Body of the Artisan[7]

A lot of what we think is gone is just hidden underneath the cement. Under the cement is the hope to bring back the ecosystem...
    —*Erik Ohlsen*[8]

As people plumb the broad body of knowledge that is humanity's heritage new syntheses of traditional wisdom and modern technology are emerging. The field of permaculture stands at the forefront of the effort to reclaim the wisdom of millennia, but it goes beyond a simple recapitulation of traditional and indigenous knowledge. To its practitioners it represents a new holistic design *science* that builds on observing the gamut of human-nature relationships through time, while still embracing the tenets of modern science.

Peter Bane, publisher of *The Permaculture Activist*, explains the synergy between permaculture and tradition: "While the synthesis of nature observation with science and grassroots activism, in a context of global resource limits, is novel to Permaculture, the elements used in its design system are in many cases ancient."[9] The coda published inside each issue of his journal offers this succinct summary:

> Permaculture is a holistic system of DESIGN, based on direct observation of nature, learning from traditional knowledge, and the findings of modern science. Embodying a philosophy of positive action and grassroots education, Permaculture aims to restructure society by returning control of resources for living: food, water, shelter, and the means of livelihood, to ordinary people in their communities, as the only antidote to centralized power. For 25 years Permaculture has combined top-down thinking with bottom-up action to make a world of difference in over 60 countries. We are everywhere.[10]

There are twelve basic principles of permacultural design described in David Holmgren's book.[11] One of the most influential of these principles is the mandate to "produce no waste," which has shaped at least two generations of activists. Capitalist ideologues have evaded this dictum by promoting anti-littering and recycling campaigns, but the permacultural creed has influenced many social technologists, from the discarded bicycle hackers to waste veggie oil biofuel developers, and the occupiers of vacant urban (wasted) lots. Many permaculture practitioners themselves are described by writer Toby Hemenway as master scavengers, "who have slowly gleaned waste and cast-offs to create charming and original permaculture sites. These people live close to the bone, and have learned to harness our culture's surplus energy and material flows as well as its social network."[12]

Another key principle informing this deeper radicalism is to "use edges and value the marginal." Conceptually, most important ideas start far from the mainstream of society, dismissed by the powerful and wealthy that benefit from the status quo. In ecological terms, margins and edges tend to be areas of maximum fertility and vital biological exchange, both conceptually and literally. Wetlands provide important buffers between dry land and oceans and rivers, harboring an abundance of life forms vital to biological processes on both sides. The edge between forest and field is another important margin in the web of life, a boundary encroached upon by centuries of urban growth towards surrounding open lands. Utopians and radicals have long dreamed of a new harmony between city and country, seeking to occupy the sweet spot between the two contrasting environments. Experimental thinking on society's margins is the fertile ground from which a radically better life is growing.

Beyond good gardening techniques, permacultural design emulates the complex interactions of sun, wind, water, plants, and animals that give natural systems their productivity. This design "patterning" applies equally to a patio garden and an entire city. As David Holmgren puts it, "Permaculture is a conceptual framework and an emerging design system rather than any specific technical or behavioral solution. Its focus is on redesign and integration of our lifestyles, livelihoods and land uses in keeping with ecological realities."[13] In fact, permaculture is but one named thread of a series of overlapping traditions and approaches that underpin the new science. Others are called sustainable agriculture, agroecology, biodynamic farming, urban gardening, seed saving, composting, and more.

Permaculture, a term coined by Holmgren and Bill Mollison in Australia in the mid-1970s, has emerged from its first generation of development to become a vital alternative to the specialized, reductionist thinking that dominates official science and modern industry. This is the mentality that, for example, chews up old-growth forests to make furniture and toothpicks. Efforts to become more sustainable lead to tree farms based on an industrial model of single species planted in organized rows to promote rapid growth. No attention is paid to the forest as a system, as an integrated ecology itself.

Permaculture has already had a profound influence on many of today's movements. In fact, the continuities between the "back to the land" movements that arose in the 1960s and today's multi-faceted permaculture efforts are many. Back to the land rural revivalists tried to replace their urban alienation with a re-integrated life in nature. Most communes failed within a few years but the exploration of tools, techniques, and new social forms continued to adapt, integrating new insights from agronomy and ecology to produce knowledge and techniques used by permaculturists today. Holmgren says "I see the ecological and social movements of recent decades being part of a continuous lineage of counterculture in the modern world... The counterculture, misunderstood and denigrated in the cultural mainstream as a failure characterized by naïve and silly ideas, has been a major source of innovation."[14] Permaculture influences innovation in agricultural re-vegetation, agro-forestry, new tree crops, organic and biodynamic methods, rainwater catchment, and whole farm planning. It promotes the resurgence of farmers' markets and the rise of community-supported (or subscription) agriculture. In new ecological housing design, permaculture promotes integration of attached greenhouses, new systems to treat waste as an organic resource, and new and recycled building materials. Additionally, permaculture activists have been key proponents of community gardens and urban farming, as well as pushing for co-housing and eco-villages which have emerged in many places.[15]

Permaculture has gained thousands of participants over the past quarter century. The founding principles continue to inspire, but there are many more variations on the core values than might have been obvious at the outset. For starters, as a holistic design system, permaculture finds itself in intellectual competition with a variety of specialized disciplines that reject the generalist values favored by the new philosophy. Unconcerned, permaculturists have developed their own programs, classes, and workshops outside of official academic institutions to promulgate their methods, and position themselves apart from the categories that dominate what they criticize as reductionist science. Their work represents one of the most articulate expressions of the epistemological shift emerging on the margins of a palpably insane, dysfunctional world order.

REDUCTIONIST SCIENCE

> Science (hypothesis-experiment-results-refine hypothesis) has taken us a long way by a reductionist approach; permacultural thinking is holistic thinking—a complement, rather than an alternative, to scientific method... The questions on which our survival depends may not be answerable in binary fashion, using scientific method to give a thumbs-up or a thumbs-down to one hypothesis at a time. Instead, we need a new method that expands the options through a more holistic, but no less rigorous, approach modeled after biological evolution: observe, design, and re-design.
>
> —*John Wages*[16]

Plenty of permaculturists are escapees from university and corporate laboratories. They do not always abandon their jobs or their credentials, but such iconoclastic thinkers usually find their work better received among the freethinkers outside than they do among their own colleagues. A case in point is that of soil microbiologist Dr. Elaine Ingham, who has synthesized a new understanding of the dependency all earthly life has on a complex underground ecological system. Soil science has suffered incomplete and misguided analysis due to the specialization of mainstream academia, and Bart Anderson describes how Ingham's work escapes the specialization trap: "The picture of the soil food web that Ingham presents seems to be widely accepted. Rarely, however, are the ideas synthesized into a coherent whole. No wonder. The concepts come from many different fields—microbiology, ecology, soil science, and agronomy. Specialists absorbed in their own fields often find it difficult to see the big picture."[17]

Ingham also developed some unconventional methods of assessing soil health by counting organisms under a microscope, and has been a public advocate for aerobic compost tea. Permaculture activists have embraced her work, as it provides some solid scientific evidence backing their long-term advocacy for soil health, recognizing the basic indispensability of healthy soil to any kind of ecological renaissance. "Rebuilding the soil carbon, fertility and water to close to those of natural grasslands and forests... is arguably the greatest single contribution we could make to ensure the future survival of humanity," says David Holmgren.[18] Our culture is obsessed with eliminating dirt, so it's not surprising that few city folk ever think about our long-term dependency on the relatively thin layer of soil from which all our food comes. Writing in the 1950s Edward Hyams made an important contribution to early ecological thinking, emphasizing in his brilliant book *Soil & Civilization* that soil is not an "inanimate collection of mineral and organic particles, but a biological, an organic entity."[19]

Renegade scientists like Ingham who avoid specialization have given permaculture its ability to produce new insights. Another basic permaculture principle is to integrate, not segregate, directly contradicting the specialization promoted in academia. As Holmgren notes,

> While the cultural harvest from specialized reductionist thinking over the last few hundred years has been great, it is the integration and cross-fertilization of concepts and ideas that is now providing the most fruitful results for dealing with the systematic problems of the environmental crisis. Much of this integrated thinking is happening outside educational institutions.[20]

The collaborative efforts of outsider scientists and non-specialists mentioned above marks this type of cross-fertilization.

Outside the constrictive boundaries of formal science and academic institutions there is also space for other frames of reference. Religion and spirituality in numerous forms have re-emerged in this historic period, including among radical ecologists and many permaculturists. It's interesting that Holmgren sees the development of a "truly holistic science" as the only way to avert a "wholesale rejection of the culture of science." He has a frankly rationalist approach, unlike the many neo-pagan, earth-worshipping advocates who often reject science and rationalism in favor of a vague eco-centric spirituality.

> Permaculture [is] firmly within the culture of science.
> It is essentially concerned with improving the long-term

material well-being of people... By using an ecological perspective, permaculture sees a much broader canvas of utility than the more reductionistic perspectives, *especially the economic ones that dominate modern society*... Permaculture attracts many people raised in a culture of scientific rationalism because its wholism does not depend on a spiritual dimension... my own interpretation of the ethical principles of permaculture rests firmly on rational and humanist foundations. [emphasis added][21]

Instead of presuming that the historic achievements of science are automatically to be respected, permaculture thinkers, unbound by careers and corporate paymasters, are reinventing scientific inquiry with fresh but still rational and demonstrable approaches. With extra-institutional experimentation going on in farms, gardens, and backyards in many countries, a new appreciation for practical work is gaining credibility against the presumed expertise of specialized laboratory investigations. Holmgren describes the work of such innovators:

This type of action research has the effect of recognizing the innovative practitioner as the creative source... The call for the development of a new field of sustainability science is a direct recognition of the failure of current scientific methods and disciplines to deal with the diverse, integrated and complex nature of interactions between humans and their environment.[22]

Wes Jackson is an *eminence grise* of the permaculture world too. He advocates an "ignorance-based worldview" as a way of going beyond the hubris of science that assumes it can always devise the next techno-fix for the mess it has already made. By acknowledging ignorance, Jackson argues humans would have to think of new questions that go beyond available answers. Most importantly for a permaculturist frustrated by the separation of knowledge into artificially distinct fields, he thinks an ignorance-based worldview "would also do the absolutely necessary job of driving knowledge out of its categories."[23] Thomas Kuhn famously investigated how scientific paradigms give way to whole new ways of seeing[24]—but not before loyalists to the old paradigm put up a mighty fight to preserve their fading expertise. The pressure permacultural and other wholistic scientists are putting on institutions is slowly eroding the mechanistic-based expertise that underpins modern life and its crises.

A compelling example of specialization-induced myopia is the notion that jungles and forests are untouched by human intervention. In fact, humans often live in these areas, where as forest dwellers they practice traditional slash and burn methods. Their work produced rich food

forests appropriate to the tropical climates in which they lived. Toby
Hemenway writes about this assumption-based blindness:

> Modern anthropologists scouted tropical settlements
> for crop fields—the supposed hallmark of a sophisti-
> cated culture—and, noting them largely absent, pro-
> nounced the societies "hunter-gatherer, with primitive
> agriculture." How ironic that these scientists were mak-
> ing their disdainful judgments in the shade of brilliantly
> complex food forests crammed with several hundred
> carefully tended species of multifunctional plants, a sys-
> tem perfectly adapted to permanent settlement in the
> tropics. It just looks like jungle to the naïve eye.[25]

A good example of a holistically-minded scientific hypothesis advanced by permacultural logic is the story of the American chestnut
tree and the passenger pigeon. Peter Bane wrote a 2003 article connecting the extermination of the passenger pigeon in the late 1880s
with the blight-induced crash of the chestnut trees twenty years later.
He suggests that the guano of millions of roosting passenger pigeons
was a crucial nutritional source for the massive chestnut trees occupying shallow, poor soils in the eastern Appalachian Mountains. When the
pigeons were wiped out, the annual shit-infusion of nitrogen-rich food
for the trees was stopped, and after two decades of weakening immune
systems, the trees succumbed to the blight. Slipping out of the common
assumption that keystone species are large predators at the top of the
food chain, Bane argues,

> I prefer the view that keystone functions can be played
> by many actors on the ecological stage: prey species,
> habitat modifiers, predators, and more... It invites free
> play of the imagination; we are in a situation where the
> scientific method alone will not save us. Great engage-
> ment by the public in scientific inquiry is desperately
> needed.[26]

There is a big debate among ecological advocates between top-down
control (predators) and bottom-up control (nitrogen effects on community composition, species abundance) and arguments on all sides
deserve close evaluation and testing. But public engagement in scientific inquiry is essential, not just as observers and testers, but as citizens
who can ask questions and shape inquiries before, during, and after
scientific experts frame the debates.

OLD SCIENCE MEETS NEW

In many fields of science an epistemological shift is emerging. Philosopher Daniel Dennett was quoted in a recent magazine article, characterizing a still common attitude among contemporary biologists: "all life is founded upon an 'impersonal, unreflective, robotic, mindless little scrap of molecular machinery'—machinery in which 'there's nobody home.'"[27] Molecular biology tells us that the nature of an organism is expressed by its genes (like a computer operating system for a living being)—a view that has crashed scientifically even while it continues to define a popular mindset driven by marketing for the pharmaceutical and genetic engineering industries.

> It is one of the more revealing paradoxes of modern science that molecular genetics, which is the poster child for the mechanistic approach to biology, shows the inadequacy of the operating-system approach. The question, 'where is the controlling mechanism?' has led geneticists back to the whole organism, as the source of unity and coherence.[28]

Robert Frenay has described how the marriage of machine-age linearity and capitalist development successfully provided the foundation for industrialism, but also systematically created unmeasured "externalities" that are now threatening the web of life. [29] Grassroots environmental political movements have been contesting capital's ability to "externalize" ecological costs for almost a half-century now. From these initiatives, new ways of thinking have emerged, not just in everyday practices, but now appearing too in high-end, advanced research in biological and ecological sciences, recasting our basic understanding of life.

One of the most basic assumptions underpinning the modern world used to be that we could clearly identify the boundary between the animate and inanimate worlds. Coming down to us from Descartes and his philosophical assertion that thinking is the essence of being, and that non-human beings are behaving mechanically, it has taken the western, scientific world a long time to get beyond this narrow dualism. The whole monotheistic world-view has always posited a uniquely dominating role for human life, relegating the "lesser" mammals and other life forms to a descending hierarchy of importance. Plants, insects, algae, bacteria, et al have been categorized as nonsentient beings.

But the boundaries are rapidly shifting. Research is unraveling the notion of "intelligence" to find so-called intelligent behavior in all forms of life. Jeremy Narby, an investigator of science, takes an interdisciplinary cruise across a number of fields with his anthropologist's eye in his book *Intelligence in Nature: An Inquiry into Knowledge.* He shakes up our assumptions about what we know and, crucially, *how knowing happens.*[30] His work, along with a generation of new thinking often castigated as "New Age,"[31] erodes the simplistic dualism putting humans above the rest of earth (this is not to say that humans don't have unique capabilities vis-à-vis other life forms—but the reverse is often true too).

Even that most successfully mechanistic of disciplines, physics, is under pressure from within. Researchers interviewed by Frenay increasingly question the existence of a clear boundary between life and non-life:

> The seamless flow of atoms from inert to living form and back again makes it hard for science to define what life is. [32]

> A pulsing interactivity also lies behind the stolid face of that reality once known as the inanimate world. As the physicist Max Born put it, "We have sought for firm ground and found none. The deeper we penetrate, the more restless becomes the universe; all is rushing about and vibrating in a wild dance."[33]

Our understanding of the process of knowing, or cognition, is also changing under a torrent of new philosophy and science. Separations between subject and object are growing blurry, while reductionistic practices defined by mechanistic assumptions are being discarded for more holistic approaches. Physicist and philosopher Fritjof Capra offers a unified theory for social and biological life in his 2002 book *The Hidden Connections*:

> Cognition is not a representation of an independently existing world, but rather a continual bringing forth of a world through the process of living. The interactions of a living system with its environment are cognitive interactions, and the process of living itself is a process of cognition... The identification of mind, or cognition, with the process of life is a novel idea in science, but it is one of the deepest and most archaic institutions of humanity. In ancient times, the rational human mind was seen as merely one aspect of the immaterial soul, or spirit. The basic distinction was not between body and mind, but between body and soul, or body and spirit... Mind is not a thing but a process... the brain is a specific structure through which this process operates. The relationship between mind and brain, therefore, is one between process and structure.[34]

These new scientific metaphors are rooted not in abstract laboratory research but emerge from a range of political and social changes underway during the past half-century. The ecological insights developed by non-scientists and the significant political opposition thrown up to un-trammeled "development" have opened space for rethinking basic as-sumptions about life. Catastrophic damage to the web of life has been condemned by critics going back decades, confronting scientists with the deathly "fruit" of their work.

In this vein, the work of agronomist Albert Howard in India in the 1920s and 1930s is a crucial foundation to the project of making visible the dire results of chemical farming, taken up more recently by Rachel Carson in her 1962 book *Silent Spring.* Howard's research among the ru-ral farmers of India led him to argue that we needed to treat "the whole problem of health in soil, plant, animal and man as one great subject."[35] Howard unsuccessfully argued against the so-called Green Revolution of chemical, centralized agriculture that forever altered the ecology of India (and the U.S. for that matter). But his work was lionized in the pages of J.I. Rodale's magazine *Organic Gardening and Farming* from its founding in 1940 onwards. When Wendell Berry cited Howard and re-viewed *Organic Gardening and Farming* in the *Last Whole Earth Catalogue* in 1971, the magazine's subscription base nearly doubled to 700,000.[36] Permaculture was one of the environmental alternatives which emerged from the first great wave of modern environmental awareness, following the Club of Rome report in 1972 (one of the first quasi-official reports to declare a "limit to growth") and the oil shocks of 1973 and 1974.[37] The desires, practices, and knowledge of thousands of people on farms and in urban gardens underpin a remarkable, unorganized, but increas-ingly effective repudiation of agribusiness.

The decades-old expansion of permaculture and organic farming is one of the material practices that have helped stimulate new ways of do-ing science. Similarly, the oil crises that started in the early 1970s and the persistent wars that sustain the petrochemical and auto industries have generated growing opposition. Grassroots experimentation in alternative energy sources has been an added impetus to new ways of framing the purpose of science and technology. Finally, growing mountains of waste generated by capitalism have generated a great deal of innovative tinker-ing as everyday people try to redesign and reinvent the material base of modern life, addressing issues from land-use to clean air and water.

All of this practical activity demonstrates an assertion made by Clif-ford Connor in his *People's History of Science.* "Scientific knowledge pro-duction is a *collective social activity*—essential contributions have been made by working people engaged in earning their daily bread, and elite theoreticians are often unjustly awarded all the credit for knowledge produced by many hands and brains."[38]

The origins of our mechanistically inspired scientific method can be traced to an earlier shift in basic epistemology. In the early 17th century natural philosophers (precursors to what we now call scientists) began to attack existing traditions based on syllogistic logic and geometrical demonstration. These techniques were centuries old, and best demonstrated in the writings of Aristotle and other ancients. In these ancient theoretical traditions direct experience was deemed an insufficiently reliable foundation on which to build a deductive system and allegedly could never have the same certainty as theory. The shift in thinking rejected received "pure" philosophical truth in favor of discovering truth through direct study of the "Book of Nature." As science historian Steven Shapin argues "Modern natural philosophers did not just *believe* things about the natural world; they *did* things to secure, to justify, and to distribute those beliefs. Doing natural philosophy, that is, was a kind of work."[39]

Like today's scientific elite toiling for corporations directly or in university labs, the work of early modern natural philosophers was shaped by the larger society and its priorities. As Shapin notes, "... if we want ultimately to understand the appeal of mechanical metaphors in the new scientific practices... we shall ultimately have to understand the power relations of an early modern European society whose patterns of living, producing, and political ordering were undergoing massive changes as feudalism gave way to early capitalism."[40] It is also important to note that just as Early Modern European social patterns were complex, the responses to purely theoretical knowledge were very diverse. The mechanistic mode that came to prevail was not the only path and its triumph was far from certain.

As early as the late 1400s and early 1500s, artisans and artists embraced the "Book of Nature" idea without turning their findings into codified mechanistic studies. Their new world view asserted knowledge derived from nature itself, a knowledge whose usefulness they demonstrated with their new ways of painting, curing illness, growing food, and much more. Their detailed observations led to the reconfiguration of knowledge as "science," a materialist method of "knowing" the world that modern historians usually attribute to Francis Bacon, Robert Boyle, and Galileo.

Pamela H. Smith, building on earlier work by the Soviet historian Edgar Zilsel, Steven Shapin, and others, delved into the materialist prehistory of science. A hugely influential, but largely forgotten character in that early history was the German doctor Paracelsus (whose full name was Theophrastus Bombast von Hohenheim). He was a major contributor to the new nature-based epistemology. We overlook him now because his long-ago embrace of a living, dynamic world lost out to the Cartesian inanimate world as machine-age science developed hand-in-hand with early capitalism. Smith argues persuasively that:

> The idea of an "active science" goes back not to Francis Bacon, but to the writings of and works of art of Dürer, Leonardo, Palissy, to the makers of the works of art that filled art and curiosity cabinets, and to the writings and persona of Paracelsus. These artisans and practitioners appealed to nature as the basis of their science... Paracelsus, Palissy, and others explicitly viewed their new science as part of a reform of philosophy. In this intellectual revolution from the bottom up, these artisans transformed the contemplative discipline of natural philosophy into an active one. Bacon's contribution was to codify the artisanal construction of knowledge that was already going on around him. In the process, he appropriated the empirical experiential knowledge, and transformed and elevated it by declaring it to be philosophy, the task of high intellect, not lowly artisans.[41]

Bacon's contribution cannot be denied, but we cannot deny either the appropriative relationship he had with the common knowledge that had been growing collaboratively in workshops among artisans for decades prior to his codification. The typical history of science that makes Bacon such a seminal figure reproduces the assumptions of the culture it serves, that individual great men are the agents of historical change while everyone else is a relatively passive observer of that greatness. That is a false story about the origins of modern science, just as it is false in today's highly collaborative and derivative world where every kind of work, scientific understanding, and practical achievement is a product of numerous people working together through time and space.

Steven Shapin's succinct history *The Scientific Revolution* intelligently situates the radical changes it promoted in their social, historical context:

> The most far-reaching links between natural knowledge and state power flowed from broad European changes in attitudes to knowledge in general and to the relations between knowledge and social order. The environment for these changes was what might be called a state of permanent crisis affecting European politics, society, and culture from the late medieval period through the seventeenth century. Some markers of that continuing crisis include the breakdown of the feudal order and attendant rise of strong nation-states from the thirteenth

century onward; the discovery of the New World and
both the cultural and the economic shocks emanating
from that expansion of horizons; the invention of printing and consequent changes in the boundaries of cultural participation; and the fragmentation of a unified
Western European religious order that followed from
the Protestant Reformation of the sixteenth century.
Each of these events, but especially the last, eroded the
authority and the effective scope of institutions that had
regulated human conduct for preceding centuries.[42]

Fragmentation and crises are again besetting the world order, and
the governmental and economic institutions on which this order is
based are becoming increasingly dysfunctional while losing credibility.
The horizontal communications potential opened up by the Internet
is comparable to the revolutionary impact of moveable type and printing 400 years ago. Today's "religion" is a blind faith in the growth of
market economies combined with the subordination of human creativity to the dictates of business, and it is being attacked or rejected from
many locations. Various fundamentalist religions are in open political
revolt against this imperial doctrine, urgently asserting their rigid beliefs against the chaotic relativity of modern life, while other "spiritual
awakenings," more loosely defined, are also flourishing in the face of a
daily life drained of meaning and human community. Meanwhile, the
material and scientific foundations of life are tangibly corroding, and in
movements like permaculture, an earth-based spiritual sensibility is reinforced by a holistic science that confronts the narrow and incomplete
"facts" of science in the service of capital.

The often derided new age enthusiasm for animistic philosophies
echoes Paracelsus in more ways than one. Ultimately, today's emerging,
holistic sense of life endorsed even by advanced biologists and physicists
turns out to be an old sense that prevailed long before literacy was common (albeit with the apparatus of four centuries of scientific and technological developments). The new science of the 17th century sought to
ingratiate itself with the religious order of its day; to do so it used a philosophy of inanimate mechanism to prove the complementary category of
external spiritual agency (i.e. God). Recognizing that purpose in nature
was noxious to true religion and the moral order of the era, Father Marin
Mersenne (1588–1648) developed a religious critique of "Renaissance
naturalism," the body of thought that attributed sentience to nature itself.[43] This 400-year-old religiously inspired metaphysics held matter as
passive and inert, and is only now giving way to a new holistic science.

However, it's not the case that the mechanistic, inanimate worldview supplanted all others. Joined with the dynamism of merchants and business, and proving itself with the dramatic results that emerged from science and technology, mechanism became the dominant paradigm. But industrialism steadily produced horrendous side effects, which in turn steadily produced articulate critics, notably such romantic revolutionaries as William Blake and, later, William Morris.

Ernst Haeckel, a leading scientist of the mid-1800s, represented an interesting bridge between pre-Cartesian animism, 19th century mechanistic science, and today's "new" ecological science. He was best remembered for his amazing scientific illustrations, and passionate embrace of Darwinism to the point of becoming an ideologue of European racial superiority and promoting his own brand of "biogenetic" racism. But his work with single-cell radiolaria, the creatures that inhabit the sea floors in thousands of variable sizes and shapes, led him to important insights into micro- and macro-structures in nature. More fundamentally, he came to describe his approach in quasi-spiritual terms:

> From my earliest youth I have yielded to the inclination
> of my heart and studied incessantly one great book...
> Nature. This greatest of all books has taught me to know
> the true God, the God of Spinoza and of Goethe... The
> unitary idea of God, which alone is compatible with our
> current conception of nature, can never recognize in
> God a personal being, or in other words, an individual
> of limited extension in space, or even a human form.[44]

The social metaphors emerging from today's new science sharply contradict the instrumental and objectified organization of human society imposed by capitalism. In place of inanimate matter, a random and purposeless nature, and humans as cogs in a machine society, a new organization of human life emerges from the vernacular ecological wisdom taking shape in the roots of daily life.

ABUNDANCE, LIMITS, AND ACCOUNTABILITY

Permaculturists are quick to recognize limits, but not because they are rooted in a scarcity mentality. As Holmgren says early in his book, "scarcity is a culturally mediated reality: it is largely created by industrial economics and power, rather than actual physical limits to resources." Instead, permaculturists see natural limits based on the solid science of the second law of thermodynamics (which expresses the universal law of increasing entropy[45]), followed by a clear grasp of the catastrophic state of planetary ecology. In spite of the grim facts, most permaculturists believe fundamentally in the fantastic abundance of the world. From a sense of true abundance, permaculturists propose asking questions the current culture leaves unasked (seeking missing feedback): How much is enough? How hard should we work? What do we need? Want? How do we measure that? What are our individual responsibilities to the common good? How shall we have accountability to each other?

Permaculture becomes most dangerous to the ruling order when it asks these kinds of questions. Capitalism depends on obscuring relationships, fetishizing objects, and inculcating ignorance for much of its power. The most basic relationship at the heart of the system is wage-labor, the exchange of work for pay. Accepted as normal and proper, this basic relationship is the daily renewal of subordination to an alien purpose. In trading our capacities for a wage we simultaneously give up control over the world our labor is making. Permaculture's adherence to the principle of self-regulation and accepting feedback, if taken literally, flies in the face of the social and economic system. Wage-labor and consumerism are mechanisms to avoid and nullify social accountability. Feedback at work consists of pressure to conform to the company's agenda and to unquestioningly carry out the limited tasks assigned. Negative feedback leads to unemployment, positive feedback is the continued arrival of paychecks. After work, feedback is limited to the banal gratifications of acquisition and consumption, freed of any connection to ecological sanity or human effort.

Our characters are shaped by these narrow options. We obliviously depend on large-scale, remote, and fragile systems to provide for our basic needs (power, water, food). But we also have a belief system that says each of us individually should enjoy near total freedom in what we do, answerable to no one else. As Holmgren sharply notes, "In a sense, our whole society is like a teenager who wants to have it all, have it now, without consequences."[46] A culture that simultaneously glorifies and fears adolescence while promoting a shallow hedonism is perfectly suited to the mass consumerism that underpins modern capitalism. It also thwarts the solidarity, long-term thinking, and deep sociability that can push life into new directions.

Capitalism's energy regime is the best example of this. Our fossil fuel binge is 150 years old now, and might go on for decades more, but will come to an end eventually. Permacultural investigations into "embedded energy" and other ways of measuring the "cost" of our daily lives leaves little doubt that the Industrial Revolution and its attendant prosperity is based on an enduring subsidy from inherited fossil fuel wealth (a "wealth" that took millions of years to store up, but only a bit more than a century to massively deplete). Even though scientists do not argue about this basic fact, it is not integrated into social policy or economic measurement.

Also, the average length of human lives is considerably shorter than the time-frame of these processes. It has been easy to push the consequences of the rapid exploitation of natural resources into the indefinite future precisely because the social system aggressively denies any but the shortest-term systems of measurement and accountability, focused mainly on capitalist profitability. Consequences such as climate change and catastrophic weather, massive poisoning of waterways, widespread erosion, and deforestation leading to desertification, all fail to register as meaningful feedback and warning signs to the entities responsible, be they corporations, governments, or individuals.

In the face of this wide-scale obliviousness and denial, permaculture and other countercultural currents advance an alternative set of values based on a high degree of personal responsibility. Observing nature and realigning our daily lives as much as possible with the energetic and biological dynamics of the long history of life on earth is a common goal. In a wage-labor society, our sense of what we "need" is continually manipulated by advertising and the proliferation of new stuff. Insofar as we think through the consequences of our use of different products or services, and adjust our sense of what we need, we start to change from "dependent consumers of unsustainable products and services to responsible producers of appropriate wealth and value," as Holmgren puts it. The key here is not just the act of "responsible shopping" but the shift from seeing the world as a consumer to seeing it as a producer. True, acts of consumption help produce the world we're in, but with much less power than the original work that shapes our choices as consumers. Further, in a world of decaying institutions ranging from government to legal systems choking on property litigation to churches hawking a hollowed out, irrelevant spirituality, we are on our own. Banding together in new circuits of accountability and socially-defined measurement point society beyond the destructive dead-end towards which capitalism hurls us.

Permaculturists, like activists in many fields, are motivated by many things beyond mere economic survival.

> We often make decisions based on good ecology rather than on economics... Similarly we make decisions based on good family, community, and worker relations... It is often tempting to incorporate as a non-profit and seek funding support. Some day we might do that. However, for now, I believe it is better to spend our time creating, planting, and teaching than raising funds.
>
> —*Darrell Frey*[47]

A willingness to ask about the purpose of work, and the consequences of different choices, leads to a creative rethinking that could be dangerous to capitalism. Ironically, permaculturists work incredibly hard, both as designers and investigative scientists, but also as agronomists, farmers, and gardeners. But that work is not driven by an unquestioning obedience to the work ethic, or by a hunger for more money and the stuff it makes available. It's a work regime that seeks to use natural processes to *reduce work*! Toby Hemenway provides an interesting example from anthropological investigation into slash-and-burn forest dwellers:

> Why replant annuals every year when you can plant trees and be rewarded over 20 years instead of one? Combined with intensely cultivated door-yard gardens and occasional permanent cropland, the swidden-fallow system offers renewable resources over the long term. It's not hard work, either: People using these practices spend no more than two hours a day tending their plants. With food taken care of, only a couple more hours a day need be spent obtaining life's other necessities, leaving plenty of time for leisure and art. Not a bad life.[48]

The first wave of permaculture in the 1970s focused on spreading its concepts far and wide, creating viable demonstration projects, and trying to shape public policy with expert opinion. The overarching assumption of early adherents seems to have been a belief that by doing good work well, the rest of the society would "get it" and come along. After a quarter century the movement has spread to dozens of countries and is flourishing in many different regions and niches. But the dominant society hasn't lost its grip on the underlying priorities, values, and decisions that shape global capitalism. If anything, the rape of the planet is proceeding at a faster pace than ever. New generations of permaculture activists have emerged to push aside the "policy wonk" approach in favor of direct action radicalism.

PERMACULTURE AND DIRECT ACTION

Second and third generation practitioners of permaculture are pushing its subversive potential to confront global capitalism, embracing contentious tactics in ways anathema to many early adherents who assiduously backed a "positive, constructive" approach to the surrounding society.

> A lot of organic farmers, permaculturists, and people in the sustainability movement are more about solutions and saying "yes."… Some permaculturists are totally against protests and direct action. Their whole piece is

to bring permaculture to the mainstream, to make it pal-
atable for middle America... It's not the permaculture
that Bill Mollison coined the term on anymore. Permaculture is a system of change that constantly adapts and
grows on its own.

—*Erik Ohlsen*[49]

New York community gardener Mark Leger concurs with Ohlsen's
take on the permacultural aversion to direct action and contemporary
urban politics. "Most permaculturists I know are technocrats in denim
and Birkenstocks. There's this whole dismissal of "protest politics." I
guess I have an EarthFirst! bent in that we should use all of the tools in
the box. I do think that permaculturists have a lot of creativity, but then
they have their own professional blinders, too."[50]

The tension between a newer generation willing to engage in con-
frontational tactics and the first wave permaculturists has been noted by
one of the originators too.

David Holmgren sees a possible split between the "invisible but influential mainstreaming on one hand, and more radical innovation and
challenge from the edge." With his overarching presumption of declin-
ing energy reserves leading to economic contraction and even fascist
politics, he thinks there will be "new opportunities for bottom-up social
processes more invisible and more subversive than the mainstreaming
of environmental innovation." In particular he points to the "Worldwide Opportunities on Organic Farms" (WWOOF) as a way to "harness
the catalytic energy of nomadic youth" towards constructive alternatives,
but also as a means for practical skills, as well as tactical and strategic
thinking to circulate among an itinerant subculture.

In the late 1990s, Erik Ohlsen and his associates launched an organization in his hometown of Sebastopol, California that organized blocks
of neighbors to have their lawns replaced with heirloom vegetable gardens. When that effort stumbled over limited resources and insufficient
follow-through by garden recipients, Ohlsen and friends took their burgeoning permaculture skills to public lands, including medians, public
grounds, and parks, eventually helping elect one of their own to the
city council. On the cusp of turning to his permaculture work (as yet
unpaid) full-time, Ohlsen and his group decided to go on a life-chang-
ing field trip.

Before I quit my job as a spa attendant in Calistoga, I
had my first global justice experience. [In 1999] part
of my Planting Earth Activation crew [proposed], "hey,
let's stack functions (a nice permaculture principle,
stacking functions), let's go visit Allen Capular (co-

founder of Seeds of Change) and get a whole down-
load of heirloom seeds and then let's go to Seattle to the
WTO." So first we stopped in Corvallis, Oregon where
we learned about seed saving and got all these seeds.
Then we arrived in Seattle. What I experienced at the
WTO–Seattle changed my life forever. Every race, every age person out together, and then the army and the
police representing capitalists... This is where I started
to weave this understanding of global capitalist control
with the solutions of permaculture.[51]

Stopping at Seeds of Change connected Ohlsen with an earlier current of radical revolt. When corporate agribusiness began buying all the
seed companies in the 1970s, some radical ecologists began seed saving.
Holmgren highlights the story of seed saving as one of the permaculture movements' early foundations.

...the saving of seed—especially of old, local and rare
varieties abandoned by agribusiness—has inspired activists, connected them to networks of seed savers, and
reawakened a cultural practice fundamental to future
survival. The rapid buy-out by the agribusiness multinationals of most of the established seed companies in the
1970s and 1980s and their promotion of junk hybrids
jump-started the modern seed-saving movement.[52]

The seed-savers might be one of the best examples of a contrary
movement embodied in the notion of general intellect. While corporations scour the world for small seed banks and companies to control,
individual gatherers, coops and collectives, and independent farmers
associations in India, Africa, and elsewhere have carefully put away the
genetic heritage of humanity, ensuring that efforts to monopolize and
commodify seed cannot succeed.

Ohlsen's connection to the anti-globalization movement soon took
on greater proportions. After watching an interviewee on TV fail to
make political points that were obvious to him, Ohlsen helped form a
group called the Green Bloc to promote the permacultural message in
larger political arenas. But unlike the first generation of permaculturists, the new activists directly confront global capitalism, recognizing it
as fundamentally incompatible with the new science and new social patterns embodied in permaculture.

Ever since my experience with WTO in Seattle I had a
need to look at the global picture and not just focus locally. I took the first Earth Activist Training with Penny Liv-
ingston and Starhawk. After that, Starhawk and I started

carving out a niche in the global justice movement. It became very clear to me that the issues of corporate control and privatization affect organic farmers just as much as they affect teachers. In the end, it's the same system and mentality which is creating the problems and the issues.

Our first big action was the 2003 Biotech meeting in Sacramento [where we skirted] the edges between social justice and direct action, and building the solution. We took over a closed one-acre community garden that was going to be built into condos. It was the oldest community garden—30 years old—and the oldest organic one. There were mature mulberries, apricots, grapes, plums, and peach trees. It was the second largest producer of oxygen in the city of Sacramento, interestingly enough.[53]

The occupation lasted into the evening before Ohlsen and a dozen others were arrested under cover of darkness. Two years later, the Green Bloc was back in action, this time at the WTO meeting in Cancun, Mexico, where they became the darlings of the Mexican media thanks to their eco-camp full of practical demonstrations of gray water systems, hand-water pumps, and rainwater catchment. More important than catching the attention of corporate media, though, was the avid participation of activists from around the world.

It wasn't just us Green Bloc'ers from the US. There were Mexican permaculturists, people from Peru, England, and Japan. There were seven different cultures represented there, designing the system. We had a group of self-identified permaculturist punks from Mexico City helping us. At one point, you've got this guy with pink hair and spikes and the whole thing giving a tour to 35 campesinos, the indigenous small farmers who had come into the camp. [They] were a bit more rancheria-style, and they loved it so much. They invited Tierra Viva (which was the name of the Mexican punk organization) to come to their communities to help them.[54]

Permaculture emerged in the 1970s outside of the academy or business world. The first generation of proponents worked hard to gain credibility and to make the new design science self-sustaining through workshops, seminars, and classes. Unfortunately this had the effect of isolating the movement in the subcultures that could afford to participate, in spite of the fact that permaculture's ultimate goal is to develop a vernacular, accessible transformation of the human relationship with local ecological reality. Later permaculturists, including the Green Bloc and many other local efforts, have worked hard to overcome this subcultural exclusivity and class bias. An Oregon group, Food Not Lawns, argues:

> The average working person today is either too poor, too busy, or both to take advantage of permaculture courses, which usually cost from $700–1200 for a 2-week course. Organic food, heirloom seed and alternative education are equally inaccessible for most families. As a result, exposure to ecologically sound alternatives is often limited to activists, students and well-to-do people. Many mainstream, working-class families are never even aware that there are simple, affordable ways to live an ecologically sound life.[55]

Taking up the challenge, many groups are now working to implement permaculture projects in cities where they can directly confront these class inequities. The Bay Area's Urban Permaculture Guild has joined an effort called the Alameda Point Collaborative in the decommissioned Alameda Naval Air Station in San Francisco Bay. Over 100 previously homeless families have been housed in abandoned houses on the former base and the Guild has spent the last two years helping them learn the basics of sustainable permaculture gardening. But it's not a philanthropic effort as much as a collaborative community building process that combines the skills of the permaculturists with the passions and skills of the new neighborhood. Together the members are designing, planting, and tending food gardens; a gazebo has been built out of available scrap lumber. New cooperative relationships are blooming among what used to be the Navy's manicured lawns, between people who were left behind by the go-go capitalist boom of the past two decades.

Finally, permaculture is not about business as usual. Permaculturists see a role for competition similar to its function in Darwinian natural selection, but their theory is much closer to classical anarchism. Erik Ohlsen makes the same connection: "Anarchism ... is really like permaculture. It's very similar in that it's about cooperation, and it's about local and it's about decentralization." Classic anarchism is also fundamentally about accountability, working in community as contributor as well as beneficiary. Permaculture also reinforces an innate trust in individuals basic to traditional anarchist thinking. As Ohlsen puts it, "I see everybody as a leader, as having a skill that I don't have. I want to see people for what their special piece is... Identifying them as an incredible resource. I think there's an anarchism in that, that's really beautiful."[56]

The conflict arising from the different paths for the general intellect cannot be addressed adequately by a reformist political practice.

Demanding change from an adaptative and coopting capitalist society is a hollow exercise when the real task is to make changes that subvert the deepest logic of that society.

Permaculture holds the promise (technically at least) of an engaged alternative to the degradation and alienation of daily life, especially in cities—to the hollow simulation that we call representative democracy. A permacultural transformation of urban life could create stacked gardens and food forests where today we have freeway overpasses and garbage-strewn asphalt housing countless private vehicles. Such a transformation would be an enormous amount of work, but an inspiring community-defined endeavor that would be light years from the stupidity and destructive wastefulness of most modern work. A permacultural agenda harbors an alternative to commodity production, a creative redefinition of work, play, and life itself. Today's permaculture is a dynamic field operating on many levels—if taken to its logical conclusions, it shapes a compelling alternative that is deeply subversive to global capitalism.

CHAPTER 5
VACANT-LOT GARDENERS

Gardening is not the revolution, nor does gardening turn every gardener into a cultural radical... Gardening...produces good food and other benefits outside the complex of exchange... Moreover, it is an art form, an area of creativity as rich and promising as any symbolic activity, and one which can roughly but easily transpire beyond the realm of representation and mediation. It can function as an important part of "everyday life" in the radical sense of that term.

—*Peter Lamborn Wilson*[1]

...the urban community garden, with its potential for feeding households and generating local cottage industry, with its power to restore a measure of community life, and with its capacity to recycle organic wastes, is thriving throughout the world: in Karachi, La Paz, Hong Kong, Nairobi, Dakar, Dar es Salaam, and Bangkok, as well as in Philadelphia, Detroit, Newark, and Los Angeles. Globally, about two hundred million urban dwellers are urban farmers. Most of these farmers are women, and they provide food and income for about seven hundred million people. Is it so surprising that urban women of color would use community gardens to repair the fabric of our inner cities? Neither nostalgic for a pastoral past, nor Luddite in its sensibility, the inner-city community garden movement restores a nature banished from the industrial city, and offers a degree of self-sufficiency and neighborhood security, achievements that elude the master plans of urban planning experts.

—*H. Patricia Hynes*[2]

Coaxing food from land is a timeless activity. To tend a patch of land, putting hands in soil, planting, harvesting food and flowers, is to join an enduring human tradition and to carry forward common skills about how to live on Earth that precedes everything we label "the economy."

On hands and knees, digging in the dirt, a gardener leaves the frenzied pace of modern life behind. A different rhythm of sun, soil, water, and growth asserts itself, a seasonal pace indifferent to the frantic demands of the clock. Our society is gripped by an obsessive awareness of "now" that reinforces a stunning amnesia for what happened last week, last year, or in previous periods of history (let alone in other parts of the world). Gardening changes that relationship to time by slowing down the gardener, making her pay attention to natural cycles that only make sense in the full unfolding of seasons and years. In a shared garden, time opens up for conversation, debate, and a wider view than that provided by the univocal, self-referential spectacle promoted by the mass media.

The day-to-day know-how underpinning gardening dates back to pre-historic times when early cultivators learned to select seeds from hardier plants, to cross-breed for useful characteristics like taste, pest-resistance, beauty, and more. Women were usually the primary gardeners, and by medieval times an oral tradition rich with botanical knowledge was a common wealth on which most people depended.[3] Many household and village necessities were produced from roots, bark, leaves, and flowers, while some people specialized in the medicinal herbs and were first-line providers of medical care until the rise of professional medicine (a social process that corresponded in time to the infamous European witch hunts attacking especially women with traditional medical knowledge).[4]

Urban gardening has its own deep roots in North American life, dating back over a century. As the industrial revolution gained speed in the mid-19th century, wealth concentrated in the hands of the early capitalist class, while the "free market" that they utterly dominated re-shaped the lives of farmers and workers everywhere. Massive impover-ishment and the rapid spread of pestilential slums in most major cit-ies were indispensable companions of the new oligarchs' concentrated power and wealth. Bankers and industrialists threw farmers off their lands, forcing them to join millions of new immigrants and desperate urban workers to compete for space in teeming tenements. "Progres-sive" reformers and rich philanthropists began to encourage the urban poor and new immigrants to "lift themselves up by their bootstraps" by starting gardens in vacant urban lots. This was part of a larger climate of reform that attempted to teach immigrants to be good Americans and the poor to be good citizens.

When the United States entered World War I in 1917 a huge patri-otic campaign was launched to "plant for freedom" and "hoe for lib-erty." Remarkably, within two growing seasons, an estimated five million gardeners produced $520 million worth of food in 1918.[5] During the 1930s Depression, self-help or thrift gardens were established across the country to provide an antidote to idleness and to provide a dignified way for people to work towards self-sufficiency. This effort took place at a time when "relief" as government cash support was more deeply stigmatized. As the decade wore on, though, the garden programs came to be mandatory rather than voluntary with slogans such as "no garden, no relief," and various restrictions on grocery orders imposed on those who had not yet started gardening. Eventually, shifts in federal policy eliminated the funding and structural support for urban gardens. Never seen as more than a temporary make-do effort, the gardens were mostly on borrowed land that was expected to become valuable when the economy "recovered," which undercut any long-term commitments to them. (This presaged the dramas that have beset community gardens in New York, Los Angeles, and elsewhere in the past decade.)

An important direct precursor to the contemporary urban gardening movement is the Victory Gardens of World War II. In Laura Lawson's masterful history of community gardening she cites a 1944 U.S. Department of Agriculture report: "By 1944, M.L. Wilson, director of extension programs for the U.S. Dept. of Agriculture, could report that between eighteen and twenty million families had victory gardens that collectively provided 40 percent of the total American vegetable supply."[6] In San Francisco alone there were some 70,000 Victory Gardens by the end of the war, a fraction of the several million across the U.S. and Canada. The know-how developed by local gardeners during the wartime effort was not entirely lost as the parks and public grounds were returned to their previous non-garden uses after the war. In San Francisco in particular, a city with dozens of microclimates and soil conditions, WWII gardeners were instrumental in the re-emergence of community gardens in the 1970s.

Gardens are patches of land containing many purposes and possibilities, and have even become battlegrounds for opposing social dynamics, pitting an insurgent autonomy against urban reformers who see gardens as useful steps towards eventual gentrification and increased land values. While contending social forces seek to control land and the political structures that administer it, space is also provided to unregulated social interaction. Gardens are important arenas for multi-generational circuits of communication, memory, and experience.

Many of the agricultural skills that help urban gardening to thrive can be traced to recent arrivals from rural areas in the South, or the Caribbean, Africa, South America, or Asia (e.g. Central Americans and Mexicans in Los Angeles; Puerto Ricans in New York and Holyoke, MA; Hmong tribesmen from Laos in Seattle, WA; African-Americans from rural Alabama, Mississippi, or Georgia in cities from Detroit to New York to San Francisco—though it is true that newcomers and ethnicities from far and wide mix in all these places too). In a recent example, Annette Young Smith, a 66-year-old Alabama native who has lived in San Francisco's Bayview district for 34 years, applied her rural roots to the rock-hard median where she lives on the 1700 block of Quesada Avenue. Since she and her friend Karl Paige started removing debris and planting a garden in 2002, the entire block has been transformed. Neighbors all know each other now, and the garden that anchors the community has won awards and attracts visitors and helpers from all around. The block is a quintessentially San Franciscan street, "young and old. Gay and straight. Black, white, Asian, and Latino. Newcomers and oldtimers. Immigrants and native born."[7] Gardening provides a common language and context in an urban environment that usually promotes private property and individualism.

Elders who have been gardening for 20 or more years, whose own forebears were often farmers, are sharing their know-how with younger generations to help extend the culture and knowledge across time and space. In the Bronx United Gardeners (BUG), long-time community gardeners are teaching young activists growing skills, but also helping the new generation sink their own roots into their community. "I started out as an activist, fighting broad ideological issues, and I wasn't very connected to my local community," explains Isabel Moore. "Through BUG, I have learned how to grow things, and I've learned more about the Bronx."… It is a sweetly reciprocal relationship as older gardeners say they have been reinvigorated by the young people who have gotten involved.[8]

In Philadelphia's Glenwood Green Acres, a renowned four-acre farm with over 100 distinct plots among North Philadelphia's abandoned warehouses and factories, the elders share a common past as disciplined, hardworking children on farms in the South with close ties to the land. During and after WWII they joined the great black migration to the north, coming to Philadelphia to work in factories, warehouses, and other "city jobs." Now in their 60s, 70s, and 80s they are anxious to share their farming heritage, especially for traditional crops like sweet potatoes, cotton, and peanuts, which had been passed down to them by their grandparents.[9]

The renewed impetus for community gardening can be traced to the upheavals of the 1960s. In *The Omnivore's Dilemma*, Michael Pollan situates the problem of choosing what to eat in a new historic context created by the industrialization of food and the rebellious malcontents confronting it. Pollen traces today's gourmet ghettoes, vegetarianism, passion for organic foods (and antipathy to processed food) to April 20, 1969 when the "Robin Hood Commission" tore down the fence surrounding a vacant lot owned by the University of California in Berkeley, California.[10] They laid down sod and planted trees and put in a vegetable garden, and declared the establishment of "People's Park."[11] One declared intention of the "agrarian reformers" with the new park was to grow their own "uncontaminated" food and give it away to the poor, echoing the 17th century English Diggers who had also reclaimed common lands to feed the destitute of their era (often themselves!).

People's Park marked the "greening" of the 1960s movements. As historian Warren J. Belasco argues in *Appetite for Change*, "the pastoral turn led to the commune movement in the countryside, to food co-ops... and eventually to the rise of organic agriculture and businesses like Whole Foods."[12] Of course this "pastoral turn" didn't happen in a vacuum. The 1960s was the period of the worst chemical warfare on-slaught in history as the U.S. tried to defoliate the rainforests of Viet-nam, poisoning generations of Vietnamese and returning GIs with Agent Orange. Pelicans and other bird populations were plummeting due to the profligate use of DDT to control insects. A massive oil spill off the coast of Santa Barbara tarred the southern California shoreline in 1969, followed two years later by a ruptured oil tanker in the San Fran-cisco Bay, ecological disasters joining the nightly parade of atrocities on American television sets that the Vietnam War was already producing. When the Cuyahoga River caught fire in Cleveland, everyone knew the world was upside down.

The successful opening of People's Park fired imaginations across the counterculture. San Francisco's Diggers had already helped shape the underground with its free stores and wild public events in 1966 and 1967. Acid tests, rock-n-roll, marijuana, long hair, and a rejection of "straight culture" fused with draft resistance, anti-war protests, and rising black and brown power movements to challenge the American Dream at its roots.

Pam Peirce grew up in Indianapolis with a good garden where her dad was a former subsistence farmer. While a botany major in 1966 at the University of Illinois in Champaign-Urbana, she violated the staid norms of depoliticized science when she "brought in pictures of de-foliation and crater formation in Vietnam and used them as part of [an] ecology presentation." Before long she dropped out of college and moved to San Francisco where she eventually authored the bible of San Francisco gardeners, *Golden Gate Gardening*.[13] Peirce describes the ori-gins of the book as follows:

> The city had a program [then] and I started a commu-nity garden on 21st and Folsom in the mid-1970s. When I moved over to Dearborn Garden there were three people left because there had been a democratic de-bate and they had voted to take the lock off the gate. People came in and stole things, so many people gave up gardening. I arrived to a vast expanse of ungardened land, several plots all full of strawberries communally

gardened, and no one to garden it! So I came in and
started gardening, and by having several plots, I learned
everything I needed to know first-hand to write *Golden
Gate Gardening*.[14]

Peirce is a crucial character in the specific San Francisco history
of gardening and food politics. Pam got her first garden in 1975 in a
friend's backyard, while she was editing the People's Food System newsletter *Turnover*. She had been an early member of the Ongoing Picnic
Food Conspiracy where she helped buy food for a whole group at the
Saturday Farmers' Market in San Francisco, and describes it as "an experiment in grassroots democracy, which is what community gardens
are too." The early history of food conspiracies and the rise of the People's Food System in San Francisco has rarely been recounted.[15] Peirce
lived through the era and in the trenches of political wars that tore
apart the movements addressing food politics. The People's Food System collapsed at the end of the 1970s, at a time when federal support
for urban gardening was radically reduced. Several dozen community
gardens were suddenly without the federally paid workers they had
come to count on during previous years. Peirce refused to see the painstakingly built and maintained community gardens disappear for lack
of infrastructural support. She made a list of local garden coordinators
and began holding potlucks, building momentum for a new nonprofit
organization to knit together the diverse and disparate community gardens in San Francisco. As Peirce tells the history:

> I organized SLUG [the San Francisco League of Urban
> Gardeners], and there were a lot of people involved. I
> was a co-founder, and I was the person who was clear that
> it had to happen... from the beginning SLUG wanted
> to do economic, social and environmental justice. All
> through the 1970s in the Food System, I was frustrated
> by the fact that people who weren't white didn't think
> that environmentalism was important to them, that it
> was a white issue. I've been really gratified to see it be-
> come an issue that other people take hold of.[16]

During the 1970s, the U.S. Department of Agriculture funded an Urban Garden Program, which provided funds for CETA (Comprehensive
Employment and Training Act) workers in most major cities. In San Francisco, Peirce was able to tap the help and supplies of the program as she
started out. In this she was far from alone. A national poll published in
1976 found that 51 percent of American families had a vegetable garden,
and of these, ten percent were in community gardens.[17] In other words,
30 years ago five percent of American "families" had a plot in a feder-

ally supported community garden. By 1980, the federal Urban Garden Program had served nearly 200,000 urban residents, including approximately 65,000 youth. In 1982 alone, an estimated $17 million worth of food was produced.[18] When Reagan became president, his administration backed the neoliberal globalization process which has had lasting consequences throughout the world. Key to that process was the shrinking of government involvement with basic needs and social support, reinforcing the stigma Americans associate with "welfare." An early reshuffling of priorities led to the federal budget for urban gardens being capped at $3.6 million per year; when a long-time congressional supporter retired in 1992 the program was entirely stopped the next year.[19] The end of government support forced gardens (and a whole panoply of "non-profit organizations") to turn to private philanthropy and foundations for support. This in turn drove many towards models of greater economic self-sufficiency, which also meant more business-like behavior. San Francisco's SLUG became more dependent on city funds, and redoubled its efforts to provide inner-city youth with training and jobs, but to some critics this also diminished their garden-support purpose.

Rachel Bagby is the founder and executive director of the nonprofit Philadelphia Community Rehabilitation Corporation (PCRC). The PCRC rehabilitates housing, turns vacant lots into community gardens, and bedecks street corners with two story murals. She rebukes a lot of housing developers for their single-minded focus on buildings. "They do houses, I do *lives*," she says. Her efforts are directed at the devastated neighborhoods of North Philadelphia. She explains the broken communities she faces. "We have almost lost two generations to dope, crime and pregnancy," which, not suffering from typical American amnesia, she squarely blames on the Vietnam War. "Men came back shell-shocked and full of dope. Came back and had lost their human feeling. Now we have babies having babies."[20] The goal of most garden activists is to rebuild human communities with the garden serving as a focal point and shared mission.

Post-WWII federal policies led to the depopulation and economic destruction of inner cities. The GI bill gave housing and college tuition subsidies to returning white soldiers. Colleges would not admit blacks and banks would not lend to African-Americans; GI loans also would only finance purchases of single-family homes, not inner-city apartments.[21] The interstate highway system promoted suburbanization and, combined with cheap loans and rapidly proliferating new housing, many white urbanites opted to move to the new suburbs. The Housing Act of 1954 funded "urban renewal" programs in most cities. Neighborhoods deemed "blighted" would be bulldozed to make way for new public and private housing. The Urban Renewal or "redevelopment" juggernaut leveled hundreds of previously inhabited inner city acres, displacing residents and often leaving the resulting lots vacant for years. In San Francisco, for example, the largely black Fillmore district was bulldozed and left vacant for a generation.

Political riots in the late 1960s also devastated hundreds of urban acres. After Martin Luther King's assassination, black communities rioted in many cities, burning hundreds of city blocks. Ongoing social discrimination and police repression in black communities provoked additional disturbances in the late 1960s. Large urban areas were devastated by fire, leaving empty urban swathes of rubble and trash. In the 1970s waves of landlord arson and abandonment afflicted many inner city neighborhoods in New York, Detroit, Newark, Philadelphia, Baltimore, Chicago, etc. In New York the city was told to "drop dead" in 1975 by major banks when it went bankrupt, squeezed between rising infrastructure costs and plunging tax revenues from abandoned and destroyed properties. Rubble-strewn vacant lots became magnets for drug dealing and prostitution and the violence that accompanied underground economies in many neighborhoods.

Depopulation, abandonment, and crumbling infrastructure frame the decomposition of the urban working class, most visible among urban communities of color, but also apparent in the atomized white-bread "middle class" lives filling suburbs around the decayed cities. Decomposition, though, is not an end point, but a stage for new growth. Faced with the destruction of communities, livelihoods, and the neighborhood-based relationships that sustained earlier generations through tough times, resilient residents began slowly to reclaim their streets. Facing official indifference or open hostility, inner city residents had only themselves to rely on as they began to sow the seeds of class recomposition. Small acts of solidarity and neighborliness were the kernels of a direct approach to the system's destructive policies.

Mark Leger moved to New York at the end of the 1980s and has been an activist gardener ever since. He describes what community gardening meant when it emerged to confront the urban catastrophe of the 1970s: "It meant people taking direct action to transform their environment. When New York was on the skids, that meant converging on trash-strewn vacant lots, cleaning them up, making them green, making them community centers where people wanted to be rather than wanted to avoid."[22]

In San Francisco, African-American men who had migrated from the deep South to work in World War II shipyards had been left unemployed by cutbacks and a shift to shipbuilding overseas. Acres of undeveloped land controlled by the Redevelopment Agency were farmed. At one point corn fields filled several contiguous blocks of the old "Harlem West" Fillmore district. Pam Peirce, scrambling in 1980–81 to find new funds to sustain the local gardens, claims that it was San Francisco's gardening program that managed to get community gardens qualified for federal housing grants under the rubric of "fighting blight," an ironic way to use the system's own twisted logic. As we'll see below, institutional support for community gardening is often based on the demonstrable rise in property values that accompanies the reclamation of vacant lots through greening projects. The "social improvement" implied by rising property values has been widely touted by nonprofit organizations seeking support for their community gardens, even if their real goal would be better understood as one of building sustainable, safe, urban communities.

In the new century plenty of urban land is still depopulated. In spite of the frenzied dotcom boom and bust that drove Bay Area property values to dizzying heights, poor, long-time black neighborhoods in Oakland remain "underutilized." About 500 parcels of land in West Oakland are vacant or unused properties, representing about 7% of the total acreage of the neighborhood. People's Grocery was founded in 2002 to bring fresh produce to the redlined neighborhoods of the East Bay far from any modern supermarkets. In a solar- and biodiesel-powered stepvan, young employees roll through neighborhoods selling locally grown fresh produce and other organic goods. Co-founder Brahm Ahmadi says, "We believe that it's possible not only to transform those lands, but to create viable food-producing farms in urban communities, and that's really a key foundation for revitalizing a local economy and increasing open green spaces in urban neighborhoods."[23]

Many community gardens grow food, but—just as importantly—they also grow community. The isolation and fear left by government bulldozers and fences, following massive capital flight and deindustrialization, has challenged those people who stay to reinvent the bonds that knit together a community. In the practical work of clearing vacant lots and planting and nurturing gardens, a different kind of working class emerges, independent and self-sufficient, improvisational and innovative, convivial and cooperative, very often led and organized by females.

Mark Leger explains, "Gardens can bring people together for community because they are a place where people meet face to face and create something together. Community unfolds from there. For me, community involves something that reflects life across all its phases. Being a child, young, middle-aged, old. Good times, bad times. Ordinary life. Celebration. Being flush. Being on the skids."[24]

At West Oakland's City Slicker Farms for the past six years Nan Eastep has worked, mostly as a volunteer, though recently she has been earning a small monthly stipend as the on-site resident (she lives in the house next door with her 2-year-old). City Slicker Farms is integrated into a small, informal network of organic urban farms stretching from the southern reaches of East Oakland up to their place not far west of downtown Oakland (where there are several small but productive gardens in the vicinity), and further north to some West Berkeley gardens. Since they started in 2005 they have helped establish 37 backyard gardens in West Oakland, cultivating nearly 8,000 square feet of land between the Community Market Farms and the backyard gardens.[25] Friendships and practical needs knit them together, as do the recently established Farmers' Markets and the People's Grocery delivery business.

As Eastep puts it:

> People come together as individuals and smaller groups and form informal coalitions, or even temporary ones. My [blood] family is distant, but I've chosen a new family for myself in my adult life, folks around here and around this project... I'm also volunteering at other gardens and the People's Grocery. It's just good to hang out with people that you have things in common with.[26]

Not far from West Oakland's City Slicker Farms is the Linden Street Garden. By providing education for children and work for teenagers and adults, the Linden Street garden has created a social structure for the area. "Neighbors talk to each other more," says Dana Harvey of the West Oakland Food Security Council. "At least on a micro-scale, it's really helped to build a sense of community."[27]

On the East Coast a nonprofit organization called *Nuestras Raices* builds community in a Puerto Rican neighborhood. It was founded in 1992 by members of La Finquita community garden in Holyoke, Massachusetts. Holyoke had a well-developed Puerto Rican neighborhood that, following the familiar pattern of the era, converted some abandoned lots into gardens. Dan Ross, Executive Director of *Nuestras Raices,* said: "The heart and soul of the organization is the community gardens: all of our projects grow out of the gardens, and all of the projects are planned and implemented by the garden members. It's not just about food. It's about building community and building connections. It isn't just agriculture, it's culture. If you recognize that, you end up being more sustainable within a community because you build greater networks and you tap into a lot more resources."[28] Again and again we see communities establish gardens as anchors to rejuvenated neighborhood life. As the food grows, so do the human connections.

In the vast empty acres of Detroit, burned down during riots in the late 1960s and never rebuilt, the city government sponsored a 1970s program called "Farm-a-Lot." With so much vacant land, the city couldn't afford to maintain the lots at public expense. Instead, residents can fill out a simple one-page application to allow land to be converted to gardens and farms. In the mid-1990s the Detroit Agricultural Network (DAN) was founded by the Farm-a-Lot farmers, Gardening Angels, and master gardeners from Michigan State University. Participants envisioned Detroit as a Garden of Eden and a gardening city rather than the urban planners vision of turning Detroit into a casino city. A DAN spokesman sums it up: "The idea is to grow community, to grow people, and to grow food at the same time."[29]

PRIVATE REAL ESTATE (ENCLOSURES) VS. PUBLIC LAND (COMMONS)

In the face of abandoned land and wrecked communities, city governments tend to look supportively on community gardening initiatives. With minimal or no financial support, but plenty of sweat equity, residents reclaim urban lands as a new commons, a place to grow food and community, while instilling the values of good citizenship. All too often, though, the new commons remain privately owned even after years of hard work and thousands of dollars of equipment and materials have been donated by neighbors and sometimes local government. Whether privately or city-owned, if the land in the surrounding neighborhood increased in value, pressure builds to sell the garden plots to cash out on its new worth. The most dramatic and contentious social war over community gardens in recent memory took place in New York City between the mid-1990s and the turn of the century, following 25 years of garden development in abandoned vacant lots.

A diverse patchwork of more than 800 community gardens took root in New York between 1973 and 1995. During the 1970s fiscal crisis, waves of arson and abandonment left the city scarred with thousands of crumbling buildings and vacant, rubble-strewn lots. By 1977, there were more than 25,000 vacant lots in New York. Littered with trash and rats, these open sores became magnets for drugs, prostitution, and chop shops for stripping down stolen cars. The municipal government spent thousands of dollars putting up fences to keep people out, but it wasn't long before activists took things into their own hands. In 1973 Liz Christy and friends started Green Guerrillas, planting a garden on an unlikely, but very visible plot at Bowery and Houston. (After three decades Green Guerrillas is a venerable nonprofit organization that has fought long and hard for New York's community gardens.)

As part of a broader social movement to redesign life from below, gardens were seen as part of an overall strategy of urban self-sufficiency. Hundreds of young radicals squatted abandoned buildings in the rough and tumble Lower East Side of Manhattan in the mid-1970s and started implementing their communalist visions. A group called the East 11th Street Movement topped one of their homesteads with a solar green-house and the nation's first rooftop windmill generator. They also installed a 300-gallon fish farm in the basement of another squat, stocked with hundreds of tilapia. While the fish farm and windmill were short-lived, the garden they started on East 12th Street went on to become El Sol Brillante, which incorporated as a land trust in 1978 and is now run by members of the East 12th Street Block Association.[30]

Early community gardeners nurtured their reclaimed vacant lots amidst crumbling, abandoned tenements full of heroin shooting galler-ies, gun-toting dealers, and high levels of street crime and mindless van-dalism. Neighbors came together to defend their new oases, creating new public lives in cooperation with each other. The pleasurable convivial-ity rooted (literally) in new community gardens soon changed how such neighborhoods were seen. Community gardens softened the harsher surroundings, encouraging more adventurous young people to move in, musicians and artists attracted to gritty urban life and the visionary poli-tics articulated by the anarchistic squatters. In a world with shrinking op-portunities for direct participation, neighborhoods with thriving gardens reinvented a form of participatory democracy:

> More than green spaces, New York's gardens are micro-cosms of democracy, where people establish a sense of community and belonging to the land. Like the antic shrines and altars they construct in their flower beds, these eclectic havens are in a very real sense churches, where people find faith—both in themselves and in their neighbors.
>
> —*Sarah Ferguson*[31]

Gentrification refers to the incoming tide of real estate speculation that started gobbling the Lower East Side block by block during the 1980s. Speculators ran into the spirited opposition of urban radicals who had spent so much time and energy carving out a semi-utopian pocket in "Loisida Libre" as visionaries called it during their struggle. When the financial and asset boom that started in the 1980s busted spectacularly in 1987, it gave squatters a brief hope that the creeping monoculture of monied interests could be held at bay. Instead, the whole process began again, with greater furiosity in the 1990s, culminating in an epic battle with the conservative law-and-order mayor Rudy Giuliani. The mayor was determined to sell off all the community gardens to real estate developers to bolster city finances. Given the tangible benefits brought to neighborhood life by the community gardens, Giuliani's single-minded determination to destroy them horrified many people. John Wright explains the underlying politics:

> The war on gardens goes far beyond short-sighted urban planning policies and real estate graft. Community gardens are targets because they are liberated zones, areas free from consumption and mediation, at a time when the very idea of urban public space is under assault. Community gardens are as much community as garden... Gardens provide a rare public place for people to meet and socialize... Many of the gardens feature sculpture, murals, music, theater, dance and poetry, precious commodities as nonprofit arts spaces are priced out of the city. In a rapidly segregating city, gardens are some of the few spaces left where people can transcend their narrow demographic boundaries in a common cause... In this world, gardens, despite their many benefits, are seen as nuisances, obstacles to profit and control, scary pagan groves that threaten the strict fundamentalism of the Market...[32]

As if he were reading from the same book, Giuliani dutifully presented the mainstream argument in the press. In January 1999, Giuliani on his WABC weekly radio show says "This is a free-market economy. The era of communism is over." A year later, the *New York Times* quotes him saying, "If you live in an unrealistic world then you can say everything should be a community garden."[33] Giuliani's rhetoric is the logical continuation of the Reagan/Thatcher assaults on the public sector, embracing fully a market fundamentalism that insists on reducing everything to a commodity for sale. As mayor, Giuliani got quoted, but it wasn't just a zealous mayor behind the attack on community gardens. A whole stratum of bureaucrats and planners understood the city they sought to engineer, based on upscale home ownership and a municipal economy fueled by luxury consumption, was anathema to the gardeners who were bringing forth quite a different life. When asked at a public hearing about the notion of incorporating portions of the gardens into development plans, New York's Department of Housing, Preservation and Development deputy commissioner Mary Bolton responded that "open space is inconsistent with home ownership."[34]

Karl Linn, a prominent landscape designer, in 2001 addressed the American Community Garden Association: "I view the destruction of community gardens that is happening in New York City as the final enclosure of the commons; following the enclosure of neighborhood streets by the automobile... With the creation of community gardens, neighborhood blocks can become arenas for a new kind of extended family living not based on blood relationships, but on friendships, mutual aid and intergenerational support among neighbors."[35]

A multi-pronged oppositional strategy prevented Giuliani from selling all of New York's community gardens. A last minute deal before a massive public auction led to the Trust for Public Land buying some 113 gardens, while several hundred more gained protection through the intervention of the New York Restoration Project. Mark Leger was deeply involved in citywide gardening politics during this era, spending nearly four years on 24/7 alert against impending garden evictions. He characterizes the final outcome this way:

> The Trust for Public Land got the cream of the crop, and the New York Restoration Project got the least desirable plots. It came down to different philosophies. The Trust for Public Land made "wise business decisions," while the New York Restoration Project acted from the principle that in a congested city, all open space should be saved. At this point, the community garden movement in NYC is very fractured and lacks a clear identity or sense of purpose. Now that the city is more prosperous, less violent, and cleaner, a lot of what brought community gardeners together in the 1970s, 1980s and 1990s is not so pressing. And with 450 gardens saved, the preservation struggle is not pressing.[36]

Another recent high-profile garden eviction took place in June 2006 in South Central Los Angeles. The Rodney King riots in 1992 left a lot of land abandoned between the black and Korean parts of Los Angeles. The city took a plot of land in the neighborhood through eminent domain in order to build a trash incinerator, but local residents successfully defeated that plan. The land lay empty, scarred and covered in crumbling asphalt. The LA Regional Food Bank's office faced the lot and proposed to the city that it be turned into a community garden. After initial success the Food Bank doubled the original seven acres with the addition of another parcel. Thirteen years later 350 farmers worked the land every day, feeding hundreds of local families, selling produce to thousands of Los Angelenos. But the original owner made a deal with a city council blind to the vital importance of this urban oasis, and regained his original title to the land. In June 2006, after a very public campaign to save the farm, sheriffs moved in and evicted direct action protestors and farmers, followed in days by bulldozers that destroyed more than a decade of urban farming and ecological reclamation. The community gardeners and farmers have vowed to retake the land, but so far have been rebuffed by courts. Though their land is lost, the community is still intact and determined to re-establish their gardens; meanwhile the South Central community received acreage in the lower San Joaquin Valley, which they have been cooperatively farming.

FREELY-GIVEN LABOR SHAPES A NEW CLASS COMPOSITION

The painstaking years-long efforts to bring community gardens to life have depended on countless hours of hard work. In a harshly capitalist society work is exchanged for money, and if it happens otherwise, it is dismissed as a hobby. Certainly many gardeners consider their work a hobby, but the urban transformation wrought over the past generation of community gardening cannot be explained as simply a lot of hobbyists. Instead, like the initiatives in other chapters, gardeners are *working* to refashion their lives in tune with their own visions, know-how, and multidimensionality. Their motivations are varied, but remuneration is seldom first among them. As we've seen already, building community is a big goal, embodying a range of needs for friendship, camaraderie, mutual aid, and ecological intervention. Later we'll examine how a new relationship to food drives a great many garden projects too. But at the root, it is a different relationship to work that inspires and sustains many community gardeners.

Pam Peirce describes how she was trapped by regular work relationships and found greater freedom as a volunteer:

> What I wanted to do was investigate things. I knew early on that if you volunteer you can do more interesting things than on a job… When you volunteer, you get to try something different. If you sit around on a job and wait for someone to notice that you can do something and give you the opportunity to do it, you might sit there forever… if you have skills [or desires] you want to develop and you're willing to do it for free, the sky's the limit.[37]

Working out of interest and curiosity and passion as a volunteer fundamentally alters the subjective experience of work. Rather than a relationship defined by coercion, by autocratic management and obedience, by the reward of wages rather than the satisfaction of accomplishing the work itself, volunteers are free to create, to cooperate, and to define the meaning of their own work. Mark Leger has volunteered in community gardens for over two decades.

> Over the years the intensity of my involvement has waxed and waned. There are times when I'm at the garden every day, and then weeks go by, especially in winter, when I hardly visit it. One of the things I like about gardening as a focus for organizing is that there's a lot of just practical stuff you have to band together to do, so ideology takes a backseat. When we get together for a garden meeting, we talk about stuff like how to organize snow shoveling for the winter. The macro stuff—like maintaining autonomously organized public spaces, food security, mutual aid—are never really part of the agenda… sometimes I long for a more sophisticated discussion than I get from my fellow gardeners or workers, who are equally caught up in *just getting the job done.*[38]

Nan Eastep was attracted to City Slicker Farms in West Oakland six years ago because she "liked the issues that came up around urban farming and community." She puts in an average of 20 hours a week, but sees it as a piece with her general engagement in the larger political and social dynamics around her:

> Being part of this project, and part of the anti-war movement, and other kinds of processes to make decisions and come together, it all just kind of melted together in my mind. Also, at People's Grocery I'm at meetings that are about process, organizational structure, and things like that. I'm interested in how long it actually takes to make something—it's just kind of grounding. Can I grow my own food? Can I make my own clothes? Can I make clothes for my friends, and if they give me some money will that pay my rent? I would like to be off the grid. I'm VERY interested in other kinds of technologies that are primitive, like composting human waste and graywater.[39]

This new relationship to freely-given work restructures relations to money and community and nature, and sets the foundation for working class recomposition in this period. Wage-workers, déclassé professionals, and escapees from meaningless drudgery forge new relationships among the organic arugula, sunflowers, and chard they cultivate in re-fashioned urban commons. Long-time residents of urban "wastelands" such as Detroit, Newark, and Philadelphia, have endured the breakup of old social webs, the discarding of organized workers, and the dissipation of families and coherent communities. Showing unheralded resilience, they have painstakingly built new circuits of communication and rebuilt relations of cooperation and mutual aid. Few people think about class composition as they're struggling to rebuild meaningful human communities, nor is their own class position much of a concern. When queried, many urban gardeners show the same confusion and reluctance to consider the class component of their work.

Discussing the issue of class, Pam Peirce, who has been involved in left-wing politics since her arrival in San Francisco, for better and worse, says:

> I grew up convinced I was middle-middle class because this is what everybody is convinced of in America. They keep trying to push that. ... My class background is so confused, which is normal. My dad grew up on a farm. His class background is subsistence farmer... my mother was an orphan... She worked as a governess when she was a teenager, she didn't finish high school... I was lower middle class. I was always getting the hand-me-downs and the bargain clothes and we lived a lot out of the garden and at the end of the month, Dad went fishing. Some people make a lot of money and work so hard to do it that they don't have any time left. All they know is to spend the money to look like they're middle class...[40]

Peirce has no doubt about the other side of the class equation: "...absolutely there's a ruling class!" Mark Leger agrees. Leger's ideas about class are fruits of 30+ years around lefty and gay politics, including a few years as a stalwart contributor to *Processed World* magazine.[41]

> Class is complicated. I tread carefully around it. I've known too many reductionist Marxists who've used the word to simplify issues and roll over differences. And I've know too many people who deny that it's a factor in anything. Maybe the best way to think about it is that there're many working classes, many middle classes, many ruling classes... I identify as a working class guy who has been a fly on the wall in a lot of different places. Being queer has meant that I've left the cultural and workplace orbit of my youth. For instance, my straight brother lives 40 miles away from where we grew up, and has the same job as my father—an air traffic controller—and is active in the union. He's one of the "working class" guys who makes significantly more than $100K a year.[42]

Back at West Oakland's City Slicker Farms, Nan Eastep talks about class:

> Class [chuckles uncomfortably]... God, that's a struggle

for me. Class is such a real thing. I've been able to transcend those categories and call myself an artist, and I
think that helps a little bit. But I'm working class…when
I was growing up I thought I was middle class, because I
didn't have a working class consciousness, even though
my dad was a union laborer. He had a sheet metal company. He owned it but he did all the work.[43]

These ruminations on class are far from conclusive, and how could
they be otherwise? The old familiar boundaries and categories have
been dissolved over the past three decades and insofar as people have
ideas about class, they tend to be awkward attempts to insert their own
lives, those of their parents, into categories received from previous historical epochs. Erecting self-definitions on unwaged platforms, which
are nevertheless still real work, poses a challenge to familiar meanings.
Ultimately these creative engagements point beyond the wage relation
to a post-economic life, animated by and under the control of freely
cooperating workers themselves.

Contrasted with the often pointless work that earns wages, gardening provides a rich variety of activities, meanings, and relationships. Patricia Hynes describes the creative project of inner-city gardeners as "a
new kind of environmental ethic and urban renewal, one based on an
urban ecology and a low-income but resilient economy. Their ecology
is predicated not on wilderness without people but on a mutuality between humans and nature; their economy is predicated on traditional
finance, sweat equity, barter, and non-monetary sources of wealth such
as networks, good will, generosity, altruism, plant lore, and horticultural
expertise."[44] Hynes describes the gardeners' deep engagement with a
new frame of reference that breaks with economic reductionism and
puts ecology and community at the center instead of an afterthought.

Gardeners are often undogmatically willing to engage people and institutions in any number of ways, both through a "traditional" economy and
through a radically decommodified gift economy. Leger points to a self-sufficient component at the core of the gardener's work:

If you're growing your own food, even giving away food
that you grow (which is the case with practically every
vegetable gardener I know worth her or his spade),
you're evading the economic system, especially if you're
using basic, non-designer tools, and you're using saved
seeds or the year-old seeds that the seed companies give
to community garden organizations. When I was unemployed last year, I basically kept healthy from the vegetables I grew to round out the rice and lentils survival
food, which was all I could afford.[45]

Eastep outlines a different definition of wealth that grows naturally, if you will, in community gardens: "There is so much wealth created from this garden, but if you measured it in dollars, it would be ignored, it would be completely inconsequential. The wealth is the relationships, and the intellectual wealth, the skills."[46]

In this respect, gardening work reproduces housework and women's work more generally. Vast efforts, crucial to survival and well-being, go routinely unmeasured, or at least under-counted by standard economic statistics. Patricia Hynes explains:

> At the neighborhood and household level, where women dwell and work on the surrounding land, they identify, collect, cultivate, and conserve large numbers of plant and animal species. Yet the value of this work, like that of community gardening, is generally not counted in the economy because such work is unpaid and not market-based; nor is it recorded in environmental history because it is considered the minor, insignificant work of many "ordinary" women and not the major, heroic drama of the rare Great Man; nor has this work been documented, until recently, by the mainstream media because the billions of examples of the "homely act of earthkeeping" as poet Robin Morgan calls her gardening, are neither grand nor romantic.[47]

Women have historically been the cultivators and gardeners that grew the vegetables and fruits. History tends to overlook this basic truth, as it also tends to frame the great upheavals of capitalist history as male-driven, even when women have fought at barricades and sacked institutions of repression, from police to church to government (e.g. the 1871 Paris Commune, the 1936 Spanish Revolution, May 1968 France).

URBAN GARDENING AND FOOD SECURITY

> The European food crisis [at the end of WWI] caused many Americans to reflect on domestic reliance on food grown far from the place of consumption, whether in other parts of the United States or elsewhere in the world. Dependency on imported food was criticized as wasteful and potentially dangerous.
>
> —*Laura J. Lawson*[48]

In 1989, thirty-two hundred volunteer master gardeners and composters in the USDA Urban Gardening Program worked with two hundred thousand low-income urban gardeners, the majority of whom were senior citizens and women of color. Together they produced $22.8 million worth of produce—all with a budget of $3.5 million!

—*H. Pat Hynes*[49]

The utopian socialist Charles Fourier argued in the early 1800s for horticulture as opposed to agriculture. He thought horticulture produced better food and, even better, it was a form of "attractive labor," magnifying the exciting anticipation of the table, where touch, taste, and smell would be given free reign. The rise of community gardens based on sociability, conviviality, pleasure, and beauty, one strand of our look at Nowtopians, echoes Fourier's utopian sensibilities.

Since that fateful invasion of People's Park in Berkeley in 1969, the dominant society has tried mightily to box in and denigrate the social movements that erupted at that time. The upheavals and radically new values we trace to the Sixties helped bring forth a profusion of new food products, markets, co-ops, etc., all rooted in that era's social refusal of bad food, unhealthy ingredients, and exploitation of nature and humans. The overt politics of that time certainly subsided, but in daily life there are continuing examples of a deep transformation that started then and endures to this day. Social workers and activists helped (re)launch inner city farmers' markets in the late 1970s and early 1980s, connecting urbanites with regional farmers. Community-Supported Agriculture links urban buyers with local farmers, allowing members to finance the coming year's crop instead of leaving farmers dependent on ruthless, profit-hungry banks. Collectives and radical co-ops in the U.S. and Europe have been saving seed, a mission paralleled by independent efforts in many countries like India and China. Urban garden organizations have sponsored regular seasonal seed exchanges to promote independence from Monsanto and other global food corporations who seek to monopolize the seed market.

As gardeners became increasingly interested in seeds, they have rediscovered old varieties of produce, "losers" to the gleaming racks of picture perfect, tasteless fruits and vegetables sold by supermarkets. When McDonald's opened facing Rome's Spanish Steps, a movement was born that calls itself Slow Food. Now in several dozen countries, thriving in Europe and North America, the Slow Food movement promotes convivial dining, enjoying the best foods and wines produced by traditional methods. Ironically, the Slow Food movement recognizes that to save heirloom species and practices people must maintain a market for those products. Thus, while rooted in ancient sensibilities about land, food, and human life, Slow Food has gained a reputation as a "foodie" movement for the wealthy since the traditional foods they promote cost more, partly because they are rare and partly because they are not subsidized by artificially cheap fossil fuel and government payouts.

Pam Peirce worked in the People's Food System and began gardening with parallel concerns about culture and human health. She recalls the early political motivations that inspired her involvement with food and gardening:

> I was part of the people that thought there was going to be big change in this country. I started working on the People's Food System newsletter, *Turnover*, and I put my all into it for 2.5 years and did illustration and wrote about nutrition, food economics, food history, and food politics and had a grand time doing it. I worked my tail off... [We had two basic constituencies:] there were people who wanted everything to be pure. And then there were the people who wanted to *eat junk food like the workers!* Neither one of them made a lot of sense to me. [I thought our goal was to] find a way to get better food to people.[50]

Food activists like Peirce deeply affected the industry, and helped give rise to new tastes and demands, first from the so-called counterculture. Eventually the demand for healthy, better tasting, organic food grew rapidly in the broader population. Industrial agriculture still provides the lion's share of food, though. Much is made of the labor-saving efficiency of industrialized agriculture, but it is a Potemkin-village "efficiency" based on massive fossil fuel inputs. In fact, the industrial agriculture system, already decried for its over-reliance on petrochemicals in the 1960s, has greatly extended its power and reach since that time. Supermarket food often comes from thousands of miles away, depending on a wide range of technological interventions to prolong it through travel time and shelf life. Heavy use of fertilizer leads to poisonous runoff clogging river mouths, while steadily destroying the soils on which it is dumped. Erosion accelerates as monocropping expands, while the shrinking biodiversity of food crops is worsened by corporate attempts to own seed banks, patent life forms, and manipulate the gene pool. Industrial exploitation of rivers, lakes, and aquifers threatens long-term fresh water supplies too. Tracing supermarket foods back to their sources reveals a convoluted tale of multinational seed companies, petrochemical inputs, shipping, packing, underpaid workers, and a food system driven by the hunger of business for profit instead of the widespread hunger and malnutrition stalking the planet.

Rejecting the technological hubris and stunning ecological inefficiency promoted by agribusiness, community gardeners have followed the earlier wisdom of such luminaries as Swiss agronomist Rudolf Steiner, English agronomist Sir Albert Howard, and the Rodale Institute's decades-long work in organic gardening and farming. Turning away from fossil fuel-based solutions, a real technological revolution of everyday practicality has been developing for several decades in community gardens. Rain water collection systems, graywater, and new composting methods (sometimes using high-tech gear), and experimental permaculture garden designs, all promise to address intractable problems that agribusiness propagandists ignore. Reinventing an intensive, local agriculture necessarily happens in many places simultaneously and over time. With new ways to garden intensively under development in dozens of cities and climates, a new agricultural biodiversity (and cultural diversity) is re-emerging from below.

Nan Eastep grew up on a farm in Minnesota, so she recognizes that small-scale urban gardens are only a start. "This is not really a solution for agriculture, just as it stands, at the scale that it's at," she says. "But it's relationship building, it's model making. So it's teaching people how to grow vegetables. And the youth that come through can see how vegetables are actually grown."[51] As urban gardeners focus on food security, surprising results are possible. Recall the tremendous output of urban gardeners and farmers during the world wars of the 20th century. In New York, according to Just Food, a nonprofit organization dedicated to improving New York's food system, 37 gardens produced more than 30,000 pounds of food in 2004. One highly productive site—Bissel Gardens in the North Bronx—harvested 2,370 pounds of food. Just Food estimates conservatively that the gardens produce an average of about 800 pounds each. The United Community Centers (UCC) garden in East New York, Brooklyn... donated more than 700 pounds of food to local soup kitchens and sold close to $4,000 worth of food at the nearby farmers' market... Some 23 resident urban growers in 12 community gardens and three upstate farmers keep the [local farmers'] market alive.[52]

The Community Supported Agriculture and backyard farm projects in Seattle, Tacoma, and Tucson successfully grow large amounts of food in small areas while addressing social inequities that corporate industrial agriculture aggravates. These three projects demonstrate that collaborative efforts among people—sharing tools, land, knowledge, labor, customers, and money—often carve out space for urban farming to thrive. This result stems from their structure, which leads people to address the obstacles common to urban food production: land tenure, food security, and economic survival.[53]

Jessica Hayes is a Boston-based environmental justice activist, who worked with The Food Project. She has a deeper political vision that connects the prosaic issues of urban gardening with a much larger agenda, illustrating a radical sensibility that sustains projects that might otherwise be dismissed as "just a garden."

> I'm looking at urban agriculture as a way to undermine the industrial agriculture system—the way that global food production works," she says. "I can fight that system until I die, but at the same time build an alternative so at some point we can just cut the global system off... Let's be really idealistic for a second and say that we were able to do large-scale food production in Boston... What would happen as far as people's demand for cleaner air and cleaner water if they saw the food they eat growing in their neighborhoods? Local food production would have an impact on the broader environment as well, by [relieving] the pressure of industrial food production [on] rural and wild lands. We could become less dependent on transportation networks, on fossil fuels, on irrigation and water infrastructure. Agriculture wraps them all together.[54]

About ten years ago, local residents from the Alemany Housing Projects, Bernal Heights, and other parts of southeastern San Francisco teamed up with the San Francisco League of Urban Gardeners (SLUG) to turn an illegal dump site into a productive 4.5 acre urban farm. For eight years they ran youth programs, training young people in organic agriculture. They distributed fresh, healthy produce to low-income residents who normally would have little access to such important staples. The farm became a cornerstone of the local community and an example of a new paradigm of urban sustainability. Unfortunately, in 2004 SLUG lost its city funding and had to abandon the farm. Without money to pay workers and run educational programs, the farm collapsed. After two years of barebones maintenance by one volunteer, a group formed to revive the farm. Justin Valone describes going door-to-door in the adjacent public housing project with an early harvest:

> Yesterday, I walked door to door, escorted by two of my youngest friends (one four, the other five), and distributed our freshly harvested lettuce, kale, and chard. I know these bundles of vegetables may be the most nutritious food in the neighborhood. People are grateful for the produce and excited to see the farm coming back to life. This piece of land holds the potential to transform the way we relate to our food. Our produce opens avenues for community interaction and facilitates understanding of how race and class affect our access to healthy organic food.[55]

Urban gardening initiatives like these embody multiple implications. First, they re-situate basic food security in local communities, or at least start the important process of relocalization and the skill development that local food security depends on. Secondly, by bringing together activists and neighbors and excluded communities, new relationships emerge based on the practical work of producing food and tending land. In an era of social fragmentation and increasing dependence on multinational food corporations these are vital counter-initiatives. The subversive possibilities embodied in such gardening projects might be a motivation for efforts to contain gardening in a smaller social terrain.

KEEPING GARDENING SIMPLE AND LIMITED

While garden promoters are proud of their grassroots activism and the self-reliance that gardens make visible to their community, garden programs also have a legacy of conservatism and paternalism.
—*Laura J. Lawson*[56]

The more I was involved in it, the more I began to understand what nonprofits do, and how they're really just an arm of city government. They're made up of generally outside people, who have a good reason to do what they want to do. But they're doing some of the city's work for them, without the city employees (that's probably a big political strategy). [The municipal government reduces] public payrolls, and can cut programs when they want to.
—*Jeffrey Miller, former board president, SLUG*[57]

Community gardens have been around a lot longer than any of the political aspirations defined since the late 1960s. We can detect the different orientations between what are called "community gardening programs" and independent community gardens. Government usually sponsors the programs with funding agencies setting up rules and providing leadership.

Gardens always face legal issues with land tenure. Basic water and compost needs bring gardeners into discussion with local utilities. These dynamics channel a significant part of the gardening movement towards institutional coexistence with the surrounding world. Urban gardens need nurturance from cheap land costs and/or grants and donations from private foundations or government agencies. In Philadelphia, e.g., it was the upscale Pennsylvania Horticultural Society that significantly supported the founding of Philadelphia Green, one of the country's largest ongoing community gardening programs with well over 1000 gardens. But the city has declined a long way since its mid-20th century heyday. In 1995 it still had 15,000 vacant lots and 27,000 vacant structures. Philadelphia Green, with an annual budget of over $3 million, started promoting collaborations with community development corporations in the 1990s. Philadelphia Green argues that gardening creates social networks that in turn get neighborhood residents to interact with each other and become involved in community improvements. Gardening activates this more quickly and cheaply than other interventions, such as housing. As Philadelphia Green's executive director J. Blaine Bonham commented, "It may be a crass fact, but gardening is logical because it works and it is cheap."[58]

Patricia Schrieber, who directs the Education Department of Philadelphia Green, sees the West Shore neighborhood in Southwest Philadelphia as a model of community gardens spurring community development. She says "In the 1970s West Shore, a ten-block neighborhood, started with window boxes, then went to trees and vacant lots. Based on the 'facelift,' a housing network organization located there to rehabilitate housing. At the Greene Countrie Towne ribbon cutting ceremony for West Shore, a banker cited the power of gardens to symbolize civic pride and tenacity and to be a catalyst for investment in the community."[59]

Seen in this light, urban gardening programs are instruments of urban gentrification. Is all physical improvement to be opposed on the grounds of "gentrification"? The problem is not making things nicer through gardens or murals or street furniture. The problem is the private ownership of land that benefits a few landlords, while pricing out the population to whom the improvements are promised in the first place. Gardening programs that don't confront private land ownership, *at least* for their own permanence, are sowing the seeds of their own destruction.

URBAN JU-JITSU

I believe a worldwide culture of resistance presently hov-
ers on the verge of coherence. The moment it begins to
come into focus at both the global and local levels, gardening will suddenly appear in its true light, as a vital
tactic of resistance, and as a means of achieving a bit of
"Utopia Now."

—*Peter Lamborn Wilson*[60]

Coexisting with and taking advantage of public resources is an ongoing challenge to independently organized community gardens.
But community gardeners can go another route, too. The creative, self-
organizing capacities that made starting a garden possible could find
a different political voice. Oakland's Nan Eastep suggested borrowing
a page from the old radical farmers of her home state of Minnesota.
"I'm into the idea of a Grange here in the urban farming movement,
resurrecting that word and having Grange Halls. Cops and politicians
weren't allowed at the Grange."[61]

Before today's extreme urbanization, metropolitan regions weren't
just centers of commerce but fertile fields, often in lush river valleys.
Even today, they have some of America's best land for sustainable agriculture. New techniques can grow healthy, thriving, fertile soil in urban
plots, which in turn makes intensive urban farming not just desirable
but more productive than ever before. Of course not everyone believes
that gardens and parks are basic necessities like food and water. Mark
Leger notes that some people "make false dichotomies—housing versus
gardens is a favorite. That's a line that the real estate interests exploit,
but also the left, many of whom would be only too happy to return to
the era of Stalinoid housing blocks. Things like charm, liveability, clean
air are frivolities. And trust me, there are a lot of ascetic leftists in the
affordable housing movement. Bless their hearts."[62] Gardening is one
thread of a new fabric of social opposition and reinvention, abandoning
the grip of guilt and sacrifice in favor of beauty and pleasure.

In fact, pleasure is probably the greatest reason to garden, the pleasure of human sociability and the pleasure of great-tasting, fresh food. A
recent convert in Montreal's thriving community garden scene writes:

My palate will never be the same again. I've come to
love gardening as well because of the kind of people
you meet... they are some of the most interesting,
free-thinking, spirited and dare I say it, down to earth
people I know. Gardening being a creative act, many
are involved in some aspect of the arts: writers, paint-

ers, musicians, dancers, etc. A lot of the time you find that you spend more time talking than actually working, but that's what it's all about too. It's a great way to find out about things going on in the city, and develop relationships and friendships within your neighborhood... Finally, community gardens make sense, offer[ing] a glimpse of what the future should be based upon: sharing in a common purpose, human interaction, safe foods and sustainable living.

—*Art Armstrong*[63]

Considering how much money is spent every year subsidizing a super-overproduction of corn and soy, there is plenty of "public" money to radically decentralize food production, even in the United States. Farmer's markets could be built in every community and big city neighborhood, while farmers could be subsidized to grow food in ways that protect land and water, and preserve open space. Publicly owned land banks could remove important local agricultural lands from the private property market in perpetuity.

Steve Frillman, current executive director of NYC's Green Guerrillas advises:

Stand your ground, pitch a tent, and invite people in who are willing to do hard work: wild-eyed idealists, pragmatists, activists, lawyers, planners. Don't get too caught up on consensus, and don't get discouraged by conflict. You can get a lot done together while disagreeing on important points along the way.[64]

For lifelong city dwellers used to food arriving in cellophane, urban gardens are laboratories where they can (re)discover seasonal foods and local plants, along with the soil and waterways hidden beneath the concrete. Urban gardening opens up new terrain—gardeners alter lands uses, people meet across cultures and ethnicities, and new ways of "doing politics" begin to emerge. Of course it remains tentative and experimental, as new relationships find their purposes, boundaries, and rhythms. But something new and important is growing in vacant lots that nourishes bodies *and* souls.

World War II Victory Garden planted in front of San Francisco's City Hall, c. 1944. (Photo courtesy San Francisco History Room, San Francisco Public Library.)

Guerrilla garden at Stanyan and Fulton in San Francisco, 2007. The absentee landlord ordered it destroyed after local neighbors spent several months bringing it to life. (All photos by Chris Carlsson unless otherwise credited.)

Community Garden on Quesada Street median in San Francisco's predominantly African-American Bayview/Hunters Point neighborhood.

Community Garden at Langton Alley and Howard Street in San Francisco. Situated in a Filipino residential area, the mural on the back wall depicts the Filipino seafarers who came to California in Spanish galleons in the 1500s.

Facing perspectives of the Alemany Farm/St. Mary's Youth Garden off I-280 in San Francisco. The freeway itself sits atop the former Islais Creek waterway. Top view looking north from across the freeway and bottom view looking south from top of hill.

EAST FOURTH STREET COMMUNITY GARDEN
.184 acre

The dedicated local residents of the East Fourth Street Garden Association have tended this site, formerly known as the Windsor Terrace Kensington Veterans Memorial Garden, since they first organized it in 1979. The garden, incorporated in 1981, has come to serve a central role as a gathering place in this community. The East Fourth Street garden has funded its operations and special projects through dues collection, flea markets, and two Mollie Parnis Dress Up Your Neighborhood Awards.

The distinction of "neighborhood" has changed over the years as populations and real estate pressures have redrawn the lines in this section of Brooklyn. Although originally part of the town of Flatbush, Windsor Terrace was subsumed under Kensington during the early part of the 20th century. The area includes Community Board 7 and Sunset Park. Windsor Terrace sits between Prospect Park and Green-Wood Cemetery, with Seventh Avenue and Prospect Park South to the north and Caton Avenue to the south.

Gowanus native tribes first inhabited this locale well before European settler John Vanderbilt took the land to build his farm. Developer William Bell bought the land in 1849 after Vanderbilt's death. Bell divided it up as the village of Windsor Terrace, inaugurating the legacy of the residential neighborhood, which remained isolated until after the Civil War (1861-1865). New railroad lines to Coney Island provided direct public transportation to a rapidly expanding list of attractions: restaurants, hotels, bathing pavilions, shops, amusement rides, race tracks, theatres, and as always, the beach and the ocean.

By 1884, Windsor Terrace had 100 residents and a schoolhouse, and by 1888, a local fire department. With the early 20th century construction of 25 two-family homes and two apartment buildings, Irish immigrants flocked to the area. Italian immigrants arrived soon after that, the neighborhood expanding with mostly civil servants: policemen, firemen, and teachers. These residents communicated through a network of friends and family to rent and sell their properties, keeping the population a fairly intimate one.

Such community oriented thinking persisted through the many changes of the next century. Established on city property, the East Fourth Street Garden uses land originally cleared of homes for the construction of the F subway line in the 1930s. Transit builders changed their plans, running the line underground where the Windsor Terrace branch of the Public Library now stands. In 1998, the Department of Housing Preservation and Development (HPD) surrendered the Fourth Street garden between Fort Hamilton Parkway and Caton Avenue to Parks. This arrangement safeguards the garden's status as a green space while leaving the administration largely in the hands of its community developers.

The Garden Association has recently completed a new concrete lining for their pond, in the back corner of the lot near the vegetable plots. Also contained within the wrought iron gates are a compost heap, a picnic area, a rock garden, a sundial, and benches. Garden members buried a time capsule in 1998 not to be opened for 25 years. Members and local school children collected current memorabilia, toys, newspapers, and family histories to preserve for the next generation's enjoyment.

Insect sculpture adorns the East 4th Street Community Garden in Brooklyn, NY.

Liz Christy Community Garden on Houston Street in Manhattan, NY.

Main Street Community Garden in Santa Monica, CA.

Brooklyn, NY.

CHAPTER 6
"OUTLAW" BICYCLING

[In] this bike subculture there's no person who is the best, who is winning, or getting the most money. It's a pretty equal community in that everyone can excel, but not have to be the top dog...

—*Robin Havens*[1]

A funny thing happened during the last decade of the 20th century. Paralleling events that transpired a century earlier, a social movement emerged based on the bicycle. This "movement" is far from a unified force, and unlike the late 19th century bicyclists, this generation does not have to rally around the demand for "good roads." Instead, "chopper" bike clubs, nonprofit do-it-yourself repair shops, monthly Critical Mass rides, organized recreational and quasi-political rides and events, and an explosion of small zines covering every imaginable angle of bicycling and its surrounding culture, have proliferated in most metropolitan areas. Month-long "Bikesummer" festivals have occurred in cities around North America since 1999, galvanizing bicyclists across the spectrum into action and cooperation.

This curious, multifaceted phenomenon constitutes an important arena of autonomous politics. The bicycle has become a cultural signifier that begins to unite people across economic and racial strata. It signals a sensibility that stands against oil wars and the environmental devastation wrought by the oil and chemical industries, the urban decay imposed by cars and highways, the endless monocultural sprawl spreading outward across exurban zones. This new bicycling subculture stands for localism, a more human pace, more face-to-face interaction, hands-on technological self-sufficiency, reuse and recycling, and a healthy urban environment that is friendly to self-propulsion, pleasant smells and sights, and human conviviality.

Bicycling is for many of its adherents both a symbolic and practical rejection of one of the most onerous relationships capitalist society imposes: car ownership. But it's much more than just an alternative mode of transit. A tall, rugged blonde man in his mid-thirties, Megulon-5, an inspirational character in Portland, Oregon's C.H.U.N.K. 666 group, declares, "We are preparing for a post-apocalyptic future with different laws of physics."[2] It sounds off-kilter at first, but there is a rising tide of local activists in most communities who accept the Peak Oil arguments.[3] Many are already organizing themselves directly and indirectly towards a post-petroleum way of life. It may not alter physics exactly, but it certainly implies a radical change in our relationship to energy resources and ecology.

The explosion of zany and whimsical, practical and political self-expression via bicycling comprises a deeply rooted oppositional impulse that challenges core values of our society. The bicycle has become a device that connotes self-emancipation, as well as artistic and cultural experimentation. The playfulness and hands-on tinkering in the subculture is spawning new communities that can be framed as emerging sites of working class re-composition.

The "outlaw" bicycling subculture has no hierarchy flowing from wage differentials and ownership, because most of the culture takes place outside of monetary exchange or the logic of business. Instead, these bike hackers are all about *doing*, tinkering with the discarded detritus of urban life, inventing new forms of play, celebration, and artistic expression. Theirs is a culture that is re-produced in action, not affirmed in acts of passive consumption. Not just an isolated geek culture, it exists in real spaces and brings people together across age, class, race, and gender boundaries.

I call it an "outlaw" bike subculture because it goes against that kind of good behavior norm that a lot of mainstream bicycle advocates promote. The outlaw subculture is not particularly concerned with wearing helmets (or even safety in general), having the latest gear, following traffic rules set up for cars, or seeking approval from mainstream society. A 2003 issue of *Christian Science Monitor* described a "mutant bike" culture.[4] Critical Mass rides have been important arenas for staking out these counter-norms in the bike scene. Crucially, this counter-sensibility has attracted legions of youth, and is eroding the nerdy image that has helped reinforce bicycling's reputation as unhip (recently emphasized in the film *40 Year Old Virgin*, for example).

It has long been a curiosity that mainstream, "middle-class" bicyclists have been obsessed with law-abiding behavior and have been so quick to denounce other cyclists for flouting their sense of propriety. Mainstream bicycle advocates maintain that cyclists as a group must be extremely law-abiding, in order to reinforce the self-congratulatory fantasy that bikes are angels in the transit universe, compared to the (automobile) devil... Once again, even among bicyclists, we run into a neo-Christian moralism that seeks to impose a black and white, good and bad dichotomy, warmly embracing those who shop and ride correctly, and casting the rest of us into a purgatory of illegality and disrespect. It's reinforced by an ideology called "effective cycling" developed by a Stanford rocket engineer (and bicycle enthusiast), which declares that bicyclists should strive to behave like cars on the streets of America.[5]

In the U.S., the prevailing cultural norm still sees the bicycle as a toy. As children we are given a bicycle when we are deemed "ready," and it is often our first experience of self-emancipation from the narrow confines of home, of our street, and of parental supervision. Suddenly, we are mobile. On bikes kids quickly expand their territories. Neighborhoods that were once far away are now close and spaces for new independent adventures open up. Who can forget the exhilarating freedom of zipping along on a bicycle with a group of friends, or even alone, at a young age? Mastery of a complex urban environment starts to seem possible as our new mobility alters perspectives, horizons, and expectations.

Of course this new freedom is tempered by streets jammed with death-dealing vehicles. Our first liberation is eventually forgotten as the promise of "true freedom" behind the wheel of a car is pumped into us before we can even walk, shaping the imaginations of children from an early age. The bicycle is usually seen as a mere stepping stone to the real thing, one's first car. And few people eschew that path and refuse to drive; for many, in spite of the financial burden, getting a car is an urgent priority of growing up, of establishing maturity. The bicycle is left behind as a child's plaything, or maybe in our overweening athletic culture it retains some use as a device for exercise. But American society, dominated by the car and oil industries for most of the past century, has been unwilling to accommodate the bicycle as a vehicular choice, as a reasonable means of daily transportation.

Nevertheless, the bicycle has been enjoying a resurgence in the past 15 years. Daily bicycle commuting has expanded dramatically in San Francisco, New York, Chicago, and other cities where the monthly seizure of streets by bicyclists known as Critical Mass has opened space and imaginations, and given people a safe and enjoyable way to reconnect with urban bicycling before venturing out on their own. For most of these new bicycle commuters, the choice is self-reinforcing. Once tried, bicycling is much more pleasant than sitting in traffic in a car. Moreover, it is much cheaper, and the rhythms of regular cycling can improve mental and physical health.

Underneath this broad move towards bicycling is a burgeoning subculture that is reaching down to kids and teens, diminishing the gender gap, and making bicycling and things bicycle-related hip in unprecedented ways. This subculture is largely a do-it-yourself (DIY) phenomenon, based on word-of-mouth, homemade zines, informal parties and events, and a deliberate sharing of basic technical know-how. The zine explosion, a quintessential DIY movement based on increasingly available reproduction technologies in copyshops and at corporate jobs since the mid-1980s, was crucial in spreading the new bike subculture. Megulon-5 attributes his own entry into the subculture partly to Greta Snider's infamous zine *Mudflap*:

> I was living in Portland, reading *Mudflap* and *BikeCult* and a lot of zines, and countercultural books. There was just this culture out there that I felt really isolated from, living in Portland. Now I don't feel so much that way, partly because I think we've —C.H.U.N.K. 666 and other people unrelated to us—made our own culture.[6]

The bike subcultures provide important social space. Unlike the chain stores and malls that dominate the U.S., the bike culture is participatory, unpredictable, and open-ended. Robin Havens moved to San Francisco in 1996, knowing no one and not yet a bicyclist. But thanks to her roommates she found herself immersed in the bike messenger scene, and before long she was publishing her own occasional zine, *Rip It Up!*, about "bikes, beer and boys." Eventually she became a bike mechanic, founded a bike repair workshop for kids in San Francisco's Hunters' Point, and now teaches bike repair as part of a public high school curriculum. She declares:

> The underground bike subculture represents self-sufficiency, self-sustainability, and responsibility... [qualities that] could definitely be attributed to other kinds of ecological activism, e.g. community gardening. I also think that the bike or the garden culture (really healthy cultures) allow for a kind of giving and receiving that you can't get in the broader society... It breaks down the anonymity of the city.[7]

The mental space opened up is one of bicycling's best kept secrets. For many, choosing to bicycle is a public act of individuation, reinforcing a self-reliant and critical mentality. Often it is the most individualistic cycling "rebels" who invest the most time and effort in new communities and institutions. On this note, Jessie Basbaum of San Francisco's Bike Kitchen says,

> Riding a bike is a very independent act. Just riding your bike around fosters a lot of self-reliance and comfortableness being alone. Riding by yourself gives you a lot of time to think, to look at things around you, so in that sense it's going against the grain a little bit.[8]

Bicycling communities are interesting amalgamations of strongly individualistic people who collaborate on self-sufficiency. Ted White, longtime bike activist and "bikeumentarist" says,

> People who are into bikes tend almost always to be in some way independent thinking and self-sufficient... I think bikes are a positive response to almost everything that is wrong with American mainstream society today. Bikes are cheap, simple, and democratic and sexy in a very different way than riding around in a car. Bike transportation is about individuality but not about excess. Bikes are congenial and social. Bikes force us to be in our bodies and help us to know and love our bodies as they are.[9]

In contrast, there are glossy magazines and plenty of upscale marketers selling bicycles and *frou-frou* lycra clothing, helmets, bike accessories and all the things you would expect a prolific consumer society to promote. But mainstream bicycling culture is largely separated from the grassroots upsurge, even if there are crossovers aplenty in the form of messenger bags, headlights, and other mass-produced accoutrements that trickle through the permeable membrane between the two worlds.

Chicago's "Rat Patrol," a self-described "anarchist group," articulates the subcultural rejection of commodification and marketing, and with it, underlines the outlaw assault on the marketing efforts to co-opt the bike culture:

The pathetic sports junkie on a bicycle is no more free than a motorist trapped in an SUV in a traffic jam... There is a void of self-doubt which athletes attempt to cover with spandex outfits and titanium objects of veneration. The sporting goods 'user' is compelled by nervous guilt to look down upon those who do not ride as fast, or as far, or as often. Persons exhibiting the following behaviors are best regarded as covert operators of the capitalistic conspiracy to further co-opt and defuse non-fossil-fueled transportation movements:

• Abnormal concern with perfect finish and perfect operation of the bicycle

• Keeps glossy bicycling magazines under the mattress

• Suggests you should buy new equipment instead of repairing old bicycle

• Always rides in superhero tights

• When riding, is more concerned with speed and distance covered than scenery or places visited

• Unable to hold a conversation unrelated to bicycles or biking

• Paranoid delusion that he/she is being persecuted for his/her hobby

• Speech is sprinkled with component brand names

• Constant desire to witness bicycle's transforming power in his/her own life

• Believes that biking is a morally superior choice, therefore befitting a morally superior attitude

• Attempts to bring bicycle-related issues into every conversation

• Awkward duck walk caused by wearing cleated bike shoes into roadside businesses

• Easily impressed with expensive equipment and celebrity endorsements

• Wears helmet even when not on bike

As you can see, these easily-identifiable symptoms of sporting goods addiction are identical to the symptoms of capitalist-driven automobile addiction. They are caused by the fetishization and worship of lifeless objects. What was once viewed as a useful tool, a means to an end, becomes the end in itself.

Should your comrades seek to impose these dangerous

ideas on you, or should you find yourself believing them, stay on your guard, and remember that these innocent-sounding ideas are in actuality part of a sinister plot to coopt the velorution. Do not let the greedy multinationals once again derail progressive attempts to save our Earth from global warming and environmental disaster![10]

The outlaw bicycling subculture is distinctly anti-consumerist. It is a tinkering culture that spontaneously re-uses and recycles in ways environmental advocates of recycling can only dream about. It is a culture that often merges bicycles with art and performance. Portland's C.H.U.N.K. 666, an exemplary and probably typical group of bicycle hackers, "acquires whatever bicycles we can ethically without spending, [or] spending as little money as possible. We cut them into pieces and weld them back together again in different configurations."[11]

In the first issue of the *C.H.U.N.K. 666* zine, a feature on one of the legendary early groups, the Hard Times Bicycle Club (HTBC) in Minneapolis, described how it has no dues, no regular meetings or rides. As the article explained, "part of the HTBC aesthetic is anti-money and anti-retail... A mechanic and artist, 38-year-old Per Hanson, is president of the HTBC... He lives 'minimally,' having few possessions and no real job."[12] The Hard Times Bike Club spread the word that they would recycle used bike parts and as a result, parts were dropped off at their garage regularly.

Martin Leugers founded Chopper Riding Urban Dwellers (CRUD), a San Francisco-based group that also puts bikes back together "artistically." As he put it:

> I like the punk rock ethics of not wanting to make money from my art... I decided I'm going to make money at my job, and I enjoy what I do (industrial design), though it's not my perfect ideal. But it gives me the ability to make crazy bikes that basically nobody wants. The bikes I make I view as a kind of sculpture... It's my totally creative outlet where I don't have to worry about selling them.[13]

Class doesn't often enter into the identities being created in these new subcultural spaces, and yet, a resilient anti-capitalist instinct runs through much of it and gets expressed in various ways. Echoing Leugers, a recurrent theme is the refusal to allow the wage-labor relationship to define one's engagement.

CRUD: Chopper Riding Urban Dwellers.

BICYCLING OUTSIDE OF THE WAGED DAY

Jessie Basbaum, private investigator, and Catherine Hartzell, immunology lab researcher, co-founded San Francisco's Bike Kitchen in mid-2003 while still in their early 20s. The Bike Kitchen quickly became a favorite haunt adjacent to Cellspace, a large community space in the Mission District.[14] Covered in graffiti, the Bike Kitchen sits in a former truck rental facility surrounded by asphalt, and on weekends, a neighborhood flea market. It's an all-volunteer space and deliberately refuses to provide paid services. "It's part of our policy not to do repairs for money... we're here to show people how to do it," says Basbaum. "It's definitely not a job," emphasizes Hartzell. In fact, if it were to become a job, Hartzell wonders "how I would feel. I don't think I would love it as much. When it's required of you, and you're not making the decision, you lose some sense of enjoyment."[15]

Basbaum described a cultural critique of wage-labor without naming it as such: "[People have] this idea that you have a job, but whatever you really care about should be your hobby, it shouldn't be your job, because then it becomes more mundane."

Bicycling subculture activists routinely work long hours for free. But they also see that wage-labor is an oppressive distraction that reduces their full engagement with their "real work." Ben Guzman, co-founder of the Los Angeles Bike Kitchen (no direct relation to the San Francisco Bike Kitchen, but the same name), works on television commercials for a living. But as he put it, explaining the relationship between his paid work and the volunteer Bike Kitchen work:

> ...my work the last few years has just been a way to get
> to be able to do the things I want to do... all my jobs,
> are just a means to get back to doing what's important.
> While I'm at work I'm taking a pause from the rest of
> the stuff I'm doing.[16]

Robin Havens explains how her paid teaching job, even though it's similar to what she was doing before for free, changes the experience of her work.

> If you're somehow making enough money to live, it's
> easy to use your extra energy on these projects, whether
> it's writing a zine—where I didn't make any money—or
> starting a bike program in Hunters Point.... I started
> that with no feeling that I needed to be paid for it. Just a
> feeling that there were kids out there that would like to
> work on bikes, that had NOTHING else going on, and
> really needed to be doing something. But after a year, I

was broke! [...] The fact that it's my primary source of income and that I'm being paid a teacher's salary, puts extra pressure on it. It makes it different from just doing things because I want to do them and I see a need. It's no longer me independently doing something that I can change at will.[17]

Insofar as creative engagement with the bike culture becomes a regular job, the radical impulses we find in the culture are dampened. But the urge to break free of the alienation and known limits of wage-work keep erupting in bike subcultures. The push-and-pull of market relations, money, and wage-work alter the experience enough that plenty of DIY bicyclists refuse to get co-opted into businesses and jobs. But the "success" of bike-subculture spaces repeatedly renews the pressure to conform to the larger society's logic of property and business.

AUTONOMOUS SPACES OR SMALL BUSINESSES?

The new DIY bicycle shops are trying to bridge class and racial divides. Facing daunting problems of sustainability they exist on the verge of co-optation. Everyday rent and survival confront DIY bikeshop staffers with the necessity of making money. This in turn pushes them towards converting cooperative spaces based on sharing and mutual aid into small businesses. The flow of cash, even within official non-profits, inexorably begins to shape decisions and behaviors. Moreover, by providing training and experience to kids (and adults), one of the ironic outcomes is to help them open the door to a "real" job.

Eric Welp, part of "Chain Reaction" in DC, describes the group's attempts to survive without

> becom[ing] a chain with a bunch of locations around the city. I think we'd just like to be stable and not have to rely on any donations or grants. It'd be great to be self-sustained and sustainable. We're not going to save the world with bikes, but we can change it by changing a kid's outlook. If we can change things to help them better understand the effect of their actions and how they can function in society, then changing our principal mode of transportation is just the beginning.[18]

Ted White recounts his experience at the Center for Appropriate Transport in Eugene, Oregon.

> When I worked at the CAT we worked specifically with so-called "at-risk" youth. I think most of these kids loved being in our bike workshop—what they did there was

tangible, it related to something real. They took metal and rubber and plastic parts, put them together, fine tuned them, and then—voila!—they had literally made themselves a vehicle for both external exploration and self-discovery.[19]

Basbaum explains how at San Francisco's Bike Kitchen "someone volunteers six hours of time to our shop and they learn, hopefully, a set of basic skills and contribute a little bit to the shop, and then they earn a frame, and build up the bike on their own. ... When someone does the earn-a-bike program in earnest and with enthusiasm I think it's very self-empowering."

Earn-A-Bike programs are running all over the U.S. Often supported by local governments and police departments, they are widely recognized as programs that help kids learn basic skills and bicycle safety, get involved in their community, and give them a means of transportation they can keep at the end of the program. The Boston-based Bikes Not Bombs is one of the organizations that have done a lot to promote the model, and they make available on their website an Instructor Training Manual.[20] Often starting with donated bikes from the police collection of recovered stolen bikes, there's no telling how far afield some of these programs can go.

Robin Havens started by volunteering to run bicycle repair workshops after school in one of San Francisco's poorest neighborhoods, Hunters Point. Later she moved to a high school in the middle of the bay on Treasure Island and has integrated bicycle repair into the curriculum in the style of a woodshop or metal shop class. She's also worked bicycling into a math curriculum and is trying to connect the Earn-A-Bike (EAB) program she started with academic subjects at her new gig.

> I can bridge the gap between an actual EAB Program and using bikes as educational tools to teach academic subjects, which is really what I get excited about. I love thinking up projects where bikes can in some way help explain abstract situations.[21]

In the case of Bicas in Tucson, Arizona, kids who have been arrested can work off their misdemeanors and infractions by enrolling in the Earn-A-Bike program. To fulfill the terms of their "penalty" they must select a broken bike from a room of over 1000 such rusting hulks, and then go about learning to bring it back to life. Once the bike is properly rebuilt, fixed, and tuned up, they have completed their "sentence" and may ride it home.

SF's Bike Kitchen, along with the Bike Hut Foundation and some other San Francisco shops, give kids a chance to earn bikes too, but without the involvement of local authorities. Often enough, once kids get involved with a bike shop experience where they are treated with some dignity and expectations, they come back for more. Pier 40 Bike Hut, founded by Victor Veysey, has been mentoring poor kids for almost a decade. Pedal Revolution in the Mission District started as a bike shop to provide training and work opportunities for homeless and runaway youth. It has since evolved into a more mainstream bike shop, but still has training and job opportunities for youth in need. In all these programs, kids in trouble get to interact with engaged and interested adults and other kids. It doesn't always "save" every kid, but hundreds of youth across the country have gotten a new start thanks to these kinds of hands-on training programs. Often enough, a seriously motivated youngster can learn real skills and go on to find employment in the growing local bicycle repair business, as, for example, DC's Chain Reaction has seen with a number of its "graduates."

The backbone of this network of under-funded, barely sustainable co-op and DIY bikeshops is provided by the outlaw bicycle subculture's shock troops—the women and men who find a way to survive on very low incomes, or who work at these shops after (and in addition to) their paid gigs. They are resourceful, politically engaged, and passionate. They challenge the transit and energy systems shaped by capitalism but cru-

Typical Saturday afernoon at San Francisco's Bike Kitchen in 2005.

cially, they are making connections *in practice* between race, class, gender, and urban life, city planning, technology and ecological reinhabitation. Ironically, by teaching kids to work for their bikes, these programs also reinforce the core values of a capitalist, work ethic culture.

Rachel Spiewak co-founded the Sopo Bicycle Cooperative, Atlanta's first DIY bikeshop, which opened its doors in October 2005 after a year of excited planning and organizing. Unlike the cities that already had an "outlaw bicycling" constituency, Atlanta's is only just beginning, the Sopo Coop being the first place of its kind.

bicycle inter-community action & salvage
po box 1811 tucson az 85702 usa
phone:(520)628-7950 fx:798-1175
warehouse:920 s.warren ave 105&106
youth bike underground; mexico co-ops

There was almost no DIY or outlaw bicycle culture in Atlanta. Critical Mass drew 60 people if we were lucky... The complete vacuum had a lot to do with our initial success. People in Atlanta are starving for this kind of thing... as an all-volunteer operation we're making enough money to pay rent, buy new tools, do bike fix-up days with children and so on... A completely overlooked basic human need is that of skills and mastery. We need it as much as we need food and shelter. I'm not opposed to new technology as such. I'm interested in calorie-for-calorie efficiency, environmental responsibility, fair labor practices, community self-reliance, and stopping the process of corporate wealth accumulation... Also I don't identify as an outlaw. I [am] a revolutionary, interested in the radical mainstreaming of sustainability.[22]

John Gerken, writing in New Orleans' *Chainbreaker* zine, describes why he is involved with the local bike co-op, Plan B (which survived Hurricane Katrina without damage, and re-opened by late October 2005).

This place is a working example of how I think things

Bicas workshop, Tucson, Arizona, October 2003.

could be different. It's a place where people can share resources, skills and knowledge, and not have to pay for every single thing. I think people can help each other out more than we're led to believe, and it feels good to also learn so much while I'm doing it.

Plan B is the New Orleans Community Bike Project. It's a DIY bike shop located in a huge warehouse near the French Quarter that also has shows, Recycle for the Arts, trapeze practice, Food Not Bombs, yoga, art shows, and other stuff. We're all volunteer, and have all kinds of tools and resources for people to use, as well as piles of parts and old frames and bikes... We don't fix your bike at Plan B—we're there to help you learn how to do it yourself... A broad mix of people does come in. It's a

Tucson's Bicas makes good use of discards for signage.

measure of success in any community project that gets
beyond its own specific community—in this case, for
the most part, scrappy young white people... I'm proud
that, while it is rooted in the ideals that are formed within my specific community, Plan B interacts with a broad
cross-section of New Orleans. Yuppies, college kids, European tourists, homeless folks, and street performers,
clowns and circus freaks, neighborhood kids. Really
people of all ages and walks of life come in.

This informal network of alternative bike spaces will keep grappling
with the dynamics of survival and cooptation. Meanwhile, they provide
an environment for people to discover their own agency, their own ability to shape life. To no small extent, these spaces are a breeding ground
for new social relations, underground media, and an alternative technological path.

BICYCLE ZINES AND WOMEN CYCLISTS

Key to the spread of the underground bicycle subculture has been
the explosion of bike zines. These journals are usually produced in
runs of well under 500 copies, often the material is handwritten rather
than typed on a computer, and the graphic quality is spotty at best. Commonly there are cartoon stories and a variety of photos capturing aspects of the local scene. The passion that zine producers pour into their
productions is itself a compelling demonstration of how hard people
will work when driven by the heart instead of the wallet. The heart-
felt stories of zinesters open up a world to their readers that cannot be
reached easily by other means, but, once discovered, exert a mighty pull
on the reader to join in.

The publisher's personality closely shapes each zine. Often enough,
the publisher writes and draws nearly all content, focusing on her or his
day-to-day experiences. A bicycling zine might detail the saga of learning
mechanical skills, working at a DIY bikeshop, and exploring strange and
wonderful sides of the urban environment by bicycle, or might provide
how-to information for traveling or commuting to work by bike, or perhaps
for discovering the thrills of riding after midnight, dating on bikes, etc.

The zine impulse is well-captured by Robin Havens of *Rip It Up*!: "It
was so much fun to do what I was doing with a bike, but also document
it. It was almost fun in the way that you write a journal and get extra
satisfaction from that, being able to look at it and read it... what makes
a good zine for me, is that it isn't super self-absorbed, that it's actually
communicating enthusiasm and energy and the idea that if everyone

was doing that, that you would have this momentum towards change, and towards curiosity and intellectual improvement."[23]

Some zines speak for local groups, like *C.H.U.N.K. 666* or the San Francisco Bicycle Messenger Association's *Cognition*. Other bike zines are love letters to bicycling and the publisher's friends in the community. *Chainbreaker*, *Mudflap*, *Rip It Up!*, *bike-not*, *Sin on Wheels*, *Biker Pride*, *V.Jer*, *Giddy Up!*, *Resist*, *derailleur*, are a few of many such zines, each unique and quirky and unpredictably particular.

Women, already present and visible throughout the biking subculture, have been foundational in the development of bike zines. The reality today is that working class politics still reinforces a patriarchal obliviousness to women's work, and considering the powerful participation of women in social upheavals—notably in the 1871 Paris Commune, mass strikes in textiles and agriculture, the Spanish Civil War, the Vietnam War, and much more—it's an ongoing puzzle to explain the failure of men to embrace and honor their female colleagues. In the bicyclig subculture, women's voices are often among the strongest, but their contributions to the bike zine world might surpass even their quantitative representation within the biking community.

Greta Snider's well-known *Mudflap*, already mentioned above, appeared at the beginning of the 1990s, during the early days of Critical Mass and the burgeoning messenger culture. In *Mudflap #6*, from around 1993 or so, she starts out with a cartoon on Equipment Fetish (*you know how it feels... there's something so good about MACHINE PARTS.. knurled wheels, dials, level meters; the KA-CHUNK of a shutter, the clicks of indexed things falling into place...*). In 48 mostly hand-written pages, Snider introduces the CineCycle and a half dozen other haunts for bike-punks in Toronto. She rants against buying stolen bikes, presents a quasi-board game about searching by bicycle for empty cigarette packs around San Francisco, writes about hitchiking, tells a story about *not* having 3-way sex in Greenwich Village, goes to a punk show with photos, and has another spread on a made-up game "Mission Gladiator" which turns out to be rather like living in San Francisco's Mission District at the time. She even introduces us to her future husband, Al Sobrante "the Gentleman Bike Mechanic," who decided to protest the first Gulf War in 1991 by repairing bicycles for free at the Humboldt State University quad every Friday. In a two page spread called "Nothing to Do in Frisco" Greta gives us photos of the New Year's Derby (drunken cyclists riding in circles trying to knock each other off their bikes), skate hockey, bike stunts, fixed gear races, illegal soap box races, and of course Critical Mass, covering in no time a whole range of activities that are the lifeblood of the 1990s/2000s underground bike scene.

Later efforts like *Sin on Wheels* by Christy Thornton in NYC, Shelley's *Chainbreaker* in New Orleans, and Robin Havens's *Rip it Up!* in San Francisco capture the excitement and passion of a lot of the women for bicycling and liberation in the new underground bike culture.

> The bike is the gorgeous steel backbone of do-it-yourself, anti-exclusionary technology, accessible to everyone, regardless of class, race, ethnicity, sexual orientation, education or physical ability. More than a means of transportation. A tool of resistance. A means of staying alive in this world… I've met some truly amazing people, and seen some of the best people I know get turned on to bikes. I have very few friends now that don't ride, and I've made so many more through riding. And, maybe most importantly, I've watched my women friends become empowered to take on the intimidating misogyny that courses through this city, using only their muscles and their willpower to push them through, to prove that they can take whatever is thrown at them… Every time one of my badass bike sisters steps onto her pedals and sets

out into the city, she's defying a culture that tells women where they can and cannot go, what they can and cannot do, how they should or should not act... She's one more visible woman, out in the streets... We're a big giant collective sin on wheels, rolling right over any misogynist fuck who thinks we can't, and pulling along any doubtful sister who's been told she shouldn't. [24]

These women cyclists are tapping a century-old history of women's liberation via bicycling. In the late 19th century, women embraced bicycling as a means of personal liberation from the limits of horse and carriage and male escorts, but even more dramatically, from the now laughable fashion constraints they faced. Abandoning corsets and full length skirts for the new-fangled invention of bloomers and shorter skirts, independent women were celebrated even in women's magazines like *Cosmopolitan*. In August 1885, Mrs. Reginal de Koven wrote, "To men, rich and poor, the bicycle is an unmixed blessing, but to women it is deliverance, revolution, salvation. It is well nigh impossible to overestimate the potentialities of this exercise in the curing of the common and characteristic ills of womankind, both physical and mental, or to calculate the far reaching effects of its influence in the matters of dress and social reform."[25] *Sin on Wheels* includes a brief excerpt from an 1896 *American Medical Association* article: "A female medical practitioner who has ridden the wheel since 1888, has expressed herself as sanguine that a healthful and comfortable dress will be the outcome of the extension of the bicycle habit among females."[26]

Thornton's zine reveals how, indeed, women's clothing *has* become more comfortable:

> ...I have this tight, short little red skirt. It wraps around my upper thighs... my long, sturdy legs emerge out from under the hem, the strong muscles cultivated on West Harlem hills. In that skirt, I feel sexy. I feel powerful. It's my favorite thing to wear riding...On my bike, my legs are my power. On my bike, my legs have nothing to do with you. Oh, they're sexy, make no mistake—and I embrace and revel in that sexuality. But I don't seem to recall having asked for your opinion on the matter, and I hardly think them being there is reason enough for you to assume you are participant in my personal celebration.[27]

Self-emancipation through sexual and gender freedom hasn't escaped the grips of capitalist society. The issues of clothing and self-presentation are inalterably snagged in the contradictions of a society drowning in softcore pornographic imagery. The resolution of gender imbalances cannot be achieved without a broad shift to a healthier culture of mutual respect and appreciation among women and men. Still, bicycling females are often at the forefront of the effort to further extend personal and social freedom. In New Orleans' *Chainbreaker,* a woman bicyclist brings up the issue of sexual harassment and speaks out to the men around her:

> Some days I feel like I can't make it a block down a street without some person making sexual or otherwise demeaning or objectifying comments at me on my bi- cycle. Things like hissing–tssssssst! like hey baby-ing me, like asking me for a damn ride (which I never really understood anyhow). Sometimes even the wrong kind of stare is enough to make me feel uncomfortable, or the sound of a car slowing down enough to ride beside me awhile. Yuck. This is what I want to say to the people who do this:

> "Realize that when a woman is on her bike, especially when she is alone, or it is at night, or when she lives in a dangerous city like New Orleans, that these comments do nothing but make her feel less safe, uncomfortable, de- moralized and uncared for, like nothing but a mere ob- ject. A nice comment could make her day, humor might even make her smile or feel better, without frightening her. But understand that if she returns your hello with a glare, that you could be the fifth or sixth guy to make some offhanded comment at her. She might just get tired of sifting through what is creepy and what is sweet and has just resorted to being mean. Understand that it is not her fault, nor is it yours. Rethink how you approach con- tact with a woman and try to do it in a way that can leave her feeling safe and positive."

> Thanks.[28]

Like a lot of today's underground bike culture, the recent flourish- ing of female cycling can trace its direct roots to the 1970s. During the emergence of mountain bicycling in Marin County, Jackie Phelan made a name for herself as a fearless and talented cyclist. Phelan founded WOMBATS: Women's Mountain Biking and Tea Society, which now has at least 250 members with the biggest chapters in Bay Area, Anchorage AK, and Albuquerque NM.

Many of the DIY bike shops around the country now emphatically of- fer women-only nights and classes. For example, Recycle-A-Bicycle Ladies Night in New York City has become a regular outlet for "women seeking not just to learn bike building and repair, but to find the confidence to be able to tackle it themselves, to understand the simple physics of driv- ing their two-wheeled wonder. Through learning collectively, women can lessen their reliance on a male-dominated service industry, lessen the intimidation factor that exists in the majority of bike shops, and strengthen the community of bike-lovin' ladies all over the city."[29] The New York activist group Times Up! also provides women-only classes, and at the Montreal bike co-op "La Voie Libre/Right to Move" Wednesday evenings are women-only.

Female bike messengers, too, have used zines to make their presence felt. Women's voices have anchored some of the best messenger zines and encouraged many more women to enter the bicycling subculture. In general, bike messengers and their friends have been prolific zine producers over the years. London cycle couriers have their own zine, *Moving Target*. *Mercury Rising* was an important journal by and for San Francisco bike messengers in the early 1990s, followed later by *Voice of Da, The Illiterate Digest, The Wall,* and *Cognition*. Most recently, some of the folks who found themselves in the middle of the largest-ever wildcat strike of bike messengers in San Francisco (at the now-defunct DMS in 2001) put out a one-shot zine called *"Operation: Courier"* that offered a survey of messenger radicalism from London to San Francisco, Portland and even Buenos Aires, Argentina.

BIKE MESSENGERS

> It's a beautiful quirk that within the confines of one of the more greedy, unnatural, heartless places on earth— the San Francisco Financial District, home of some of the biggest planet-raping corporations known to man: Bechtel, Chevron, BofA, General Electric, etc.—there exists a subculture of crazed, anarchist individualists who get to break laws for a living. In our society of technology-run-amok, the fastest way to transport material downtown is still on a bike... the scene [is] a complete oasis from the shallow values of western society. Money, status, looks, power? Fuck that—how about a game of spokepoker, popping a wheelie on an Aerobike, climbing up the Marlboro Sign, a new copy of Huffbo Chiente, a housewrecking party, or ditching a motorcycle cop in a parking garage?
>
> — *America Meredith* [30]

Unmistakably distinct, the bike messenger subculture has fueled the broader outlaw bicycling subculture. In an era when working-class culture has become invisible in TV land and malls, bike messengers (or cycle couriers as they are known in some places) are a lively and self-conscious community of workers. Messengers are mostly young, often in rebellion against boring 9-to-5 office work or the drudgery of factory life, and embrace the free and mobile daily life of messengering. Ironically, they play a crucial role in the interstices of late capitalism, whipping across town with signed contracts, checks, contraband, and various types of Extremely Important Packages.

Their working conditions are famously free but extremely dangerous. Death on the job is a daily threat as they hurtle through financial district canyons, weaving insanely through urban gridlock. Between the punk music underground and the coded lingo used over the dispatch radios, plus the distinctive garb (an anti-uniform of sorts), messengers set themselves apart from mainstream America. The rugged individualism and militant independence of many of the personalities drawn

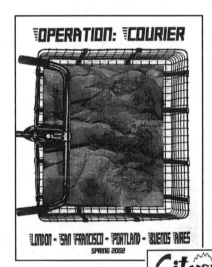

to messengering makes the effort to organize collectively doubly difficult. Still, over the past 20 years independent organizing efforts have emerged here and there, notably in New York City and San Francisco.

In San Francisco the S.F. Bike Messengers Association (SFBMA) was formed in 1991. It set out to improve conditions for bike messengers and to help sustain the local culture. *MessPress* was a small zine promoting the SFBMA, and later that same year *Mercury Rising* began publishing, too. The first issue humorously declared that it was the official publication of the San Francisco Bike Messenger Association, "a new organization that has existed for over 40 years. We pay our dues everyday." A lead article decried the imminent plan to eliminate bikes and walkers from the Special T messenger workforce; an inside piece by Fur told how he flyered the messengers at one company to refuse an imposed commission cut since, if they caved in, the new lower rate would soon be imposed on messengers at other companies, too. Running through a number of reasons why he took it upon himself to organize, he concludes "in a way, we all work for the same company," indicating a growing consciousness among messengers in San Francisco and beyond.

> As messengers, we are a highly visible community whose future depends heavily on the promotion of bicycles, check?! Every day more people everywhere are realizing the advantages of pedal power, yet many remain discouraged by a society largely ignorant and hostile towards bicyclists and their rights. Buckling under to the interests of big business, our government continues to reinforce this nausea with sexy oil-guzzling energy and transportation policies that perpetually subsidize the freeway gridlock libido cancer industry... Get the Fuck Outta My Way, it's high time we added our chain driven ambition into the mixin'... think about it! A network to keep us informed, active and unified would benefit us greatly. A voice for our anger, an effective vehicle for our bicycle moxie!

> Our bicycles afford us a healthy self-determination and a liberty to move about freely that is indeed revolutionary. It is time to demand a change in misguided transportation policies—time to recognize the bicycle as America's true Freedom Machine![31]

In spite of resistance to traditional unionization, messengers have proven quite able and willing to organize themselves as a culture. One of the charismatic characters behind *Mercury Rising* was Markus "Fur" Cook, who worked hard before his premature death (in 1996) to build messenger self-awareness and self-reliance. As a main writer and organizer with the zine he touched many lives. Like people in other lines of work messengers often extend themselves beyond their money-making lives. Cook (who played in a band, L.Sid, and co-published *Mercury Rising*) captured the larger dynamic of working several jobs to be fully alive in a 1992 interview: "For those of us playing music, that's not anti-work either. It's another job. Lots of messengers are working incredibly hard on all kinds of things after [our] 10 hour days."[32]

Outside of work, the culture has spawned a number of annual rides and semi-regular events. A "messenger gang" called H@nx has been hosting the Russian River Ride for over a decade, a weekend-long excursion to the old-fashioned working class resort along the river, some 75 miles north of San Francisco. On or near Groundhog Day every year, the SFBMA stages the "49-mile Ride," and a hardy few actually manage to traverse the entire hilly route of 49 touristic miles, making sure to tag the Seagull signs along the way with an SFBMA sticker to prove they were there (the larger number of riders barely cover eight miles over a day of heavy beer drinking and pot-smoking). Semi-regular "Alleycat Races" pit messengers and anyone who wants to compete against one another in combination scavenger hunt/bike races, a type of event that also takes place in other cities. Messenger culture overlaps with dozens of punk bands, as many musicians work as messengers for their "day jobs." A CD of local messenger bands came out in 1996 with the punning title of "Pothole."

The summer of 1996 saw the 4th annual Cycle Messenger World Championships in San Francisco, held for the first time in the U.S. after starting in London and going to Berlin and Toronto in previous years. It has become the huge annual contest and party for bike messengers worldwide, providing a handy reason to travel far from home, and an incredible mechanism to share skills and experiences across cultures and languages.

In 1996, working out of a chaotic office in the Civic Center of San Francisco, volunteers from the messenger community met for months to pull off the event. In spite of many people who thought it would never happen due to the chronic disorganization and inebriation of the local scene, the event was a huge success, staging events and parties over a week-long festival in August 1996. The culminating party following the August Critical Mass quickly became a local legend.

A decade earlier, in the mid-1980s, the Independent Courier Association was formed in New York City after Bob McGlynn, then working as an NYC messenger, put out a flyer titled "WAR!!—City Council Vs. Bike Messengers" explaining the city's plan to enforce license plates, uniforms, and special ID cards. The newly-formed ICA was unable to prevent the passage of the law, but by agreeing to participate in its implementation they managed to render it meaningless. By the time it took effect in January 1985, no more than a quarter of working messengers obeyed any part of it, and almost none complied with all the new rules. And there was no enforcement either, so it soon blew over. The ICA folded by the late 1980s and nowadays New York has its own New York Bike Messenger Association.

In a 1985 summary of this story, McGlynn concluded:

> Wouldn't it be interesting if "ignorant" and "unorganizable" messengers might be among the ignition points of a future rebellion against this dollar- and object-centric society, and for a people- and life-oriented one? Imagine a coalition of the street (couriers) and office (secretaries, computer programmers, etc.)—Yo! It's the Revolution! OK, OK, so it's a silly fantasy, but such wild imaginings have a habit of becoming very real in history a la France 1968 or Poland's Solidarity. If the farmworkers out west could get organized, why couldn't we?[33]

Formal unionization has made few inroads, though the Teamsters, Service Employees International Union (SEIU) and the International Longshore and Warehouse Union (ILWU) have all managed to organize workers in some companies. The ILWU in San Francisco is well known as a bastion of progressive unionism and when the San Francisco Bike Messengers Association decided to affiliate with the union there was a lot of hope. Already there was a general upswell of organizing amongst local messengers in many companies, and before long a major

S.F. Bike Messengers rally at The Wall on "10-9 Day," Oct. 9, 2003.

wildcat strike erupted at Dispatch Messenger Service (DMS) on January 12, 2000. (DMS had set out to consolidate dozens of small messenger companies around North America, the UK, and Australia, standardize the management model, and make a good profit.) The DMS wildcat was not under the auspices of the ILWU and it didn't take long for serious tension to emerge between the self-directed wildcatters and the union reps who felt they should be setting the pace. The strikers held their own, though, and won major wage increases and other concessions (thanks in part to brief follow-up walkouts in the ensuing year) before the company went bust in late 2001.

In 2004 the ILWU ended its relationship with the SFBMA, on the grounds that the messengers weren't doing enough to organize themselves. The union's strategy had been based on its own history. Longshoremen were a notoriously intermittent and transient workforce before their coastwide uprising in 1934 led to the creation of the independent ILWU two years later. Starting in the late 1990s, the union sought to organize messengers sufficiently to be able to set the price of labor industry-wide. But that attempt was thwarted by the delivery industry's resistance, taking full advantage of the weak enforcement of labor laws to prevent organizing. Also unhelpful to the union movement were the steadily emerging independent courier companies, often self-managed by former messengers who preferred to break out on their own. These companies "cherry picked" the most lucrative clients, and enjoyed the relatively better wages and conditions that came with self-employment, and so were uninterested in an organizing campaign that sought to stabilize the industry from below.

Of course, people come and go from bike messengering, and the future of workplace organizing among bike messengers is probably more similar to other low-wage, contingent and precarious workers than not. New entrants in the business nowadays often have a foot in the broader outlaw bicycling subculture. Even back in 1992, a messenger working on *Mercury Rising* articulated a radical vision that transcended the normal labor organizing paradigm:

> In utopia, there're no cars. Down the middle of the street, we're gonna tear up all the asphalt and there's gonna be gardens and orchards and you can just grab a peach as you're riding by. Everyone's gonna work 20 hours a week at a job they find meaningful, and they can change jobs throughout their lives if they want to. And everyone is gonna get taken care of, maybe no one will have a lot of stuff but everyone will have shelter, everyone will have food—if they get sick, they'll be taken

care of. You'll be able to walk everywhere you need to
go, you really won't even need a bicycle.[34]

Messengers will keep rediscovering their power until they find a way to
consolidate it. Editorializing in 2002, messenger organizers wrote:

> There's nothing stopping messengers from demanding
> more, except cynicism and disbelief. Disbelief in our abil-
> ity to coordinate strategically and disbelief in the potency
> of collective action. These (dis)beliefs serve only those
> who profit from our labor. As workers, we can either con-
> tinue to accept living at the mercy of the bosses and cor-
> porations that exploit us, or we can explore our power,
> take calculated risks, and act strategically to make gains...
> which brings us to the reason for this publication. What
> unfolds in these pages is the sense of possibility, with mes-
> sengers at the center. The experiences of messengers or-
> ganizing in San Francisco, Portland, and London against
> the bosses, and in Argentina against the government, are
> inspiring and instructive. These messengers have imag-
> ined something better.[35]

As cities continue to promote traffic congestion with short-sighted
accomodation of cars and parking, messengers will fill an important
role in the interstices of urban life. The wild individualists who hurtle
through clogged streets may not conform to traditional concepts of
"working class." Nevertheless, they are a self-conscious and vibrant link
between the outlaw bicycling subculture and the sprawling 21st century
logistics industry.

RIDES

...all you habitual motorists are suckers.
You've been hoodwinked. Your automobile is expensive, annoying, and anti-social. My bicycle is cheap, fun and at times,
a traveling party.   —*Resist #42*

The bicycling subculture is action-oriented. A
lot of energy can go towards fixing and ac-
quiring bikes, but finally it always comes down
to riding them. There are countless recreational
bicycle clubs around the United States but they
tend to be remarkably apolitical, except for occasional forays into lob-
bying to demand a rare road closure for a race or ride. Moreover, their
members are not famous for hanging out together, working together, or
having any other existence together beyond the club rides themselves.

But the outlaw bikers have forged new communities out of hundreds of theme rides, "derbies," races, rodeos, even bicycle polo, bicycle rodeo, and bicycle ballet in San Francisco. Messengers in New York and San Francisco spontaneously asserted their strength in large group rides in the late 1980s to avoid municipal regulation and harassment.

The New York Independent Couriers Association swung into action in 1987 when Mayor Koch announced a 90-day experimental ban of bikes from central midtown Manhattan. Groups of 30–400 messengers organized "work to rule" rides up 6th Avenue and down 5th.[36] These courier rides took place fifteen years after large rides in 1972 demanding the elimination of cars from Manhattan, in one of the first late 20th century upsurges of bicycle activism. A similar mass ride appeared in Berkeley, California in 1971, as part of the early eco-activism of the "sixties."

In San Francisco the 20th anniversary of Earth Day was celebrated in 1990 with a big ride through the city, under the slogan "Bicycles Aren't In the Way, Bicycles Are the Way!" Months later cyclists converged on the big anti-Gulf War marches in January 1991, acting as scouts and roving bands of cycling protestors. A group of 50 cyclists even rode 65 miles from Santa Cruz to join in. Later that year the Bay Area Bike Action Winter Solstice People-Powered Parade rolled through Golden Gate Park on December 21, protesting the prevalence of auto traffic in San Francisco's premiere public park. Cyclists have been campaigning for over fifteen years now *for* a Park and *against* a Parking Lot.

Critical Mass erupted out of this climate of politicized bike rides and direct action. The first "Commute Clot" took off from the foot of San Francisco's Market Street on September 25, 1992, about 50 riders strong. After a couple of months of the "organized coincidence" growing steadily, riders dubbed it "Critical Mass" after a comment in Ted White's "bikeumentary" *Return of the Scorcher* about bicycle tactics in China. It has since spread throughout the world and has appeared in over 400 cities on five continents. It is still a magical monthly occurrence in San Francisco, routinely drawing over 1,000 riders, and sometimes several thousand.

The full history of Critical Mass has been told elsewhere.[37] Among the different threads of the outlaw bicycling subculture, Critical Mass represents the most public demonstration of the subculture's existence, and its most overtly political expression. The monthly drama of a mass seizure of the streets by bicyclists is unique in many ways. It has no official organizers or leaders and thus is a monthly experiment in spontaneous self-organization. It has more of a celebratory tone than one dedicated to protest, but both realities coexist. More subversively, it is a *prefigurative* demonstration; it puts into practice a new type of public commons, created and animated by human conviviality, the kind of life usually promised "after the revolution." It escapes the logic of commodification entirely. No one has to buy anything to participate, and there is practically no hawking of wares around the event. Rolling down the street in a new mobile community, Critical Mass has pioneered network swarming as a political tactic, albeit a tactic employed to no instrumental purpose.[38] Critical Mass's amorphous and prefigurative qualities militate against making demands, declaring an agenda, or seeking specific goals (at the same time, hundreds of political ideas, campaigns, and slogans have been distributed during Critical Mass rides, including e.g. "Bicycling: A Quiet Statement Against Oil Wars"). Instead, an unpredictable number of citizens come together freely each month in cities large and small to begin living the life they can only dream about the rest of the month.

City life based on bicycles, walking, and well-developed public transit is a dream in America, but the bicycling dream becomes real every month during the brief minutes Critical Mass fills the streets. The right to assemble and to engage in free speech also get exercised each month, highlighting a diminishing public life through dramatic public action. Critical Mass exceeds simple civil libertarian behavior, though. In gathering dozens, hundreds, or thousands of cyclists month after month for over a decade across the world, a social space has been opened up in which further networking has flourished. The bike ride is the premise, but the deeper transformation of imaginations and social connections is hard to measure.

Clearly bicycling is on the rise, and other bike rides have emerged in the wake of Critical Mass, as have dozens of new associations and initiatives. In Chicago a campaign to "Depave Lakeshore Drive" bubbled out of the Critical Mass community. Chicago has also staged a "Bike Winter" festival, held annual auto-free art shows, and organized dozens of theme rides, including a lengthy ride along the old canals and railroad right-of-ways. In Bloomington, Indiana, cyclists have held midnight full moon rides over the past few years, as they have, too, in Austin, Texas. "Midnight Ridazz" take over the streets of Los Angeles in the middle of the night, too, on themed rides for more than a year now, slowly mapping the entire city of Los Angeles.

In August of 2002, the New York Bike Messengers Association hosted the first annual Warriors fun ride—all night, from the Bronx to Coney Island. Maggie Bowman described the scene at the beginning of the ride, a rainy night.

> The park is filled with approximately 500 warriors, loosely sectioned off by gang, 83 gangs in total... We make our way around the park checking out the competition. The Fearleaders, Los Banditos, the Aliens, the Turf, the Ridge Street Wrenches, the Pelham Park Ten-

Image by James R Swanson, San Francisco Critical Mass 2002.

nis Pros, the Flatbush Dandies, the Electric Vikings, the Ghost Riders, the Furies, the Killer Clowns, the Riffs, the Rotten Apples, the San Francisco Cutters.[39]

In San Francisco an ongoing series of cultural bike tours began in 1993, inspired by Critical Mass. The first ride visited three dozen community gardens (out of a citywide 110 or so) in the southeast part of San Francisco. After a few more informal tours, the local bike advocacy group began sponsoring them, and has had a wide variety of rides over the past decade, including tours of ice cream parlors, gay history, labor history, a Freeway stump tour, and more. In Los Angeles, a Tour de Tamal took riders to a half dozen tamale parlors around the town.

Annual Bikesummer festivals in San Francisco, Portland, Vancouver, New York, and Los Angeles have brought thousands of people onto bicycles and into contact with the whole gamut of bicycling culture—from mainstream to decidedly "outlaw."[40] In Los Angeles, some of the Bikesummer organizers put on an event in March 2004 called "More Than Transportation" which centered around bicycles and DIY punk culture, which in important ways set the stage for 2005's Bikesummer there.

Zany clubs and their events have created their own cultural whirl. In San Francisco, the motley crew of Cyclecide has developed a full-scale Bike Rodeo, including pedal-powered rides, derbies, races, bike toss, and more. C.H.U.N.K. 666 in Portland is famous for their Chunkathlons, with tall bike jousting and beer-soaked races, while other outlaw cyclists have developed what's become known as "zoo bombing": hurtling down a major local hill, often in the dark on various altered bicycles. As they bring their "rodeos" and festivals on tour they spread the subculture further by continually introducing new people to the values and experiences. The wild creativity of the Cyclecide mechanics in San Francisco and C.H.U.N.K. 666 in Portland and elsewhere underscore a profoundly creative engagement with bicycling technology.

CONTESTING THE TECHNOSPHERE

Popular culture has tended to treat developments in science and technology as automatic processes, almost natural, that proceed independent of human choice or will. The elevation and inaccessibility of scientific expertise has been an important method for "naturalizing" capitalist modernization. Most of us are mystified about scientific research and the choices that produce the technologies shaping our everyday lives. And instead of the "excess of leisure time" promised by early theoreticians on widespread automation, the escalation of technology in the workplace and industry frequently leaves people unemployed, or else much more tightly controlled and regulated within their workplace environment.

Modernization has consisted overwhelmingly of a systematic process of deskilling human labor. In pursuit of profitability and competitive advantage, capitalists and technologists have focused their efforts

(right) a bike lift during the July 2003 Critical Mass in NYC that concluded the month-long BikeSummer there (above). Below is the logo for BikeSummer in Los Angeles in 2004.

Photo by Suzahna Poliwka

on controlling the labor process, transforming living humans into cogs in an enormous machine. To the greatest extent possible, knowledge and skill are taken out of the workers heads and hands and implanted into the machines. The workday itself has been both lengthened and intensified. Some labor processes are now designed to extract 56 productive seconds of each 60-second minute in the workday, thanks to the time-and-motion studies known as "Taylorization" after their early 20th century inventor, Frederick Taylor. During the past 25 years the eight-hour day has been lost to most people.

Humans make the technosphere, of course. Though people may be deskilled on the job and turned into keyboardists, dial readers, "checkers," they retain a great deal of creativity outside of the workplace. Practical technical knowledge is disseminated faster and in higher volume than ever before over the Internet. Communities like that of DIY youth, have rejected the culture of expertise; objects are being re-imagined and re-purposed. Nowhere are these processes more apparent than among the outlaw bicycle subculture where the proliferation of skill sharing and repurposing is rampant. Objects made to be used in one way are constantly being re-imagined and re-purposed to new uses.

The bicycle often inspires rapturous enthusiasm for its simplicity and efficiency. Bike aficionados find it easy to see the bicycle as a model of appropriate technology more generally. Eric Welp of Washington DC's Chain Reaction says:

> We're dealing with a self-sufficient, efficient, simple motion machine; not a perpetual motion machine. It's a pure, simple technology... I appreciate the use of bikes in terms of benefits for the community, human well-being, self-empowerment and all that, and those are good values to apply to the idea of technology, but I think that sometimes technology has lost site of its basic purpose in terms of those values. So the shop is an important reminder of how technology should be.[41]

Given the tendency to see the bicycle as an uncompromised form of transportation technology, bike advocates have tried to extend the relationship to associated parts and devices. In an issue of *C.H.U.N.K. 666*, the whys and wherefores of "gear" are addressed at some length. "The corporate slimelordz of America have fixated upon gear as an easy method of sponging money from yuppies and yuppy wannabes." Though they refuse the marketing juggernaut knocking at the edges of their culture, CHUNKsters have developed their own argument for "gear" that also eschews the total rejection position that some adopt.

Rising from the homebrew gear kit, we have the refunc-
tionalized gear, gear which has either been adapted to
its purpose or which would normally be retired. The
majority of headwear fits this category. Garage-sale bicycle and motorcycle helmets, football, army, and construction helmets, and even Viking helmets with added
straps have served to encourage dwindling collections
of brain cells to retain their coherent mass. Ski or avia-
tor gogs with a handkerchief taped to the bottom protect the sensitive face when diving (or being thrown)
through plate glass windows.[42]

Many of the prominent activists in the subculture turn out to be newly
adept at working with tools and mechanics. "I didn't become a mechanic
until after I'd become a bike nut," says Robin Havens, "technology can
empower people because they can use it as a problem-solving tool. I see
technology as being much more useful to me than I did before. When I
say 'technology,' I mean in a limited sense, I mean tool use and such."[43]

Other bicyclists agree. For example, Ben Guzman says that "it was
through bicycling that I developed tinkering. In college I did an art piece
about how my father didn't teach me about cars, because he didn't know
about cars, but how that's so *not*-male. But it was through bicycling that I
learned how to do things."[44] Jessie Basbaum has a similar tale. "I was not previously mechanically inclined... to someone who has never put a wrench
on a bike, it's this utter mystery, it's like magic. But after having some basic
skills everything makes sense, it all fits together in a logical way."[45]

The technological self-sufficiency that bicyclists can achieve stimulates broader development. As bike mechanics become demystified to
technology and tinkering, a critical engagement with technical systems,
broadly construed, easily follows. Once expertise in some technological
areas is demystified, other mystified hierarchies of power are more easily
seen through, too.

In New York, Bill DiPaola helped start the bike activist group Times
Up! He became a plumber after becoming chastened at his own lack of
practical skills. "I realized if you want to do something, you just can't be
sitting in a room and talking about the philosophy of it. You have to know
how things work and you have to be able to get your hands dirty. I'm not
very happy with a lot of the new activists I see, that don't really understand
mechanics... I'm happy whenever I see a new person in the group who's
got a skill."[46]

In the dissident subcultures that bicycling touches, there is a common undercurrent of anti-technology ideology. Basbaum explains:

... A lot of the people in the bicycling community and

a lot of the people coming to our shop, and who love bike mechanics, really have an anti-technology bent, you know? These are people who don't like cars, who don't like television, that kind of thing, [but they] like organic food and all that. It's healthy technology I guess, to put a term on it. Gardening and bicycling versus automobiles and monoculture. Those are two types of technologies, technology that's in theory sustainable and environmentally friendly [and a technology that isn't].[47]

But Megulon-5 of C.H.U.N.K. 666 counters the idea that bicycling technology is simplistic and an obvious sustainable good. "It's a technology that a lot of people don't see that involves steel foundries and rubber plantations and oil extraction." His own experience of the recurrent anti-technology line leads him to argue,

I'm not only pro-technology, I'm anti-anti-technology... I'm willing to make distinctions about the use of technology. I'm willing to distinguish between cutting your tofu jerky with a knife or stabbing me with a knife! That's technology... Technology is not a thing, it's a process. And I'm for the development of technology... there's a lot of people who want to turn to a pastoral, neolithic, paleolithic, level of technology, and they're "against technology." But what they're really against is a certain level of technology... the plow is ok, paper clips are ok, the telegraph maybe, bicycles yes, but no steel refinery. Wooden bicycles are good. They've never ridden a wooden bicycle, but they want to... As I got more hands-on I became more realistic. I don't think of bikes as the cure for society's ills so much anymore,... everyone's living in a factory that moves people. So I see bicycle technology as a way to escape, or help escape that...[48]

Sharing information and technical know-how creates new circuits of knowing, of trusting, of social verification, and finally and most importantly, of self-confidence. In Los Angeles, Ben Guzman had a typical experience with someone who had no knowledge of bike repair, but also felt alienated culturally.

This guy didn't want to talk to me, and he didn't want to really ask me for anything, but he's like, "yeah man, I need a tool to do this thing," and you're like, "yeah, man, well you can come in and do it." He's like, "oh man you have to show me..." and I'm like "That's what we do, come on in." So he comes in. Once he pulls off the crank arm, he walked outside the door to his friend, and he's like "Check it out!" Removed his bottom bracket and swapped it. And then he came back the next day. On Thursday he's back going, "Oh man I want to do this, and I want to do that!" And then what's cool is you have him interacting with this woman, that he would never interact with, but [now] we're all buddies because we ride bikes.[49]

An unexpected, but perhaps unsurprising, result of bike tinkering is the emergence of new communities. One common glue in working class cultures, especially but not exclusively among males, is the ability to engage in tech talk. Bike Kitchen's Basbaum concurs: "Talking about bikes, absolutely, I've made friends through the shop and so have other people, strictly based on bikes. Of course it bleeds into other things. You can talk about bikes for a long time, but eventually it's like 'so, where do you work?'"

Eric Welp in DC describes the role of shop talk this way:

Shop talk sort of gives us all a common ground in the shop working with each other... it gives the kids working in the shop confidence to be able to communicate and talk knowledgeably about bikes with these folks who they might not otherwise interact with. It gives them a sense of pride to be able to help other people in their neighborhood with repairs and explain things to them. Self confidence: It's amazing, you see it everyday working with innercity youth.

For example, Jimmy, he was one of the kids we had in a class. When he started, he was just a really skinny, shy kid. Now, it's amazing, you can talk to him about bikes and he is actually passionate about it, and he is extremely articulate with customers. I think he's really developed confidence as a mechanic, so he's a great example.[50]

Not content to buy and ride a bicycle, outlaw bicyclists have banded together to reconstruct hybrid bikes in all kinds of shapes and sizes from the junked bikes littering any city. The widespread rehabilitation and sharing of discarded bikes is common in many cities. Outside of economic logic, bike co-ops have institutionalized skill-sharing, training, and experimentation with technology that already has given rise to a whole subpopulation of tinkerers and appropriators. Ultimately, their practice portends a practical engagement with the technosphere more broadly, perhaps eventually addressing the shape and direction of scientific research itself.

CLASS COMPOSITION AND COMMUNITY

> There's very little doubt in my mind that the way our soci-
> ety works is dictated by corporations. Ultimately our lives
> are run by commerce and corporations that drive it, and
> the politics that shape corporations' behavior. It's all cap-
> italism I guess, it's all an exchange of money... I'm defi-
> nitely not working class. I mean I work but, I don't work
> a blue collar job... My upbringing was probably upper
> middle class. My parents are scientists at UCSF. I don't
> know what economic class I would fall in.
>
> —*Jessie Basbaum*[51]

As described in the first chapters, combined with an amnesiac culture that disdains history, the American working class does not consider itself *as such*. Self-definition is increasingly established *outside* of
wage-labor, and, given the stupidity and pointlessness of a great deal of
the work people do as wage-laborers, this is a very healthy response.

The bicycling subculture is but one of numerous examples of people
assembling themselves into new constellations, creating new ways of as-
sociating that escape the familiar bounds of mid-20th century, "middle-
class" America. The new bicycling subculture is one of the prominent
examples of the gradual re-composition of the working class in North
America (although the emergence of the bicycling subculture is also a
European phenomenon, and can be glimpsed in South America and urban centers in Asia too). This does not mean that self-aware workers are
embracing bicycles as a strategy of class resistance in a capitalist world
(although it may be largely true that these are wage-laborers who are
deserting the economic constraints imposed by car ownership). What it
denotes is a process by which people who survive through selling their
time and skills in "normal" jobs are connecting with each other *outside*
of that process through association with the bicycling subculture.

Bike Kitchen's Jessie Basbaum says:

> We've created a space where all different people come
> through; people that wouldn't normally associate with
> one another. You meet people and other people meet
> people and friendships are made... we've created a
> space that fosters people helping one another.[52]

These new relationships constitute a new kind of community—a much
over-used word, but one that denotes re-emerging class groupings in col-
loquial terms. In these new communities bicyclists provide each other mutual aid, self-education, critical engagement, camaraderie, and, ultimately,
solidarity.

Megulon-5 explains the community he's a part of in Portland:

> Everyone in the Chunk 666 community for whatever
> reason—cheapness or ideals or just bike obsession—has
> [escaped] being a chump about the car culture. Usually
> they have the same kind of nonsubordinate [attitude]
> to [The Machine]. Part of my view of the role of Chunk
> 666 in the bike community is we do what we do because
> we love it. Hopefully we can get people together to have
> a fun time involving bicycles, low technology or high
> technology, and drinking beer, hanging out on the
> street. Like the Family Truckster, a long bike with a grill
> on the back. We'd park it somewhere on the sidewalk
> and start grilling burgers and drinking beer, and people
> come over and hang out with us. One of the best things
> about the Chunkathlon [a zany gathering of bikers on
> improvised choppers who participate in beer-soaked
> races, jousting matches, and fire-leaping stunts] is that
> we own the street. We have a block party to close off the
> street, but long after our permit expires we are drinking
> beer around a bonfire in the middle of the street.[53]

The anonymity of modern urban life forces people to invent new forms of interaction. Instead of workplace or neighborhood as the basis for relating, the bicycle subculture has created a variety of events and gatherings where people connect. Los Angeles's Ben Guzman sees the new community as central.

> The community is so much fun. We hosted a *Tour de
> Tamal.* Everyone chipped in some money, and we went
> on a ride and ate tamales all over the place... Riding a
> bike is part of a community, and you wave hello to every-
> body you see that rides a bike. It's the biggest punk rock
> thing to be a community... The giant city of Los An-
> geles is saying "don't be part of a community, don't in-
> teract with each other, don't be happy, don't commute
> on a bicycle"... If you do those two things, interact with
> each other well and ride a bike, those are the biggest
> extremes you can pull off in LA.[54]

Bill DiPaola of New York's Times Up! gives community a similar importance.

> Community means a lot to me, personally. It's every-
> thing. I'm surrounded in the East Village... we actually
> help save the community gardens, and we have com-
> munity spaces. We are nothing, the bicycle community
> in NYC, unless we can organize. We cannot organize

unless we operate in community spaces. There's a big public space issue in New York, and we're using a lot of the community gardens, the community spaces, the parks, to meet and talk about these things... With class we try to say "everybody is acceptable in our group." So when I hear the word "class" I think we need to break that down, but not in a negative way.

As a long-time activist on the left, DiPaola struggles to overcome the baggage of past efforts. He rejects outright the labels "working class" or "middle class": he says, "Those are just labels that are created by the corporate media."[55] But DiPaola is quick to agree that there is a *ruling* class.

Ben Guzman, on the other hand, enthuses about his own growing awareness of class:

I've heard and seen the statement forever, that "there's no war but the class war." In the last six months, I finally figured it out, and it's TRUE!! I grew up in a middle class neighborhood... I choose to ride a bicycle and then people say "oh, you choose to ride a bicycle because you're allotted the choice to ride because you come from a certain class." Everybody in my class is NOT riding a bicycle by choice. Everybody else in my class is driving a car because they haven't even thought that there's a different choice... what's happening with the Bicycle Kitchen, is we're breaking down the classes. Everybody rides a bike. Or if they want to, everybody CAN ride a bike.[56]

Of course there are plenty of low-wage workers in LA or SF community on bicycles (especially Spanish and Chinese speakers) who are not closely connected (yet) to the outlaw cycling subculture. But at this early stage of the culture, the boundaries of the subculture are far from fixed. New hybrid identities and relationships are easy to foresee. Portland's Megulon-5 explains why outlaw bicyclists' values are distinct from mainstream America's:

Being a bicycle person turned me into the kind of person who saw the value of spending a lot of time doing something I liked, as opposed to spending more money... yeah, it changes what you do, and also it often involves your doing it with your comrades... [it creates] a social process, not necessarily "all for one and one for all" ... but a competition and cooperation together for resources, mostly cooperation. I'm a craftsman. I think most people are surprised if they meet me in the context of C.H.U.N.K. I'm a very anal retentive, uptight, and stable type of person. I'm a computer programmer.

He also elaborates on his own lack of clarity when it comes to the idea of "class," but as he describes his ideas he tells us something about the values and self-awareness of outlaw cyclists:

> I don't even know how I define "class" myself, because I'm not much of a political thinker... a lot of the people riding bikes don't want to be riding bikes. They are not excited about the fact that they're riding a bike to work. I recognize that it is class that puts them there.... [and] that our class is what gives us the opportunity to be Chunk 666. Most, but not all, have an upper middle class background. They all have a comfortable enough life that they can spend time doing this. They can play. They can live in Portland and have jobs that involve riding their bikes to work, for example, or spend time looking for a job that will give them that. Mainly, we're all just young slackers without kids, so we can mess around. Lots of us are broke, but I don't think any are poor. Someone might not be able to buy the beer one night. Most of us are living in cheap rooms in rundown houses, but nobody's worried about being homeless. [57]

Martin Leugers of the Bay Area's Chopper Riding Urban Dwellers (CRUD) escaped his very poor family life in Ohio as a child: "My parents always tried to appear, not well off, but like they had no problems when they clearly had HUGE financial problems. My dad was unemployed most of his life but too proud to ever get public assistance, which they probably could have got, and my mom was a teacher at a Catholic school." Now Martin is a well-paid industrial designer at a small consulting firm in Silicon Valley and has the freedom to work on bikes for fun. He says "I avoid any appearance of being wealthy. I definitely do identify as déclassé."[58]

Jimmy, a young African-American man working at Chain Reaction in DC, explains his own sense of class:

> I'd say I'm probably in the lower middle class. You gotta work, and if you're makin' it all right and the work's not too tough, you're sorta in the middle. Lower class means you don't have nothing. And middle class pays the upper class by consuming all the upper class's goods made by the lower class. But nobody is better than anybody. I don't think about [class] at all.[59]

Like Jimmy, bicyclists usually don't think or talk about class. Race, on the other hand, comes up more often, partly because a lot of the activists running alternative bike shops are white, and many of the kids who gather at such spaces are black and Latino. Among the young, motivated, usually white activists, a self-conscious sensitivity to racial diversity has taken root. No doubt better than an oblivious blindness, this contemporary race awareness has its own crippling presuppositions. Atlanta's Spiewak describes her frustration at a recent "BikeBike!" conference workshop in Milwaukee:

> We were subjected to a rather offensive anti-oppression training done by folks from Colorado. There ain't no black folks in Colorado. Those kids had no frame of reference [and] it didn't speak to our experience in the South... We have race dynamics that are completely different from other places typically known for DIY bicycle scenes. In Atlanta, black folks and white folks interact with each other [and] often work together. We talk about our differences, and it's okay... in Atlanta we know that skin color does not dictate consciousness. We offer a neutral space where we are kind to everyone. We don't front and we don't tokenize... Do we build community? That's what people tell me they are experiencing![60]

Part of what makes the independent DIY bike shops so interesting is the diverse crowds you might find there. The harsh self-segregation of U.S. culture starts to erode when black kids and middle-aged white men spend evenings helping each other fix up their bikes, or when an elderly Chinese man helps some Latino kids get their wheels on. These tentative and hopeful new relationships open a space where the age-old racism that has divided U.S. workers from each other again and again can lose its hold, or at least loosen its grip. A new comfort across racial boundaries can only help promote a more profound social solidarity that challenges class society at its roots—in our daily work lives.

* * * *

No one wants to think of themselves as low class. The dignity of being "working class" is a lost cultural concept and no amount of demands for "respect" can overcome the abject stupidity and routinization that has destroyed the dignity of work itself. So most workers don't want to think about class. We each examine our own lot in life and reasonably conclude that we're somewhere in a sprawling "middle" between Learjet luxury and total destitution. Given the fact that the poorest 10% of Americans are still "richer" materially than two out of three of the world's population, that idea has some objective truth.

But this so-called middle is in fact a broad working class made up of wage-laborers in innumerable occupations who receive a wide range of salaries and benefits under many different conditions. The micro-stratification of the U.S. working population puts everyone into the subjective position of being able to imagine falling down or climbing up a notch or two (or several). People see themselves as "middle class" as a way of avoiding the plain everyday truth of living in class society, but most people's lives are overridden by the shared reality of wage-labor and a feeling of basic powerlessness. Part of the reason people's identities are defined so much through shopping and consumer choice (rather than, for instance, occupation) is the steady dilution of class consciousness and the successful implantation of the concept of the "middle class." But insofar as people are creating meaning by *doing interesting things* outside of the job, they are slowly creating new ways of understanding their own lives and the communities and the class in which they are lodged.

The common resistance to thinking about class shows up again and again in assertions that in the bicycling subculture they are "breaking

Every year on Groundhog Day, Feb. 2, or the nearest weekend day, the San Francisco Bike Messenger Association sponsors a drunken ride along the city's famous 49 mile scenic ride.

down" class, that "everyone's welcome" and so on. In fact, the subculture demonstrates a healthy impulse towards free association and mutual aid. Going back to Marx or even Kropotkin, we can see that in a real sense these are the stirrings of individual and social revolt against being reduced to "mere workers," to being trapped in the objectified and commodified status of labor power.

The invigorated subjectivity of outlaw bicyclists is apparent in their full engagement, their humanity and their urgent need to define their own culture, to make their own lives' meaning directly and cooperatively. From these myriad experiments new ways of living are being created in the here and now, which not only make life better immediately, but in crucial ways are laying the social and technological foundations for a post-capitalist life. Resilient individualism insisting on a cooperative, shared future illuminates the subjectivity that might finally overthrow a society that has reduced us all to mere objects.

(right) screen print patch from San Francisco's Cyclecide, a group that scorns bicycle safety! (below) a tall-bike joust along Brooklyn's East River at NYC's Bikesummer in 2003.

San Francisco's Cyclecide stages semi-regular Bike Rodeos, with choppers and Tall-bikes, pedal-powered merry-go-round and ferris wheel, jousting, Huffy toss, art bikes, and beer-soaked good time for the whole family!

CHAPTER 7

FREE FUEL: THE TINKERER'S GRAIL

My involvement in biodiesel is a direct response to 9/11... biodiesel has this tremendous potential because America is a car society. It is a tangible change that people can make, it is here today.

—Claudia Eyzaguirre[1]

Biodiesel is great fun. It's empowering. Nothing feels better than tooling down the highway with the knowledge that you are free. Free of Chevron. Free of Mobil. Free of George Bush. Free of the Saudis. Free of the whole sorry lot. ... vegetable oil [is] here now. It works. It's renewable. It's sustainable. It smells good. It creates jobs in the United States. And there is no war required to get it.

—Lyle Estill[2]

Biodiesel is my most quixotic dream come true... Biodiesel is cheap. You can make it yourself. It smells like your favorite greasy donut shop. It's noncarcinogenic. Most important, since my conversion to biodiesel I am no longer an accomplice to the human and environmental destruction caused by oil exploration, transportation, and policies... Biodiesel reduces carcinogens of truck exhaust by 90 percent, carbon monoxide by 43 percent, and particulates by 55 percent, according to conservative figures released by the EPA.

—Claudia Eyzaguirre[3]

Fry-O-Diesel in Philadelphia... are the folks working with trap grease as a feedstock. Since people will pay to have their trap grease hauled away, it would seem to be the holy grail of biodiesel.

—Piedmont Biofuels[4]

In the past half-century a desolate architecture oozed over the North American landscape. Petrified rivers of asphalt bisected fields, bridged rivers and imposed a cloverleaf-shaped model of on-and-off convenience. Ostensibly serving a mobile culture of increasingly free individuals, the interstate highways, like the 19th century railroads before them, are the transportation infrastructure that shapes countless human experiences. From the suburban "edge cities" that have risen to supplant the dense urban lives that grew around railroad stations, to the vast factories and workshops that employ millions in producing and servicing cars, parts, fuel, and roads, not to mention all the health care work dedicated to handling the death, mayhem, and illness caused by cars, our lives are heavily influenced by the car. Most of us can hardly imagine life "auto-free," even if we don't understand how to fix and maintain cars ourselves.

In our car culture, sidewalk mechanics are a mainstay of modern life. Boys stand around watching their fathers or older brothers or neighbors as they crawl under cars, digging into the opaque mysteries of the internal combustion engine, and generally making a mess of themselves. This romantic male subculture is the stuff of legend; for many men their first car is a contemporary right of passage. Learning to fix one's own car, or at least check the oil and tires, is to carry on a (false) tradition of rugged self-sufficiency deeply embedded in this culture. The car has long been a bastion of do-it-yourself tinkering and mechanical play. It is somehow appropriate that one of the most creative and productive technology revolts of our times has burned brightly on its margins.

The sustainable biofuel boom of the past decade is a remarkable example of a passion-driven, grassroots techno-scientific movement, a decentralized, self-directing research and development program that thrives outside of normal business models and without the supposedly indispensable profit motive as its "driving" force. The expression "sustainable biofuel" indicates that there is more than one kind of biofuel. In fact, there are different approaches even within what is clearly the "alternative" to the mainstream. Biodiesel and biofuel cooperatives have formed, some to make bulk purchases of fuels for their own members, others to learn and teach how to convert engines to run on straight vegetable oil (SVO). Diesel engines can run most biodiesel fuels with no alteration, but for those who want to run "straight vegetable oil," some modifications are required. Different degrees of fanaticism or commitment lead some activists to insist on 100% biodiesel (as opposed to the B5 or B20—5% or 20% biodiesel mixed with regular petroleum-based diesel), straight vegetable oil, or fuel derived entirely from discarded, waste vegetable oil (French fry oil is a favorite).

Big Capital in the form of such firms as agribusiness giant Archer-Daniels-Midland or oil company Chevron have invested hundreds of millions of dollars in new ethanol and agrofuel processing factories in the past three years. The news has been filled in 2006 and 2007 with reports of a burgeoning industry of biofuels or agrofuels, derived primarily from sugar cane, and oils from corn, soy, palm, and rapeseed. This heavily capitalized approach to biofuels seeks to maintain much of the existing structure of modern life, simply replacing gasoline with some kind of biofuel.

Lyle Estill, co-founder of Piedmont Biofuels in North Carolina and a prolific philosopher of the movement describes the two approaches to biofuel this way:

> One is comprised of those who are motivated by sustainability. We are the ones who preach conservation, who cry out for local economies, and who focus mightily on reducing our ecological footprints. Another stream is commercial biodiesel, which is motivated by greed and shareholder return. Biodiesel by the balance sheet allows for the importation of soybeans from Ecuador, the freighting of used fryer oil through the Panama Canal and the deforestation of the rainforest for oil-rich palm plantations.[5]

A decade ago, biodiesel and straight veggie oil advocates were anxious to get the word out, but now their attention is shifting to finding ways to promote a sustainable and local approach to the new fuel economy. Their efforts point to a different path, and are reminiscent of past technological choices.

In the face of the imposing edifice of our technological environment, it is easy to forget that most familiar devices are historical accidents that prevailed in a clash of inventions backed by different powerful interests. Basic electricity could be DC rather than AC, engines could burn peanut oil instead of gasoline, cars could run on electricity instead of fossil fuel, we have (or had) VCRs instead of Betamax (now we've got five versions of DVD!), and so on. The biofuels movement is new but the technology is not. At the end of the 19th century many people were working on different designs to power individual vehicles. Rudolf Diesel invented his eponymous engine and expected it to run on vegetable oils, which would promote local self-sufficiency against the coal and steam railroad monopolies of that time.[6]

Kept alive during the 20th century by nonconformists, techno-cranks, and tinkerers, biodiesel was sustained in isolated, often rural places. Starting in the wake of the 1974 oil crisis, some scientists and academics in Idaho and Colorado discovered ways to make biofuel from waste vegetable oil (and eventually practically anything with fat molecules). Building on that, other scientists in Missouri and Iowa extended the research, which was eventually taken up at the National Renewable Energy Lab in Colorado.[7] After the first Gulf War (1991), a new generation disgusted by the violence underpinning the oil economy was looking for alternatives.

In 1994 five women from San Francisco took off in a standard Chevy diesel van, cadging used fryer oil as they crossed the continent and promoting waste product as fuel along the way. In *Fat of the Land*, their documentary of their trip,[8] we are introduced to Louis Wichinsky, an elderly inventor who has run his vehicle on vegetable oil for years, as well as Lee Conneh, a young man with a fierce gaze, who defends his freedom through self-sufficiency: he has modified his car to run on a veggie oil/ kerosene blend. The "Fat of the Land" trip inspired dozens of imitators in the following years, most notably Joshua Tickell. Tickell began experimenting with vegetable oil to fuel his van in 1996, later gaining fame as the first "Veggie Van." Tickell went on to publish what many consider the bible of the biofuels movement, *From the Fryer to the Fuel Tank*.[9]

The environmental movement originally emerged clamoring for clean air and water and to protect public health from the toxic waste produced by industry. In pursuit of a more coherent approach, ecologically-motivated activists moved up the chain of production to challenge technological choices, rejecting glib assertions of inevitability. The "oil crisis" of 1973–74 heightened awareness of society's structural dependence on oil and fossil fuels. While some directed their new consciousness to an attack on Arabs, progressive activists saw the twin monsters of militarism and multinational oil and car companies as the chief enforcers and beneficiaries of an increasingly catastrophic approach to planetary life. The oil/petrochemical industries and their voracious *raison d'etre*, the car, were identified as key culprits in many ecological and social problems.

Another campaign in the 1970s focused on energy production opposed nuclear power. Anti-nuke eco-activism spawned other initiatives; anti-toxic waste campaigns dovetailed with a growing anti-sprawl, smart growth sensibility, and for a brief time at the end of the 1970s it seemed that a real ecological transformation might begin. Solar energy briefly flourished, only to be stymied by government withdrawal of support (under the Reagan administration) and squelched by industries still profiting from fossil fuels and from ongoing state subsidies going back generations. Oil price manipulations during the last quarter-century intermittently stimulated and then stymied efforts to develop alternative fuels. In too many cases oil companies actively thwarted renewable energy technologies.

PROLIFERATING CARAVANS

Whenever the news crews want to cover alternative fuels, they gravitate toward those who have converted their vehicles to run on straight vegetable oil. It's wacky enough to get noticed, and the public often is introduced to bio-fuels by a bunch of nutty kids in a bus powered by vege-table oil. The "I'm going to get a bus" crowd include[s] many people I have talked to who are about to sacri-fice a portion of their young lives to travel around the country on a biodiesel powered bus. To evangelize. And spread love. And help the movement along.

—Lyle Estill[10]

At the dawn of the 21st century strange vehicles began crisscrossing the desolate interstate landscape. Sporting stickers such as "vegeta-bles give us gas" or "ask me about veggie power" a growing number of bio-fueled cars, trucks, and buses began to appear. Rediscovering the early 20th century experiments in engines and fuels, and tapping into a small network of tinkerers scattered around the country, a grassroots movement began using biofuels, from various blends of biodiesel to re-cycled waste vegetable oil.

Converted school buses became the vehicle of choice for college stu-dents and other young people who sought to claim power from the pre-ponderant oligopolies controlling oil and car production. Embracing a "hippie" aesthetic in slogan-decorated school buses running on straight vegetable oil, a coterie of dumpster-diving, eco-freak survivalists have toured North America promoting their vision of a sustainable, locally-produced clean(er) fuel. Joshua Tickell's "Veggie Van" traveled 10,000 miles across the U.S., powered by biodiesel that he made en route. By the summer of 2003 many more such projects were embarking from college campuses and enclaves of alternative culture. "Project Biobus" carried thirteen Middlebury College students from Vermont to the west coast during the summer of 2003. Two years later the "Clean Fuel Caravan" joined a dozen such projects together, including the Veggiebus, the O^2 Collective, and the Mexican Bus. A Sustainable Solutions Caravan in 2003 made the first ever biofuel journey from California through Central America on two 40' Gillig schoolbuses running on 100% vegetable oil. The two-bus tour ran through California, Mexico, Guatemala, Belize, El Salvador, Honduras, Nicaragua, and Costa Rica, and carried a 25-person team of sustainability experts, eco-technologists, farmers, performance and media artists. Logging over 35,000 miles on veggie oil in its first year, the "Unifried" 40' school bus has been touring the continent since the summer of 2003, promoting biofuels. Biofuels4Schools is a project dedi-cated to converting fleets of school buses to biofuels. Dartmouth Col-lege's "Ultimate Frisbee" team converted a bus for a 6-week, 10,000-mile crosscountry trip in 2005. That's just a random sampling of the several dozen such projects out there.

Not every caravan is staffed by college students on a break, but mostly it is a young crowd in their twenties and early thirties. You might say this is the Lorax Generation, after the 1971 Dr. Seuss children's book that gave trees a sane voice against rapacious exploitation. The first wave of ecological activism was largely focused on laws and governmental policy. The largest environmental groups set up shop in Washington D.C. and grew comfortable as institutional players at the seat of power. Meanwhile, under the radar, basic assumptions about nature and biology were adapting to ecological awareness. In countless schools kids were taught to think globally and act locally by planting trees, working in gardens, saving local waterways, cleaning beaches and parks, etc.

Now, biodiesel conversion is making its way into public school life. In 2006, 11th and 12th graders at Mansfield High School in Massachusetts began converting an old school bus into a vegetable oil-powered "Cool Bus." The kids are doing the work on the interior and reconfiguring the engine. And they are doing it through classes—such as auto shop, chemistry lab, art class—which are all about participating. Julianne O'Donnell, a senior, says "I love it because we're not learning about global warming from a textbook; we're actually working on a solution."[11]

Rock musicians have joined the movement, too, sensing the growing "hipness" of biodiesel. Rock tours have always been strange hybrids of pop culture "rebellion" mixed with ruthless business savvy. In the summer of 2006 several multi-band tours converted their buses to biofuels and embraced a zero-waste approach to their food services, all to further promote new ways for the American Way of Life to switch to greener foundations.[12]

A more hand-to-mouth merger of entertainment and biofuels is found in the Big Tadoo Puppet Crew, founded by Jonathan Youtt and Emily Butterfly in San Francisco. Youtt explains how he came to be involved:

> I first learned about it about four or five years ago when I watched *The Fat of the Land,* and then I met the Veggie Van guy...I'm using the alternative fuel movement to bring a grassroots puppet show across America on a shoestring budget, at a time when the gasoline prices are going through the roof for the rest of the country. In our small RV we installed a third storage tank with a heating element in it... we put veggie oil in cold, and we drive for an hour and at our leisure we get out, do a little demonstration at the truck stop or the rest area: "Hey folks, you want to see veggie oil?" And we've got the puppets... Anywhere I go I'm talking about it, I'm bringing other people on board as potential converts, and inspiring them to take action, and reminding them

that for 400 dollars and a day's work, they can start driving away on free fuel.[13]

The past few years of biofuel proselytizing across the country has triggered many more initiatives. In the summer of 2003 when I interviewed them, Bianca Sopoci-Belknap and Ben Gillock were students at Antioch College in Ohio. They bought a diesel car in order to drive to the west coast starting point of a cross-country bicycle ride they were joining. Ben was an environmental studies major and had spent some time at Greaseworks, a biofuels cooperative in Corvallis, Oregon. Bianca embraced it too, because as she put it, "It's a trend, a feasible alternative that's been proven because of those other cross-country trips."[14] They bought a kit from one of the small companies that have sprung up, and did their own biodiesel conversion.

Bianca's parents grew up in the sixties "and were very much involved and impacted. They've always had really progressive opinions." Ben's mother worked for the lefty Catholic Charities while he grew up, and both Ben and Bianca landed at Antioch, one of the more well-known progressive colleges in the country. Their story represents a generational continuity of the values that the right-wing media echo chamber has disparaged for years as the "sixties." One of the hidden stories of this subculture, along with the other ones examined in this book, is the extent to which they are historic movements that have been developing out of sight for decades. The so-called drop-outs from "middle class" life didn't disappear and certainly didn't abandon their idea that life could and should be very different from the empty affluence and alienation normalized by American society. Along with other subcultures described in this book, the biofuels movement marks a creative alternative that has gestated for over a generation. The people touring in biofuel buses are carrying out a deep campaign to change life.

Latter day hippies are far from the only ones to "get on the biofuel bus." As biodiesel neophyte Ben Gillock discovered in 2003, "it's a bunch of Republicans, it's a bunch of homesteaders, it's a bunch of libertarians."[15] Even at the Berkeley Biofuels Collective, "we attracted people to our collective who weren't necessarily just like Samaratin social conscious do-gooders. They were people who were fascinated by gaskets and liquids and submersible pumps, and moving fluid around."[16] Backyard mechanics, a mainstay of American working class life, have been seduced too by the allure of converting vehicles to run on free home-brewed fuel. Dozens of efforts across the country are experimenting with making fuel, inventing technologies to scale up production, perfecting standards for content and performance, and embracing cooperative and collective structures to further challenge the corporate model.

A major impetus for the spread of the biofuel idea beyond the touring of demonstration vehicles has been the dissemination of technical knowledge over the Internet. Because they are motivated by ecology and a political vision of new ways of engaging with technology, biofuels developers are enthusiastic practitioners of open source philosophy. As Youtt told me, biodiesel is "like shareware, like Linux, it's an open source paradigm of abundance, not scarcity."

The *Fat of the Land* women, having learned from Tom Reed of Agua Das and their own limited experimentation in the mid-90s, freely shared everything they could learn about biofuels and waste veggie processing. Most of the pioneers in this field have been ardent about sharing and remaining open, much as the free software developers have fought encroaching business norms in their field.[17] Lyle Estill makes the analogy explicit in this excerpt:

> We have played a role in the "open source" nature of grass-roots biodiesel. Instead of waiting for patents and hiding our secrets, as a community we tend to push whatever we have learned out to the net—from which everyone can help themselves to information. You see very little proprietary action in the backyard... You are not going to find yourself signing a lot of non-disclosure agreements. Rather, you are going to brush up against experienced geniuses that will readily tell you all they know.[18]

Ben Gillock learned a lot from various biofuels discussion lists. "It's one of the few really great uses of the Internet that I've seen so far. It's not flaky [or] weird, people actually make connections [and then] volunteer their time and energy to help you out with something."[19]

> Whereas biodiesel is like a nascent Microsoft, expanding rapidly into a new market through a forced consensus of standardization, the straight-veg culture is closer to the Linux of alternative fuels. There are no rules or patents. Information and techniques are swapped freely. It is, dare I say, open source—a grassroots, exploitable energy, which is one of the reasons its users feel so empowered: Anyone can join in, and the raw material is waiting to be hauled out of parking lots nationwide.
> —*Joshua Berman*, LA Weekly[20]

Claudia Eyzaguirre, the biodiesel activist mentioned earlier, has been a key organizer in the Berkeley (CA) Biofuels Collective. She describes how anyone who enters the biofuels world with the wrong (proprietary) approach can get ostracized:

> People say, "Oh that guy, he just wants to open a biodie-
> sel business," and he's given that Berkeley scorn for be-
> ing a for-profit business. And those people have failed;
> what we've seen in just two years is that those people who
> haven't embraced the community and opened up their
> information and opened themselves up, have failed.[21]

To be sure, the same people promoting biofuels grew up in an era of
unprecedented material wealth. A majority of their cohort became shoppers just as avidly as their forebears. For all too many people, separat-
ing their garbage for curbside recycling is the extent of their behavioral
response to ecological awareness. A significant and growing minority
understand that the challenges we face require a more thorough-going
transformation. In the proliferating biodiesel and veggie oil caravans a
new generation of activists found a technologically creative way to address
this transformation. The sudden biodiesel business upsurge since 2005 as
evidenced by tax credits, major corporate investment, and big agriculture
support—forces this kind of activism to refine further its philosophy and
message. Biofuels drivers say they've found a viable alternative to petroleum oil, but a debate has erupted challenging the notion that any combination of biofuels can wholly replace all the ways we now use oil.

> Climbing out of a dumpster, setting down our rotary
> pumps and searching for clothing that is not grease-
> stained, [we] are startled to find we are promoting a
> "techno-fix." We find ourselves pitted against scientists
> who are busy calculating the number of BTUs that can
> be extracted from the biota on an annual basis, and
> comparing that to the amount of fossil energy neces-
> sary to power the global economy. We stand accused of
> using valuable food to power vehicles.[22]

Alarming news reports have given impetus to this concern. In the
Guardian of London writer John Vidal reported that in 2005 a third of the
U.S. corn crop went to ethanol, a 48% increase over the previous year. A
UN report predicted that Brazil and China could double their 50 million
acres dedicated to agrofuel production in a decade. Brazil has 120 million acres that could be cultivated with agrofuel crops according to the
Inter-American Development Bank while an industry lobby is targeting
379 million acres in 15 African countries. "We are talking about expro-
priation on an unprecedented scale. It is likely to mean the privatization
of communal land, farmer evictions, rising food prices, competition for
water resources, and the cutting down of forets and conservation areas,"
said Teresa Anderson of the Barcelona-based group Grain.[23] Against this
global shift the small producers in the U.S. who helped establish the tech-

nology and the market face pressure to be the latest "techno-fix," as Estill details. Grassroots businesses

> like Yokayo and Piedmont Biofuels now find themselves in an interesting trap... We've moved from being a little quirky to being a techno fix. We never intended to scale up to meet America's fuel needs. We want to keep sustainability at the fore. I'm not sure we could be a techno fix even if we discarded sustainability, and the fact is that we are not interested in doing either one.[24]

The committed activists know well that changing fuels is a non-solution unless structural changes are also embraced. In an online discussion one writer said:

> What gets lost in the mad scramble to popularize the "quick fix of the moment" (see hydrogen two years ago) is that the real long-term and ONLY fix for our dire overuse of transport fuels, whether fossil or not, is increased energy efficiency, better mpg, more mass transport, a paradigm shift in the way we think and live.[25]

Changing our everyday relationship to transportation and fuel is the goal of the sustainable grassroots wing of the biofuels industry. Ben Gillock sums it up well: "I don't think bio-diesel or SVO is going to transform the world or end our oil addiction. When people use it or come in contact with it, it transforms the way that they relate to their fuel, to energy, to the idea of fuel source."[26] It is this conceptual shift that underlies the importance of biofuels, whether or not people embrace any specific alternative fuel. This new mentality grows naturally from doing the work directly, from the material experience of demystifying the source and function of fuel, from Do(ing)-It-Yourself (DIY).

DIY: TINKERING TOWARDS APPROPRIATE TECHNOLOGY

> The nice thing about biofuels is that you can build your own refinery in your garage. If everyone did that we would have a shot at changing our typical energy infrastructure to a micronodal system that might be borderline sustainable...If you don't like to plumb things, pass on building your own biodiesel setup. Welding also is helpful. Carpentry too. Successful backyarders tend to be handy and to have a lot of tools. The movement is populated by expert scroungers, recyclers, inventors and generalists who put the average homeowner to shame.
> —*Lyle Estill*[27]

The active sharing of information and expertise has stimulated invention and innovation. Crucially, this body of work demystifies an important piece of the techno-apparatus on which our lives depend. Anyone who wants to learn can find a wide range of sources, many which have already gone through an extensive process of trial-and-error. But because it's done openly and collaboratively, it alters the material experience that participants have. The competitive drive, insofar as it exists, stimulates a jocular and collegial effort to make improvements instead of cut-throat schemes to dominate and conquer.

Technologies depend on interaction, communication, and cooperation, and in the case of biofuels the *social process,* rather than isolated geniuses or capital, is driving innovation. The divergent paths confronting biofuels parallel the contradictory trajectories embodied in the idea of General Intellect. A consciously transformative agenda based on self-reliance, self-education, self-confidence, and cooperative collaboration faces a corporate model of centralized private property and profit-driven decisions. Centralizing corporations and governmental agencies hide knowledge, and suppress diverse approaches and techniques. End users are expected to be ignorant and helplessly dependent on opaque manufacturing systems. The grassroots biofuels movement is driven by the opposite logic of openness, free sharing, and a trust in oneself and each other to solve problems and make good choices. As Bianca Sopoci-Belknap discovered, you enjoy a palpable "independence and freedom [when you] get your own fuel from a local source and don't have to pay for it. Just put in a little time and energy and know that you're the one who made that fuel."[28]

With this new hands-on engagement with fuel-making comes a different way of thinking about the social and ecological relationships embedded in technological choices. Sara Hope Smith co-founded the Berkeley Biofuels Oasis. Her decision to open the Oasis reflects her commitment to appropriate technology, a concept that gets its meaning from long and in-depth examination of how different choices affect daily lives, local and global ecology, and more. Sara Hope Smith grew up in a family that she guesses owned over 100 cars during her childhood, her father being a classic sidewalk mechanic, so she gained a lot of self-confidence around technology. "I love gadgets and the things that make things happen easier… I figure out the easy, quick way to do things."[29] But the Oasis is far from convenient—customers had to bring 5 gallon containers and fuel their cars in a cumbersome process of pouring fuel into those plastic jugs and then into their cars (in September 2007, the Oasis opened its first pumping station). Something more than ease motivates the community of early biofuels users. For Smith, it's a moral decision:

Like the organic foods industry, people make a moral decision to go into biodiesel. Whatever angle they're coming at—better cleaner environment, not wanting to be part of the petroleum industry any more, opposing wars for oil, making biofuels themselves, escaping the corporate chain—it's self-empowering. Bringing the power back to individuals and away from remote corporations is a key thing.[30]

The Berkeley Biofuels Oasis represents a step away from total self-reliance for its customers, but just barely, and only quite recently. Biofuel pioneers trade gas-pump convenience for dirty, inefficient, but self-satisfying work. Ben Gillock says, "The labor is in collecting and finding grease. Instead of paying 2 bucks a gallon, you're working for it." For early adopters, there was a lot of greasy work preparing the fuel and getting it into the car. Bianca tells it this way:

Cars also meant you had to get filthy, really greasy. It was sloppy, and that was really good too, because that's the truth about these things. They're a lot of work, they take a lot of energy and thought and all those things, and they're also not always fun. Sometimes it's miserable, and you're exhausted, but you've got to filter grease, or you have to clean out your filter, or something like that.[31]

This kind of work reinforces a subculture that prides itself on a certain willingness to sacrifice and even suffer, which helps participants feel different and, too often, morally superior to folks who don't want to get down and dirty in pursuit of ecological sanity. Biodiesel scribe Lyle Estill nails the problem:

I wonder if in the process we are leaving the majority of people out of the sustainability equation because we demand they do everything themselves. Perhaps renewable energy in all its forms is too closely tied to an individual's ability to do the work and that connection could leave sustainability in a DIY ghetto.[32]

Sara Hope Smith's Biofuels Oasis is but one of dozens of new businesses sprouting up between individual self-sufficiency and a "pure" business model geared towards profits. Before analyzing the contradictions inherent in the institutionalizing evolution of biofuels it's interesting to note that the existence of this entire field is a product of resistance.

The presumed democracy we live in provides no political mechanisms for people to evaluate and to choose technological paths. Corporate and university laboratories funnel research and development towards priorities shaped by perceived market opportunities or government funding. The research is ultimately designed to stimulate private business too, but with invisible public subsidies to cover research and development. The only time science and technological choices are subjected to any kind of popular opinion is when dissidents have sounded the alarm to provoke political opposition—and most of the time that opposition appears long after the early research and development investments have made the approaching technology seem "inevitable."

A growing subset of the ecology movement has brought forth the idea of "appropriate technology," which is a vague way of suggesting that technologies should be subjected to democratic evaluation. Though we've made little progress in reshaping how scientific inquiry is decided upon, or in creating political systems to choose technological paths, in the proliferating grassroots technology movements, appropriate technologies are being grown from below. Bianca Sopoci-Belknap illustrates this emerging sensibility:

> A lot of things having to do with industrialization are just way beyond me, and have made me frightened and skeptical. Mechanical things that I create, adjust, and adapt myself, help me overcome intimidation. Just opening up the diesel engine car and knowing that all the parts clearly interact with one another—all I had to do was learn the relationship between those parts, and then I could do anything I wanted to! Appropriate technology gives everyone a feeling of control. It's something they're using but it's not controlling them, it's not overpowering them.[33]

The sustainable, small-scale part of the biofuels scene is not ecological just because it gets dirty and does-it-itself. An important motivation for many has been to reclaim resources from America's enormous waste stream. Most Americans try to recycle paper and bottles but the landfills are still filling up and a solid waste crisis joins the numerous other eco-disasters dominating our near-term future. Biofuels developers outside of big corporations have urgently embraced waste vegetable oil as the best source for abundant, free, local fuel.

A great deal of innovative DIY tinkering is based on reclaiming abundance from the rivers of waste produced by capitalist life. As Sara Hope Smith puts it: "There are so many things that are tossed aside that are still useful and wonderful. When you start reclaiming, nothing is trash and everything has value. We live in SUCH an abundant world. It's incredible!" Diesel engines themselves can be seen as a reclamation project. Ben Gillock: "I'm using technique on this used piece of equipment that we saved from the junkyard, it's the diesel engine from the past."

Even animal byproducts can be put to use as a fuel source, as San Francisco's Department of the Environment is trying to do with a local renderer.[34] Estill urges biofuels producers to avoid getting trapped by Big Soy or Big Corn or any other potential feedstock provider. "Let's stay feedstock neutral. As producers, all we need is a fat. Give us a glycerin molecule with a few carbon chains and we can make fuel."[35] Moreover, when the feedstock is taken from waste instead of fresh agricultural produce, Estill rebuts the rising objection to pitting fuel against food: "When we jump into a waste stream, with our 55-gallon drums and our canoe paddles, and set out to meet our family fuel needs, we are not contributing to world hunger."[36]

In Europe the notion of producing energy from waste is much more advanced. In Zurich, Switzerland, five Kompogas plants ferment organic scraps from homes and restaurants to produce fuel for 1,200 cars and trucks, including, ironically, the local McDonald's fleet. The methane/CO_2 output from this process produces 80% less smog-creating chemicals than gasoline and is carbon neutral. A private company, Kompogas makes auto fuel and compost and also earns money by collecting urban biowaste.[37]

Burgeoning use of biofuels brings interesting questions to the surface. How much work does it take to get fuel? What are the ecological impacts of different methods of producing fuel? Of producing different kinds of fuel? Imagine how different our technosphere might be if all the work we did were subjected to those kinds of questions. What part of our current apparatus would we think worthy of pouring more work and time and resources into? How much could we live without while at the same time increasing both our real wealth and our quality of life? These are the kinds of questions that arise naturally from a culture of DIY, where rational decisions about how to spend time and resources confront the individuals who will actually perform the work.

An online discussion produced the following intelligent overview of how we might think more clearly about our energy choices:

> Overuse (waste) of biofuels is no more morally or ecologically acceptable than overuse of fossil fuels; perhaps even less acceptable because every soybean or kernel of corn you burn on your way to the mall could have had an alternate life on someone's dinner plate. Both petroleum and biofuels are incredibly energy dense resources whose best uses society needs to decide upon in a rational manner that maybe shouldn't boil down to sale to the highest bidder.[38]

THE WORK OF BIOFUELS: MAKING AND UNMAKING CLASS

> People rush to biodiesel in search of community. Our
> pumps aren't as fast, our conversations are longer, and
> our connections with one another go way deeper than
> what you will get at a typical gas station fill.
>
> —*Lyle Estill*[39]

U nlike the frayed relationships characteristic in most workplaces
these days, deep and exciting connections are growing among
"biofuels people." Paralleling the self-confidence reinforcing
itself through DIY tinkering, cooperative networks not only meet practical needs but become the basis for friendships and community. Starting
out as a simple request for help with converting waste veggie oil into fuel,
or where to find a part, soon leads people to visit each other's homes,
knitting their lives together more vividly and with more depth than the
shallow, temporary connections typical among coworkers, neighbors, or
people who meet shopping.

Relationships that form in voluntary association around practical activities like making or providing fuel are immediate and engaging. Isolation starts to crumble. Being part of a subculture of *technovative* creativity
stimulates the mind and the heart. You aren't just passively accepting what
fate has dealt out, you are choosing to do real work for your own purposes,
work and purposes shared by like-minded folks who become a new community, helping you in your own efforts as you are helping them.

At the Biofuels Oasis in Berkeley, a steady stream of customers pull
up to get their brew. A casual familiarity, a familial glow, imbues the exchanges between buyer and seller. The economic exchange is a minor
irritant to the warm enthusiasm, mutual curiosity, and genuine interest
that constitute the real exchanges at the Oasis.

> Just for people to be able to meet face to face at The
> Oasis has been a gift. Hooking people up and making
> connections has been part of the synchronous energy
> here. We have forums and discussion groups and cre-
> ate community… in community, people take you for all
> your quirkiness and for who you are. You're accepted
> and appreciated for whatever it is… AND a) you show
> up for others and b) they show up for you. That's com-
> munity too, being there for each other.
>
> —*Sara Hope Smith*[40]

Claudia Eyzaguirre affirms the drive for community and solidarity
underlying biodiesel in Berkeley. "The guiding light of our culture is

that it should be fun and we're building community… there's this whole network that's just forming."[41] The community begins around the machine and the fuel that makes it go.

As noted earlier, cars have long been a quintessential arena for working class tinkering and play. As automobiles have become more computerized and less simple, the old familiar self-sufficiency that many people gained from maintaining their own vehicles has diminished. Tinkering and perfecting your own machinery and making yourself more independent are bedrock values of American workers. If you can fix a machine yourself you are admired for the skill and the relative autonomy it provides. Mechanics, plumbers, electricians, and carpenters all have useful skills and exemplify a practical self-sufficiency that many yearn for, especially the millions who can't fix a thing because they've been running computers, working in shops, hotels, or with "information." Largely white-collared and affluent enough to feel "middle class," these workers don't hold long-term jobs and tend to move a lot. Hopping laterally from employer to employer and community to community, they are living out the extreme fragmentation and class "decomposition" several decades of economic restructuring and globalization has imposed. Neighbors are at best short-term acquaintances who come and go before relationships can deepen.

The biofuels community fills an empty space for many of its adherents. Biofuels activism has introduced a way of regaining some self-sufficiency along with the connectedness that accompanies mutual aid and sharing skills. New friends form in the activities—the real work—that people engage in freely, not for wages or monetary gain but for motivations spanning ecology to morality, health to self-sufficient simplification.

Working for a wage reduces work's purpose to an undignified, shallow monetary reward. Work done for its own sake is fundamentally different. Defined by the person doing it, deemed good and necessary on its own merits, un-waged work fulfills and confirms a multidimensional sensibility, providing a whole range of feelings and experiences beyond the narrow instrumentalism of work for money. Freely chosen work is always more satisfying to do, a source of pleasure that few other human activities can match. The quality is "better" too, because everyone does their best work when determining their own purpose and pace.

Organizer Claudia Eyzaguirre offers a nuanced appraisal of her different relationships to paid and free work to capture a common experience:

> If you work for your avocation, your passion in life, by the function of it being work, you no longer enjoy it. I hate work. A lot of people hate work. You [can] separate your vocation and your avocation and get paid for one and work at the other one with a freedom of spirit.

That's been my attitude towards biodiesel. Some people talk about your work being your passion... I don't think that works. Because once something is constricted by "you have to be there" and you put a monetary value to it (at least coming from a lefty perspective), that taints it, right? ...[Biodiesel] validates my time. During the past two years I've done something really impressive. Everybody in the Bay Area now knows what biodiesel is, and a lot of people are driving on it. The Berkeley Biodiesel Collective is largely responsible... [42]

Antioch student Ben Gillock describes a similar dichotomy between work for money and his biodiesel work, which he labels a "hobby."

I never really had a hobby where it is a significant and regular part of your life and it's where your mind travels to. [Biodiesel] became that way. I was thinking a lot about cars and engines and studying it and putting a lot of work into something that wasn't yielding a paycheck or anything like that.[43]

The diminished life we're left as workers in an alien system we unconsciously call "the economy" drives increasing numbers of us to do our "real work" outside of its logic, for our own reasons and in cooperation with people who also "get it." Biofuel activism demonstrates this logic, but it also shows people moving on this path without necessarily thinking about it that way ahead of time.

Ben Gillock discovered a far from homogenous population in his on-line investigations as well as in his encounters on the road with bio-fuel enthusiasts.

On these biodiesel forums people are talking mechanics, ideology, technique and they have relationships with one another. They go visit each other and talk shop. It's built up around what they're doing and what brought them to do it. It's an interest in independence, an interest in novelty...[It] is not a like-minded place when it comes to politics. It's people who share this interest in working with stuff, which for [them] is a fundamental value. Being able to work with a car, the underside, come up with something interesting, innovative, put it together and do it like RIGHT, so it works.[44]

But the blue-collar manufacturing working class is only a small fraction of U.S. society now. Mechanical dexterity is less common these days, partly because a lot of people have never been exposed to the basic workings, never been taught how to analyze and troubleshoot machinery. We are encouraged to be dependent on experts. And a lot of technology is complicated enough to be kept deliberately opaque behind trade secrets and copyrights. Or designed so whole "black boxes" are swapped out if something breaks, instead of trying to fix the specific malfunction.

After the early days of widespread tinkering and hands-on innovation, the people getting involved with biofuels have slowly shifted away from the mechanics and towards the environmentalists and activists. Claudia Eyzaguirre describes such a shift in Berkeley:

> We began as a user-producer coop and had this physical space where people tinkered around. We're not attracting the diverse sector of people that we were before. Now we only get the people who want to work for biodiesel because they believe in working for a cleaner environment.[45]

Grassroots biofuels boosters don't usually hail from the blue-collar part of society. A lot of them are educators, computer workers, performers—a range of "middle class" occupations. Because of this the director of the San Francisco Department of the Environment could tell a local newspaper, "It's seen as a boutique fuel for people who can afford it, and we want to make it a fuel for everyday people."[46]

As noted elsewhere, "middle class" refers to a well-paid strata of the working population subject to the same precariousness and instability as anyone working for wages. But there's more than one "middle class" as Eyzaguirre notes here:

> Because I'm middle class the amount of money I make doesn't matter. Much more it's about the circle that I travel in [where] life is so good and comfortable that you don't need to have that much money... There's two kinds of middle classes. There's the middle class that I'm in, where there's tremendous luxury. I'm not working today and I have on $80 sneakers. (But certainly not as wealthy as people who are rich.) Then there's the other middle class, who maybe have a few more things than me, but not that much. But they're at work right now, working all the time. Some people out there [are] working to pay off their $350 car payment every month and other people aren't, [even though] they are essentially living in the same economic strata... when you come into this world with blessings then you have the luxury of working to make other things better. I'm not spending every minute scrambling to keep my head above water.[47]

Choosing exodus from much of the work and trappings of "middle class" success, Eyzaguirre and other biofuels activists find themselves wealthy with free time and use it to do unpaid work. Curiously, this biofuel "techno-rebellion" has erupted from people who resist class as a useful category. Eyzaguirre answered my query about class with "It seems like a really old-fashioned word, one that's gone out of style." Sara Hope Smith expressed her own ambivalent ideas:

> Class. It's a division that we all ignore… I'm kind of con-
> fused now, because I thought as a kid that I was grow-
> ing up middle class but my dad was a probation officer
> and we were a pretty working class family. My grandpar-
> ents on my dad's side were both schoolteachers. On my
> mom's side not so working class, more white collar. [48]

The folks I spoke with mostly thought they were middle class. Jona-than Youtt, the charismatic founder of San Francisco's Cellspace before he co-founded the Big Tadoo Puppet Crew, told me "I grew up middle class. Working class was always more like blue collar and my dad wasn't blue collar. He was a public defender in a very expensive city [though] we didn't have much disposable income …"[49]

Ben Gillock declared "I'm definitely upper middle class. [As] a straight white male, I can't imagine a situation that I really wanted to ac-cess where I wouldn't be able to. My grandfather was a CIA agent, my dad started [out] working class but now he's very much upper middle class. Education is the key that separates working class from middle class."[50]

Openminded curiosity is a rare quality in our culture. Some get fully involved in developing a critical sensibility, sometimes through formal education, but just as often through life experiences. Sara Hope Smith's attitude to work, not constrained by the insecurity many feel, demon-strates a similar curiosity:

> I look at work as ways of getting paid to learn new things…
> I am not insecure enough about my ability to make mon-
> ey that I'm going to settle for stability and security over
> my sense of what feels right and what feels good.[51]

Biofuel tinkerers and activists are producing new kinds of work, and most importantly, new kinds of work-based relationships. The open source, cooperative, and collaborative practices that define the best of the field dovetail with similar practices in other grassroots movements that re-ject the limited choices imposed by contemporary capitalism. An *a priori* class consciousness is not motivating this, but clearly a new kind of cama-raderie and shared sensibility is growing among the adherents of sustain-able biofuels, based on practical work. The new communities and values are not limited to biofuels either but connect, sometimes quite overtly, to similar counter-movements in software, agriculture, and bicycling.

BIG CAPITAL VS. SUSTAINABILITY?

Despite the chemical kinship connecting biodiesel and straight veg, there is bad blood between the camps. Biodiesel has green roots, but it is becoming a big business, with lobbyists and backers like the American Soybean Association and petroleum distributors who have their infrastructure in place to cash in on the booming demand... and [the National Biodiesel Board doesn't] like the free agents out there tinkering on the side.
—*Joshua Berman*, L.A. Weekly[52]

The deeper I get into the industry, the more biodiesel starts to take on that taint of everything else.
—*Kumar Plochar, Yokayo Biofuels*[53]

Biodiesel is a gateway drug to sustainability.
—*Sara Hope Smith*[54]

After a frantic decade of freewheeling experimentation and exploration (most dynamically and creatively among backyard brewers and artistic mechanics), the biofuels movement is starting to have *commercial* success. A large market of public vehicles is beckoning. School districts and municipalities, public transit and utilities across the country are gradually converting their fleets to biodiesel. Federal tax credits available since the beginning of 2005 have given official blessing to the industrial "invasion" of biofuels.

Major agriculture and oil multinationals are making investments and strategic plans to absorb the emerging biofuels market. Chevron and BP[55] are jumping in while agricultural giant Archer-Daniels-Midland recently chose a refining manager from Chevron as a new CEO. Advertising campaigns tout their sponsoring global corporations for far-sighted engagement with alternative energy sources. Faced with growing demand for biofuels to replace petroleum, industry and government seek to integrate these fuels into the status quo. If biofuels can be controlled from seed to pump by the same interests that already own our existing dependency, it will indeed "take off," at least in its bastard corporatized form.

It seems to be happening. In Germany, output tripled between 2002–2005 to apx. 450 million gallons. According to Javier Salgado of the leading European ethanol producer, Abengoa of Spain, when crude oil sells for $70 a barrel (it hovers around $60 at this writing) unsubsidized biofuels can compete with petroleum.[56]

Technical problems with biodiesel get more attention than they perhaps deserve, but it's true that some conversion efforts run into trouble. Unlike gasoline, pure 100% biodiesel sometimes causes engine problems (although aficionados will assure you that there should be only improved performance with biodiesel). In 2003 the city of Berkeley switched to pure, veggie-based biodiesel for its vehicles, but that experiment failed after two years, largely because of mechanical problems associated with the fuel. In March 2005 Berkeley downgraded from 100 percent biodiesel to a 20 percent blend.[57]

The bigger problem is how the growing market penetration of big capital will shape the technology to its own interests. Eric Bowen is a San Francisco Biofuels Collective member, and advisor to the city government. He understands how large businesses take over markets from smaller ones:

> Big-Ag biodiesel makes community scale biodiesel more challenging. If and when we see a biodiesel supply glut, Big-Ag will flood the market with cheap biodiesel. It will want to maintain and/or expand its market share and will be able to operate with little to no margin because of its extensive non-biodiesel revenue sources.[58]

Lyle Estill points to an important piece of the competitive puzzle: "Organic produce and biodiesel share similar market plights. Both are in spaces where the 'competition' has successfully externalized their costs. Big Food and Big Oil have figured out how to get society to bear their costs in ways that do not show up in the price of their products."[59]

Most biodiesel proponents promote co-ops or at least small business models for their industry. The harsh embrace of multinational capital has not been their goal. Berkeley's Eyzaguirre explains:

> Our original idea is that we'd be this user-producer co-op and we'd all meet our fuel needs by making our fuel and working together, but our philosophy was that we would be creating decentralized resource control and building community, including the environment. One of the big problems initially was that there was no supply. The only way to get the supply in the U.S. in 2004 is through somebody supplying it as a business... The idea of biodiesel appeals to some people much less from a social justice standpoint than it appeals to me. They see it as a business opportunity.[60]

Jonathan Youtt has been active in the Bay Area for the past few years and his view of the industry is still largely co-op oriented. "There are individual user co-ops around the Bay Area (Sonoma County, Mendocino, Marin). Either they bulk buy biodiesel and then give it away to the members at cost, or they collect it as a group, do the conversion, and it's just for the users." In North Carolina, Lyle Estill and the folks around Piedmont Biofuels maintain their co-op approach, which in practical terms means that as they make their plans, they have different goals than a typical expanding business. For example, several years ago they "successfully resisted the desire to scale up and devoted ourselves to perfecting small-batch processors that could meet a small number of drivers' needs using local feedstocks."[61] But just a couple of years later, when an expansion became necessary anyway due to surging interest, they still define their purpose differently.

> Today our little biodiesel co-op meets the fuel needs of
> a couple of hundred families. We are building a plant
> that will meet the needs of 800 more. Scaling up for us
> means meeting the needs of *a small community that is in
> search of a different way of being.*[62] [emphasis added]

Cooperatives and collectives have represented an alternative to business-as-usual for millions of American workers going back to the 19th century. Countless co-ops and collectivized small businesses have flourished and collapsed over the past century. The notion that a self-managed business, whether co-operatively structured or as a collective comprised of equally responsible members, can escape the ruthless logic of capitalism, is a persistent dream of people who create these alternative structures. The Berkeley Biofuels Oasis is dedicated to showing that "it is possible to do business in a different way and it is possible to do things on a basis of love and caring and trust and community and integrity, as opposed to greed and a bottom line of money. So no we're not expecting to get rich off biodiesel."[63]

But the well-known difficulties that face any small business (shortage of capital, insufficient markets, limited advertising budgets, etc.) are not overcome by "caring and trust," even if community and integrity can be sold to specific marketplace niches. The internal politics of any co-op or collective are as coherent and sound as the personal relationships among its members. Usually, the pressure imposed by the need to pay for space, wages, etc., relentlessly drive even the most altruistic of efforts towards the same kinds of business behaviors as any other business. The iron rule of the market is inflexible and unforgiving. Grassroots biofuel pioneers face the classic capitalist dictum—grow or die!

More and more individual proprietors are entering the market as small businesses have started to compete with the first wave co-ops, and are thriving in the space between self-sufficient tinkerers and earnest environmentalists. Kits are now available from a variety of companies. Here's a quick synopsis of the growth of one of them, Greasecar, in Massachusetts.

It starts with founder Justin Carven learning about biofuels at Hampshire College in 1998. He spends time at college working on modifying inventor Carl Bielenberg's tropical seed oil engines. Carven graduated in 2000 with his BA in mechanical design. He rented a small workshop in 2002 in Florence, MA. By 2004, Greasecar was getting 50–100 telephone calls a day. In June 2004 Greasecar moves to a 4000-sq. ft. location in Easthampton, MA. In Spring 2005 sales skyrocket, revenue increases 350% that year. During 2005 it expands to 14 employees and by the end of 2005 they have caught up with the backlog of orders.

Greasel Conversions, the company Ben Gillock and Bianca Sopoci-Belknap bought their conversion kit from, is still flourishing too, but have moved to Springfield, MO and changed their name to Golden Fuel Systems. They are shipping conversion kits and solar installations as well, branching into other parts of the alternative energy business.

In Los Angeles, Lovecraft Biofuels has made a splash with Reagan-era Mercedes Benzes that it converts to straight vegetable oil. Rocker and blogger Danita Sparks wrote about Lovecraft in the summer of 2006:

> I'm talking about *a lot* of these cars and all of them looking rather stately save for a bumper sticker in the back window that reads, "Fueled By 100% Vegetable Oil." I was intrigued and soon stumbled upon the source of this mystery. Lovecraft Biofuels, on Sunset Blvd., is a trip. It is absolutely *packed* with multi-colored and custom painted Mercedes. Brian Friedman converts diesel engines to pure veggie oil cheaply and guarantees his work from soup to nuts. His business is absolutely booming! The car is great. Runs smooth and smells like popcorn cooking. When I first heard of this Biofuel/Biodiesel stuff it seemed like a big pain in the ass. Now there is a sea change going on.[64]

Biofuels activists are defining a sustainability standard for the industry. At the 2005 "shadow conference" in San Diego while the National Biodiesel Conference went on nearby, attendees agreed to start an organization to defend and advance sustainable fuels policies. There is also a plan to create a "Sustainability Rating," presumably to help biofuel buyers spend their consumer dollars on an alternative political path.

But collectively the grassroots biofuels movement faces its own crisis of sustainability. As the major multinationals invade the market niche they have painstakingly cultivated over the past decade, the values and practices that have shaped this alternative business are likely to be overwhelmed by the much larger capitalists and their ruthless practices. The required commitment of time and energy from dedicated activists is itself difficult to sustain over longer periods. Piedmont Biofuels' Estill describes the problem:

> Because we are a co-op with worker-members, we are populated by volunteers and have the same problem as churches and homeowner associations and every other volunteer group on the planet, which is that a small core group does most of the work.[65]

For those individuals who find themselves in that indispensable core group, their lives get eaten up by the organizational, social, and business demands that fall on them. At the Biofuels Oasis, Smith admits, "I have not had the downtime that I used to have. I'm working twice as hard and making a quarter as much money as I ever used to... Everybody I know doesn't have the time they used to... I am definitely making social sacrifices to be here."[66]

An abiding problem confronting projects based on volunteers and a core group of overworked regulars is time. If a project manages to last beyond months into years, the most minimal overhead costs have by then already imposed business-like issues and responses. With increasing work to satisfy the record-keeping tasks of any lasting group (mailing lists, tax forms, etc.), it grows more difficult to cover the drudge work with volunteer labor. Once someone starts getting paid, the informal hierarchies that have self-managed until then begin to shift. The eventual end point of this process is a more normalized business structure. Whether it is a for-profit company or a nonprofit organization, survival is the first goal, followed, if successful, by expansion. The initial inspiration, freedom, and collaborative excitement wane over time to be succeeded by the pursuit of success, however defined. Starting from the deep pleasure of a shared mission the project becomes mere enterprise. Boisterous excitement is reduced to business. Community becomes commerce.

The drive for community and innovation also inspires thoughtful activists to redefine their mission in ways that escape the narrowing imposed by commerce. The emerging philosophy of permaculture, a systemic rethinking of how we produce, use, and live with the biological wealth of the planet, provides a broad frame of reference for growing numbers of biofuels adherents.[67]

At the Biofuels Oasis, Sara Hope Smith describes her parallel interest: "I got myself educated, right as I was moving in this [biodiesel] direction, in permaculture. [It shapes] the longterm view of what Bio-Fuels Oasis is going to be. My partner Jennifer and I are both permaculturists. As you walk inside, we've used wheat gluten paint with natural pigments on one wall, we've got Elize plaster on the other wall, so we're working that end of it. I think those things are really woven together and form each other."[68]

Another example is Common Vision, a nonprofit organization operating since 1999.

> Common Vision fuels all of its vehicles on Recycled Vegetable Oil, a clean-burning and renewable substitute for diesel fuel... Common Vision has found that the principles of permaculture are not only important in gardening and landscaping but also as design principles for all aspects of our organization and lives. They represent the underpinnings of our sustainability education programs.

> Permaculture-based education enables emancipation from dependency to direct and active participation in the creation of the most basic aspects of human existence—food security, energy, and shelter. The creation of local systems of sustainability is a ritual of reclaiming production of basic needs through ecologically inspired designs of interconnected resource flow. It serves as a potent tool in the development of a culture that lives in harmony with each other and the earth. [69]

Key elements of a sustainable vision come to light in the grassroots biofuels ferment. Unsurprisingly they overlap with fields covered in other chapters in this book. The dynamism of both technological innovation AND community cohesion among biofuels activists depends on open source philosophy. In practical terms this means a rejection of trade secrets, owning ideas, hiding research from potential competitors, and a practically unconditional willingness to share knowledge and help each other. A politically informed embrace of working with waste underscores many initiatives, an approach that harmonizes with a broader permacultural focus on resource cycling. A prominent piece of the capitalist economy is its ability to hide the mountain of waste it creates, but biofuels developers have embraced the waste stream as a rich resource of feedstocks from which to make fuel.

The brilliant minds and big hearts of feisty, innovative tinkerers and biofuel inventors might bring forth something much more than just a new way to power private vehicles. There are many paths that depart from any historic moment and our time is no exception. Contesting the meaning and purpose of our looming fuel conversion is a front line in the much larger project of reconceptualizing what we know about lives on this planet. Imagine instead, working from the cooperative, generous values that spurred this decade-long insurgency, biofuel activists are part of a radical revolt of the Nowtopians. Not just replacing fuels but replacing and transforming our society, our relationships with each other, with nature, with our own tools, and with our infinite possibilities. It is a lot to ask, but in a way, the challenge before us is to think *big enough* for our historic time. The people who have challenged the rapacious behemoths of multinational oil and automobiles are not daunted by the scope of the task ahead. Among the increasingly self-conscious strata of technologically subversive workers, the biofuels proponents have already created compelling examples of what is possible. How much further they and we can go remains to be seen.

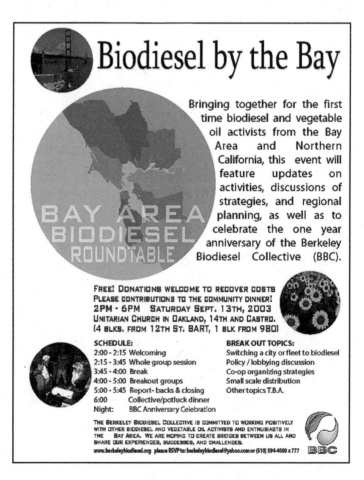

Biofuel bus caravans have helped promote biodiesel and other alternatives to gasoline, now being distributed more widely. Meanwhile, at a Berkeley, California biofuels vehicle show, locals get out to kick the tires and peer into engines.

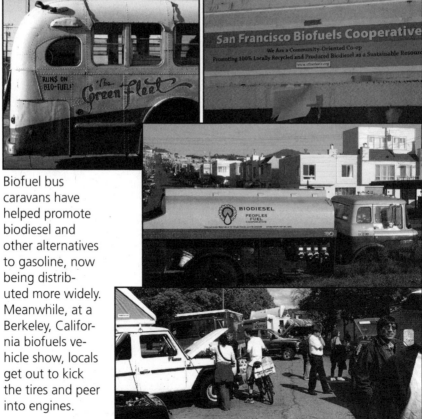

CHAPTER 8
VIRTUAL SPINE OF THE COMMONS

The open source community is pretty much tech support for the revolution, if you will, or tech support for the new society.

—*Will Doherty*[1]

...It is the machine which possesses skill and strength in place of the worker, is itself the virtuoso, with a soul of its own in the mechanical laws acting through it... The science which compels the inanimate limbs of the machinery, by their construction, to act purposefully, as an automaton, does not exist in the workers' consciousness, but rather acts upon him through the machine as an alien power... The production process has ceased to be a labor process in the sense of a process dominated by labor as its governing unity. Labor appears, rather, merely as a conscious organ, scattered among the individual living workers at numerous points of the mechanical system; subsumed under the total process of the machinery itself, as itself only a link of the system, whose unity exists not in the living workers, but rather in the living (active) machinery, which confronts his individual, insignificant doings as a mighty organism.

—*Karl Marx*[2]

The Internet is an ongoing creation of a staggering, unmeasurable cooperative effort by an unknowable number of contributing workers. It is several decades old, but expanding continuously, always reaching more people and more places, affecting ever more aspects of life and work. This world-spanning system of wires, circuits, microchips, machines, and frequencies shaped by global capitalist imperatives provides the physical foundation for the automated office and far-flung capitalist managerial control. The physical network has also facilitated an unparalleled and largely unregulated proliferation of communicative relationships which themselves are producing unprecedented connections, movements, behaviors, and social knowledge.

The Internet balances on radically opposite assumptions about the material basis of our lives. It is a curious hybrid of money-making business and a sprawling gift economy of avid writers, programmers, designers, and inventors, mutually dependent while working (often unconsciously) towards antagonistic goals. Private ownership and its foundational fear of scarcity push the Internet to extend and intensify the exploitation of human labor. The commodity form is imposed on the "products" that traverse the Internet, while wherever possible human connections are reduced to mere transactions. Elsewhere, the integration of computers and information technology into material production greatly intensifies the exploitation of human work, expanding production systems geographically and temporally while ever more tightly subordinating individual workers to rhythms and expectations beyond their comprehension or control.

The Internet also reveals a nearly limitless abundance that stimulates sharing and cooperation for its own sake, a digital commons reinforcing human interconnectedness and interdependence. In a late capitalist world of numbing barbarism and alienated isolation, the powerful allure of meaningful communication inspires passionate engagement and remarkable time investments by millions. This participatory commons harbors every kind of human relationship, from the banality of buying and selling to the unconstrained sharing of poetry, art, music—any kind of expression that depends on communication. A post-capitalist life founded on generalized abundance is prefigured in self-expanding autonomous communications spaces on-line. But that is only one possible future, and far from inevitable.

The two opposed visions of the Net co-exist in tense mutual dependence. Equipment vendors, infrastructure owners, and increasingly, retailers require users by the million. Netizens can only exist with an elaborate technical infrastructure maintained—in this society—by private capital and nation states. Nevertheless, the infrastructure can be used to attack capital's control both directly and indirectly. Activist programmers use free software to provide communications infrastructure to oppositional groups fighting cultural and political battles. Indymedia centers and blog sites provide open publishing platforms for independent opinion, and noncommercial news reporting. Thousands publish photos, music, and writings for free distribution on the Net. Millions share thoughts and experiences via email and private discussion lists, plenty of it publicly posted, too. Self-organized and self-directed independent programmers spend endless hours working to produce "elegant," free software, often trumping commercial competitors in design and capabilities.

The Internet can be stuffed into the tiny box we call the "Market" or it can prompt a revolutionary redesign of how we do what we do, and how it fits into an urgently needed planetary ecological renaissance. In the first decade of the 21st century, social forces are pulling in both directions. The Internet—and the creative, often unpaid software work that makes use of it—is evolving amidst an epoch-shaping fight over the purpose and status of this new arena of human socializing. Prolific free communication on the Net constitutes an ongoing material experience unlike anything available in pre-Internet societies. Its practitioners are learning something new about cooperation, sharing, and collective and derivative social endeavors. Furthermore, the quasi-communistic results of free software production (even the more business-oriented open-source projects) are an ongoing affirmative "NO" to the shoddy quality and profit-distorted work undergirding commercial software produced at large corporations.

Abundant on-line creativity demonstrates the social nature of modern work more clearly than ever before, even though most work has always been dependent on social cooperation. Much of the Net has grown on the foundation of free software, leading in turn to the crazy proliferation of new creative uses, predominantly outside of exchange or commodification. All these daily acts of communication and creative sharing facilitated by the Net escape the capitalist imperative to measure individual work, pay for some tasks and not others (and at inexplicably divergent rates), while continually haranguing people to accept a "fair day's pay for a fair day's work."

Maurizio Lazzarato notes that "waged labor and direct subjugation (to organization) no longer constitute the principal form of the contractual relationship between capitalist and worker. A polymorphous self-employed autonomous work has emerged as the dominant form, a kind of 'intellectual worker' who is him or herself an entrepreneur, inserted within a market that is constantly shifting and within networks that are changeable in time and space."[3] In other words, economic life has been transformed by an increasingly blurred line between work as life-activity and work for pay. Individuals often produce work that is shared freely in one moment and then sold to an employer another. Though a majority of people do not work in computer- or Internet-related business, the growing precariousness of fixed employment in most fields parallels the relationships emerging in on-line and related work.

A BRIEF HISTORY OF THE INTERNET

Computers developed after WWII under the control of the military and large defense corporations like Raytheon, Honeywell, and IBM. By the time of the social upheavals of the 1960s, computers were equated with government and big business, sprawling bureaucracies with pernicious agendas. The original network of computer communications (called ARPANET) was set up by the U.S. military in conjunction

with a select number of elite universities and contractors. The purpose
of this system was to facilitate communications among researchers and
analysts, mostly working on advanced, often secret government weapons programs or basic research that would eventually lead to strategic
advantage in war and peace. Eventually, parts of the network became
more open, allowing professors doing unclassified work to use it for
collaborative communication. Throughout this era few imagined the
future role of the Internet, and no one attempted to impose a private
property model on the system. By the time a Swiss technician wrote out
the specifications for what became the World-Wide Web in the early
1990s, there were already thousands of users who were accustomed
to unfettered communication via email, discussion lists, and bulletin
boards. But we're getting a bit ahead of our story.

In the U.S., an explosion of underground newspapers and FM radio
(corresponding to the political revolts of the 1960s and 1970s) provided
a model of open and unfettered media that challenged the hegemony
of daily newspapers, formulaic radio programming, and the three television networks. Hundreds of underground newspapers gave voice to
the social revolts erupting during the era but could not alter the cen-
turies-old logic that gave freedom of speech to those who owned the
press, leaving most people to be passive observers. By the mid-1960s
high school students were graduating who had learned to do basic programming in early computer languages like FORTRAN and COBOL
on punch-card machines. Plenty of them soon sported long hair and
beards and sought a role in the explosive social movements of the time.
Computing philosopher Eric S. Raymond described the moment: "The
theme of computers being viewed not merely as logic devices but as
the nuclei of communities was in the air... 'Fellowship' would resonate
all through Unix's subsequent history." Unix was a software operating
system developed at Bell Labs by Ken Thompson, originally. It went on
to become the diffuse site of much early software experimentation and
collaboration.[4]

By the mid-1970s some of these early "shaggy hippie and hippie-wan-
nabe [computerists were giving] Unix software development a countercultural air, as Unix hackers reveled in the sense that they were simultaneously
building the future and flipping a finger at the system."[5] Meanwhile, on a
separate track, hardware hackers were building experimental machines,
trying to get access to the computing power they then could only vaguely
imagine. The Homebrew Computer Club fanatics became the most famous
of the new groups of tinkerers. Using parts scrounged from corporate and
university labs and available in hobby shops, they competed to build small
computers. The first Apple computer emerged from this ferment at the

Homebrew Club. In retrospect we can see that the personal computer arose from the parallel streams of microcircuit miniaturization, independent invention, and creative engineering.

Contemporaneous to the Homebrew Club's gathering of nerdy engineers and tinkerers, another group of brilliant hippies and radicals, some overlapping with the Homebrew crowd, were busy writing software programs to make possible a new kind of public computer network. They called it Community Memory, and they envisioned a kind of information flea market, but when they saw the unexpected uses to which the system was put, the idea got bigger. Community Memory could be a system that would escape the control of the government or large companies and bring powerful computing power to the hands of everyday people. An experimental version in 1973–74, based on a Xerox Data Systems 940 computer (a 58 MB hard drive the size of two refrigerators was acquired for $20,000!), had generated fantastic enthusiasm among its Berkeley and San Francisco users. The Community Memory collective retired that system after its early experiment, feeling certain that there would be a great public demand for their vision, consisting of public terminals connected to a state-of-the-art computer (that they were also building). The collective believed that computers and computing technology would be kept exclusively in the hands of large corporations, government, and the military, and never envisioned that computers would escape their control and become personal consumer items.

They wanted not only to outflank corporate America and the military-industrial complex, but also to enhance and supercede the forms of underground media that had been so influential in the preceding decade. Rather than a one-to-many broadcast model that newspapers, radio, and television all reinforced, they imagined the Community Memory system as one in which everyone could speak to everyone without mediation. Community Memory was to be a place where people could write their own news stories, engage in philosophical debates, post notices of events, items for sale—basically it was the Internet as we now know it, except that in the 1970s hardly anyone thought computers would become so small and powerful that they would be individually owned as consumer goods. Journalist Joyce Slayton recently wrote a retrospective on Community Memory:

> Techno-optimists and futurists we were, with Marxist communalist yearnings," says Jude Milhon, the feisty programmer known in some circles as St. Jude who joined the project soon after it was launched. "The idea was to make a new medium so useful, yet so yummy, that people would use it again and again, but whose

use would inevitably create this new sort of communal family. Mark [Szpakowski] added in the concept of the organic exchange of information, Ken [Colstad] formulated ideas about forms of economic exchange made possible by the new medium and I saw the possibilities of governance via conversation. But the users opened up many new avenues themselves, seeing it as a medium for art, literature, and self-promotion.[6]

The Community Memory collective embraced the open Unix operating system, wrote a state-of-the-art relational database program as well as a cutting-edge program for packet-switching networks, which they eventually sold to a number of large corporations in the hopes of financing their altruistic goals with the filthy lucre of their enemies.[7] Community Memory went on through the 1980s, eventually supporting a public network around the East Bay that had a dozen computers. Their efforts to capitalize on commercial software largely failed and their skilled programmers eventually scattered to the many new computer companies in the area.

A key reason that Community Memory did not live on is that they were founded on the belief that the personal computer would not become a common household item. In fact, small personal computers didn't immediately find a big market, but by the mid-1980s they started to, driven by the IBM Personal Computer and Apple's MacIntosh, along with the indispensable operating systems that made them useful.

Interestingly, the personal computer's success parallels a shift in capitalism. While the personal computer took shape, mass consumption based on uniform products and Fordist factory production began to give way to a rapid proliferation of niche markets, small batch production, and an ideology of human potential that bolstered an individualism defined primarily by shopping choices. The post-Fordist organization of work promoted a service and information-based economy with a much greater use of temporary and contract labor. This new style of work held increased expectations of what workers should *think and feel*, rather than just what they *do*. Referred to as "affective labor" by some theorists, it was summarized as a question of attitude in the 1980s magazine *Processed World*.[8]

Apple took full advantage of the cultural legacy of computing, with its strong anti-authoritarian roots shaped by cultural rebels like the 1950s Beats and 1960s Hippies. In Apple's original 1984 marketing campaign, a yellow spandex-clad, muscle-bound blonde bombshell ran into a stadium of drab masses to hurl a huge hammer into a screen broadcasting a Big Brother-style leader, shattering oppressive authority, freeing everyone to embrace their new power by buying a Mac. This heavy-handed symbolic co-optation flaunted capital's power to absorb opposition and turn resistance into energy for its own further growth, a key aspect of its continuing survival.

Around the time that the personal computer found its first big markets in the mid-1980s, Richard Stallman launched the idea of free software. His story and that of the early development of the General Public License (GPL) and the GNU/Linux free operating system have been told at great length in dozens of books and articles, all readily found online. Julian Stallabrass describes Stallman (and by extension hundreds of other computer nerds) in a 2002 article: "…waist-length hair, flowing beard, brown polyester trousers and ill-matched T-shirts."[9] He was born in 1953 and grew up as a relatively isolated math whiz, avoiding the 1960s protests to end up at the MIT Artificial Intelligence lab. His cohort at MIT was passionately committed to the sharing and collaborative processes that were the foundation of their research. When software started becoming a business and copyrights were used to lock up source codes, Stallman adamantly refused to go along. "For programmers like Stallman, this was an assault on what they most cared about, as material that they had worked on for years was snatched from their grasp—an act analogous to the enclosure of common land."[10]

The Free Software movement ironically used legal means to achieve their goals. They created the General Public License, ensuring that work created for the commons would stay there, and that any derivative work based on it would have to join it in the uncommodified digital commons.[11] When the Linux operating system (based on the "GNU Not Unix" operating system, a totally rebuilt-from-scratch system similar to but different than Unix, under a General Public License) emerged and began to chip away at Microsoft's monopolistic domination of personal computer software in the early 1990s, a number of competitors discovered a new business model. Eric S. Raymond published "The Cathedral and the Bazaar" in 1998, promoting the idea of "open source" as a way of pushing the efficiency of free software while uncoupling it from the anti-propertarian values promoted by Stallman and his followers.[12] Since the late 1990s the open source concept has spread far and wide, almost obliterating the subversive movements that called for Free Software. Even in its free form as General Public Licensed work available to all, it has been embraced by most large computer companies. Like a poker game of "Texas Hold'em," companies use the "cards on the table" (the growing body of free and open source software) to seek commercial advantage in technical knowledge and ideas, while charging money for everything they can (particularly organization and technical support).

The rapid expansion of the Internet has provided a means for software development to accelerate, both due to the greater ability for long-distance collaboration and to the rapidity with which new software can be distributed to the public on-line. Regardless of an ideological commitment to "free," (or lack thereof) these twin developments have helped to radically reduce the price of software, providing access to thousands of new programmers and technically skilled people. Plenty of developers realize that giving away their work is a way to gain renown quickly—and thus market advantage—serving a practical rather than ideologically motivated purpose. Still, underlying the steady expansion of the Net and its available tools is also a cultural impulse seeking a break from the deadening logic of capital.

MAKING TECHNOLOGY SOMETHING NEW

> Today, as in the past, technology is still a main metaphor for intellectual and cultural work. There is a hegemonic metaphor haunting media criticism and network culture, curating and the arts world: that is Free Software. We hear it quoted at the end of each intervention that poses the problem of what is to be done (but also in articles of strategic marketing.), whilst the twin metaphor of open source contaminates every discipline: open source architecture, open source literature, open source democracy, open source city and so on.
>
> —*Matteo Pasquinelli*[13]

Movement-oriented computerists have tried to solve the tension between the original Free Software concept and business exploitation under the rubric of "open source" with the broader title FLOSS, meaning "Free-as-in-Libre and Open Source Software." Initiatives across the planet have embraced this. FLOSS projects tend to fall into gaps where private developers haven't dared yet to tread, whether in promoting free Wi-Fi networks, internet telephony, providing computerization to poverty-stricken communities in the North and South, etc. One such project is OpenMute, associated with the cutting-edge journal *Mute* in England.

> The OpenMute project started in 2001 to provide FLOSS communications web tools to cultural and community groups, with an understanding of their shared circumstances: limited resources, mixed levels of computer skills, and often little experience of the networked communications that FLOSS facilitates. As an advocate

of the public domain, OpenMute adopted FLOSS as a tactical media toolset for its ability to challenge the ongoing conversion of everyday knowledge into property. Shared conventions from daily life can be borrowed and patented just because they have been replicated in computer code... FLOSS and its associated strategies are a way of opposing these exploitative types of property and social relationships."[14]

Since the first efforts of nerdy engineers, everything from the personal computer to social networking software represent *political actions* by programmers and engineers. These creative acts are sometimes conceived as explicit contributions to "the revolution," and at other times they are accidental or unconscious. If taken together they have promoted a more diverse and distributed information commons than might have existed if technological development was left to the monopolistic corporations and the military that had controlled computing until the late 1970s. The largest part of on-line content is still noncommercial, and more often than in other spheres of contemporary life you readily can find *anti*-commercial expression. That noncommercial content, though, anchors whole industries of capitalist business, from the telecom operators selling bandwidth, to the publishing companies providing tools and space to make audiences for advertisers (e.g. Blogger, Myspace, Youtube, etc.). A profitable business model arose by placing things people have been making privately for a long time (personal diaries, novels, photos, ramblings, poetry, school gazettes, etc.) in a public context of advertising and ecommerce, and then working to make those public, commercial platforms as monopolistic as possible.

Richard Barbrook was one of the earliest to identify communistic values operating within the logic of the digital commons in his 1994 essay "The High-Tech Gift Economy." He describes how non-market values slowly accreted among the growing community of Net denizens:

> From scientists through hobbyists to the general public, the charmed circle of users was slowly built up through the adhesion of many localized networks to an agreed set of protocols. Crucially, the common standards of the Net include social conventions as well as technical rules. The giving and receiving of information without payment is almost never questioned... Everyone takes more out of the Net than they can ever give away as an individual.[15]

Barbrook understood even in 1994 that the dynamic struggle underway was between the embedded gift logic and the growing efforts of business and government to commodify the Net. What was emergent then, and is still with us today, is a strange hybrid of mutually dependent economic forms. Few Net users are reluctant to use market resources and government funding (when they can get them!) to pursue their "potlatch economy" of free exchange online. Corporations try to colonize as much as they can, while the insidious pressure to survive economically forces many digital innovators to seek business models for their ideas. The reimposition of a regime of property is, according to Barbrook's essay, the main strategy through which capitalism tries to bring the anarcho-communism of the Net back to its scorched earth.

The wrestling match between fee and free unfolds above a ceaseless wellspring of creative energy. An authentic, uncoerced motivation continues to fuel free software work, continually refreshing its fundamentally anti-authoritarian character. Stefan Merten of the German group Oekonux describes the process:

> ...the organization of the production of Free Software differs widely from that of commodities produced for maximizing profit. For most Free Software producers there is no other reason than their own desire to develop that software. So the development of Free Software is based on the self-unfolding (from the German term "Selbstentfaltung," similar but not completely the same as "self-development") of the single individual. The form of non-alienated production results in better software because the use of the product is the first and most important aim of the developer—there simply is no profit which could be maximized...

> Free Software is both inside and outside capitalism. On one hand, the social basis for Free Software clearly would not exist without a flourishing capitalism... On the other hand, Free Software is outside of capitalism because of the absence of scarcity and [because it is based on] self-unfolding instead of alienated labor in a command economy. This kind of relationship between the old and the new system is typical for germ forms...

> There is simply no reciprocity [in Free Software] and even better: there is no need for it. You simply take what you need and you provide what you like... Not by chance, this reflects the old demand "From each according to his ability, to each according to his needs.[16]

Many overlapping debates have erupted among cultural and political theorists about the nature of the Internet as a new public commons,

the labor process that sustains and expands it, the unpaid cultural production that largely fills the bandwidth, and much more. Some have
responded to the communistic (or anarchistic) theories of the Internet
by arguing that the free labor that fills the Net is an example of the
increasingly blurred boundaries between work and life that is characteristic of the post-Fordist regime. From this point of view the free labor
functions something like housework or having children, as a necessary
subsidy to capitalist accumulation, a vast source of uncompensated human labor that is essential to the full functioning of a sprawling social
factory. Moreover, the production of cultural commodities subtly ex-
tends a logic of commodification over an expanding range of human
experiences. Tiziana Terranova, one of the sharpest theorists of network culture, eloquently describes the way late capitalism makes use of
the reservoirs of free labor that have appeared on-line:

> Rather than representing a moment of incorporation of
> a previously authentic moment, the open-source ques-
> tion demonstrates the overreliance of the digital econo-
> my as such on free labor, free both in the sense of "not
> financially rewarded" and of "willingly given"... Free
> labor is a desire of labor immanent to late capitalism,
> and late capitalism is the field which both sustains free
> labor *and* exhausts it. It exhausts it by undermining the
> means through which that labor can sustain itself: from
> the burn-out syndromes of Internet start-ups to under-
> compensation and exploitation in the cultural economy
> at large. Late capitalism does not appropriate anything:
> it nurtures, exploits and exhausts its labor force and
> its cultural and affective production. In this sense, it
> is technically impossible to separate neatly the digital
> economy of the Net from the larger network economy
> of late capitalism. Especially since 1994, the Internet
> has always and simultaneously been a gift economy *and*
> an advanced capitalist economy.[17]

But political radicals can't leave it at that, since the work going in
to the Net clearly has multiple meanings. Writing a review of the *DATA
Browser 01* collection,[18] Trebor Scholz argues that the same work is creating subversive alternatives to existing power systems.

> Within the cooperation commons people create and
> distribute content. This overwhelms traditional compa-
> nies that cannot match the massive amount of free con-
> tent created by a multitude of user communities. These
> cultural reservoirs and much of cooperation-enhancing
> technologies allow the like-minded to connect and share

knowledge. This has the potential to undermine the content hegemonies of universities, museums, companies,
and the military. Knowledge pools put in place unorth-
odox knowledge economies. They are communal exchange spaces that allow anyone to re-use/share and edit
content. Users move away from systems of production
and distribution that are based on market relations.[19]

The political goals that animated Community Memory thirty years
ago have been fulfilled in ways that were unimaginable at that time. Writing in *Computers & Society* in 1975 Michael Rossman, a friend of Community Memory, hopefully described the implications of the CM vision: "The
system democratizes information, coming and going. Whatever one's
power status in society—titan of industry, child of welfare recipient—one
can put information into the system and take it out on an equal basis. It
is a truly democratic and public utility, granting no one special privilege."
Although this sounds terribly quaint now, after 15 years of the worldwide
web's expansion, the democratic, participatory nature of the web far exceeds the wildest fantasies nurtured three decades ago.

The infrastructure provided by the Internet has facilitated protests
and movements while fostering radical decentralization and local control. Movements and campaigns that might have labored in total ob-
scurity find a global network of interest and support. Slowly but surely
the new transnational and asynchronous networks are shaping up as a
real alternative to traditional political forms. It's difficult to imagine,
for example, the Zapatistas avoiding massacre without the global attention they gained through savvy use of the Internet. The February 15,
2003 global anti-war protests brought out between 12 and 20 million
people in what is widely acknowledged as the largest planetary protest
ever held, an event self-organized largely through the Internet. "Fourth-
generation warfare" like the insurgency in Iraq shares "open source"
characteristics, and has bedeviled advanced military machines unable
to adapt to the new flexibility.[20]

But the Internet itself is only an environment of possibility, and it
has taken countless hours by thousands of dedicated technical workers
to make the resource effectively useful for a wide variety of "alternatives." With the creation of practical tools, political groups of all stripes
have staked out an on-line presence, augmenting their campaigns, gaining new adherents, and spreading their message in ways that far exceed
the limitations of pre-Internet society.

Will Doherty is a founder of the Online Policy Group (OPG), a web-
based organization founded to provide Internet services to dozens of
small dissident groups and social hubs, controversial entities who might

otherwise be censored or locked out if they had to rely on commercial hosts (its motto is "One Internet, with Equal Access for All"). Like the free software developers who keep improving the GNU/Linux operating system, the OPG is maintained by a group of programmers who are committed to building software tools better, not because they want to sell them, but because they want to continually improve and expand the usefulness of the tools they provide for free to the groups doing political work they support.

Doherty used to work for Sun Microsystems, and later, after abandoning the corporate world, did a stint at the nonprofit Electronic Frontier Foundation. He has spent more than a decade working on practical tools and campaigning for policy changes to promote a more profound democracy. He has worked long and hard for greater openness and transparency, in terms of software but also for his own vision of a restructured polity in the future: "Whatever shape this takes in the future, agencies responsible for various parts of making sure that we can live comfortably should be accountable by being open and transparent in their operations and methods and decision-making."[21]

Another project that has been made possible by the free software movement is called Localharvest.org. Founder Guillermo Payet explains "Local Harvest is infrastructure that produces a community, providing a virtual meeting space and a range of services to small food growers." Payet is a Peruvian immigrant who came to California to work as a programmer, eventually starting his own business after a few years in the cultural desert of Silicon Valley. In Santa Cruz he established a thriving Internet service company, prospering during the dotcom boom only to collapse a few months after the dotcom bust. After his frustrating life in Silicon Valley hell, he was especially missing the diverse and tasty foods he had grown up with in Peru. During the years his business thrived, he and his half-dozen employees filled the gaps between commercial jobs with a project to connect farmers and local markets, figuring a website could become a useful hub for direct connections. After five years, Local Harvest is thriving, with nearly 10,000 active members (farmers' markets, farms, local small grocery stores selling locally produced goods, or similarly oriented restaurants, even people producing specialties in their backyards from honey to kimchee).

Payet describes how using free software underpins his work, making this free resource for thousands of farmers available (instead of being a pay-for-service site as it might have been had it emerged from commercial motivations):

> What I'm trying to do is to help build an alternative
> food system that is away from agribusiness, from cor-

porate supermarkets and all that. With Local Harvest I leveraged open source to do something with just one guy and a half an employee... the reason why I can do so much is because it's not just myself, I'm leveraging the efforts of thousands of people in the open source movement. Local Harvest is about helping people find their local sources of food... The main goal of Local Harvest is healthy farms, not necessarily organic... [We are doing] social activism. The second goal is environmental activism... The real activism is in helping design new systems that are self-sustaining.[22]

The grassroots biofuels movement is another example of a self-sustaining system supported and expanded by the Internet. When Nicole Cousino and her friends first started researching how to convert waste vegetable oil into biofuel, they spent hours tracking down contacts and making telephone calls. Dozens of phone conversations with a scientist in Colorado slowly walked Cousino through the steps of transterification back in 1994. Within a few years websites were popping up with elaborate how-to information, and by 2003 hundreds of people were involved in the technological tinkering and, crucially, communicating it openly over the Internet (see "Free Fuel: The Tinkerer's Grail" chapter for a full discussion of the biofuels movement).

Ed Phillips is a seminal contributor to on-line discussions on free software and the social paradigms it has helped shape. He also works as a programmer, using free software tools exclusively and he contributes to free software projects. In conversation he emphasized the DIY skills that both create and are created by the infrastructure:

As an open source developer [you develop] do-it-yourself skills, and the confidence and the power to seize the means of production, and get stuff done that you need to get done. So that if the existing infrastructure were to have a crisis or existing systems were to go into a crisis mode you could assume some responsibility for your own survival and for the betterment of others, without need of these institutions. You're a fashioner rather than a mere user.[23]

Payet is a natural born technician, the kind of person fueling the political use of the Internet in addition to the technocultural rebellions appearing all over the emerging commons.

Since I was a little kid I was always a big tinkerer. I always like to get to the bottom of it. That's what I like about open source is that you can get under the hood. My work is technically interesting. It's about optimizing

things, making things a lot smoother, easier, getting rid
of bureaucracy. I'm a very good engineer.[24]

This kind of hands-on capability alters one's relationship to technology more broadly, demystifying concepts and languages that often stop the less technically adept from engaging at all. Phillips told me, "[My attitude towards technology has] changed dramatically in a lot of ways. Through the free software community and all the people I've met and all the things I've worked on over the years, I've gotten to understand a lot of other technical disciplines and areas and become much more comfortable with other technical domains."

How can so many skilled workers spend so much time doing free work? What is their motivation? If Terranova is correct to argue that free labor is a desire immanent to late capitalism, we might assume that this is an automatic urge independent of specific desires and purposes. But it's not that difficult to see how the structure of work pushes talented people to find fulfillment outside of paid work's limits. A hard look at our culture quickly reveals the vast gaps between what our society dedicates itself to and what it *would* focus on if our goal was a good life for all. In an atomized world increasingly drained of social meaning and shared purpose, these dynamics create a lot of refugees from "normal life."

THE COGNITARIAT WORKS FOR FREE[25]

I had a real crisis of confidence in what for-profit corporations are doing, and more specifically how the products of my work were used. At Sun [Microsystems] I figured maybe 40–60% of my work was being used by the Defense Dept. and Intelligence agencies. I didn't feel too good.

—*Will Doherty*[26]

One of the motivations of hackers is pleasure, the pleasure of programming, programming as hobby. However, even if "hobby" is the term they usually use, it does not correspond to its common usage. As Eric S. Raymond notes "It is very amusing to be a hacker, but it's an amusement that demands a lot of effort."[27] Linus Torvalds [the former student who wrote the software kernel that joined GNU to make the new operating system GNU/Linux], speaks of it similarly, "Linux has mostly been a hobby (but a serious one, the best of all)."[28] He goes even further, affirming pleasure as a central value, "but Pleasure with a capital P, the Pleasure that

gives meaning to life."[29]... Among hackers, what links
is of course a common production, but above all the
pleasure of programming and the recognition of that
pleasure by others. The notion of work changes, it is no
longer toil, but work as passion, self-realization.
—*Matthias Studer*[30]

It can be said that the networked organization gives back
to the employee—or better, to the "prosumer"—the
property of him- or herself that the traditional firm has
sought to purchase as the commodity of labor power.
Rather than coercive discipline, it is a new form of inter-
nalized vocation, a "calling" to creative self-fulfillment
in and through each work project, that will now shape
and direct the employee's behavior... "the networker"
is delivered from direct surveillance and paralyzing
alienation to become the manager of his or her own
self-gratifying activity, as long as that activity translates
into valuable economic exchange, the *sine qua non* for
remaining within the network.
—*Brian Holmes*[31]

It's difficult to imagine anyone working for free if they didn't have
food to eat, or shelter or other basic needs covered. Computer workers have enjoyed the advantage of having relatively rare skills during the
past decades, and for many this has meant high wages and benefits, and
in some cases, an unusual freedom within the work process. The path
through computer work has led to great wealth and a foothold in the
ruling class for the parvenus of the Net. But the vast majority have had
to contend with temporary and insecure employment contracts, absurd
deadlines, lousy tools, and all too often, embarrassingly bad products at
the end of a project.

The commercialization of software production is the root cause of
these negative qualities, even if it has provided relatively high pay to
some. Corporate managers have been trying to wring greater productivity from the herd of cats known as programmers for a long time, but
it's only with the advent of outsourcing to India and China that they
discovered the leverage they've had for much longer over workers in
other fields. The opacity of programming work has frustrated efforts to
control it historically. Some years ago "object oriented programming"
was developed to facilitate a kind of Taylorized division of labor among
programmers, but also to further obscure the ultimate purpose of the
larger programs that the individual "objects" are meant to facilitate.

Anger at stupid, degrading managerial practices has driven plenty of programmers into working on projects in their spare time for their own creative and professional satisfaction. Countless others have been motivated by the realization that their work's purpose was directed at murderous weaponry or ecocidal technologies over which they have no say. In response, they make their skills available to projects dedicated to fighting corporate and government programs. It certainly cannot be claimed that all the dedicated free software programmers have been motivated by a desire to overthrow capitalism. A more common political stance is some variant on a libertarian individualism that resists Big Brother. But the desire to do good work for a good purpose is a very common quality among disaffected computer workers, and in the free software movement they have been welcomed with open arms.

Many programmers crave artisanal commitment to quality work, instead of being forced into programming abstract modules. As Doherty reports, "many of the programmers, [while] not necessarily opposed to commercialization, just like [free software] because of the elegance of the methodology."[32] Nothing pleases a talented code writer as much as making (or even discovering in others' work) "elegance" in form and function. One of the peculiar ironies of modern capitalism is that it exhorts its workers to work hard, but it structures labor processes to control and limit the creative potential of its employees. Commonly the drive to do "good work" is ignored or suppressed by corporate behemoths, hemmed in by maladaptive bureaucratic structures geared to self-referential plans and immediate, short-term stimulation of stock prices.

To voluntarily leave behind the security of a steady paycheck is a difficult choice for most people. Some wait until they've saved up enough for a good period of time off, others try to combine paid work with unpaid work. "I'm not independently wealthy so I do feel much more secure when I have a paid job that's keeping things going while I'm also able to do this unpaid work," Doherty told me. He is a seasoned activist, going back to his teen years almost two decades ago, splitting his time between paid work and unpaid activism throughout his life. He captures the sensibility that motivates people in all kinds of oppositional movements:

> Somehow it always comes back to the paid work and the passionate work. I think people are very fortunate who find complete alignment of their paid work and their passionate work. I don't know how often that happens, especially for people that have a social conscience. I don't think it happens very often... I operate as much as I can in a kind of post-capitalist world... I spend a lot of my time doing work that I don't expect any kind of remuneration for, just because I think it should be

done.... I don't like money. I don't like the whole system of using money. If there was a way I could live without dealing with money, I would... What I'm getting is a
sense of self-satisfaction.[33]

Doherty left his job not long after I spoke with him, unsure of what
would come next, but wanting to move on. He did not have much sav-
ings to fall back on, so he would soon be seeking employment again,
like most computer workers who have been well-paid but are facing increasingly precarious and uncertain futures. Doherty appreciates where
his skills have gotten him, and takes on some responsibility from that:

I don't really feel like I identify with a particular class.
Because of my class position, I have a certain luxury to
work on certain types of work, and so I feel a certain
social responsibility associated with it.[34]

Guillermo Payet of Local Harvest comes from a fairly upper-class
background in Peru, but since he came to the U.S. he's been a salaried
programmer, an owner, and now works for a nearby University on their
technical support infrastructure. Like most folks I interviewed about
their work, he resists classification:

I don't really think in [class] terms. But if I had to put
myself somewhere, I'd say middle class... The fact that
I come from a background where I lived in a stratified
society where I wasn't in the fields, trying to figure out
how to make enough money to eat. I'm aware of that.
In that sense, yes, I have the luxury of being able to do
activism because basic issues are taken care of.[35]

Payet did his time in the corporate pixel mines and has no plans to go
back, even though he endured a year-long period of great uncertainty in
which he almost lost his home to foreclosure. "I didn't want to get a job
because I didn't want to be part of the whole corporate world again. And
also because if I did that it would just suck my life out... I worked for the
corporate world for a while, and it sucked, it felt dry and meaningless."

Resisting this experience in his work for Local Harvest, he fended
off some Seattle bankers who saw in his website a great business opportunity. He had a meeting with them, but realized they would take his
work and turn it inside out by implementing some kind of distributed
food warehouse where the food products would not be shipped directly
from farmer to consumer, through their website sales. Payet refused: "I
couldn't believe that we could focus on the bottom line, and not see it
get perverted... the point really is to redesign our culture."

Working on Local Harvest is so satisfying. It is work that

is really making a difference. When I work for somebody else, it was always like what you do to pay the bills.
It's good work but it's not where you heart is. You're just
doing it to make money and then you go and your real
focus is what you do outside. . . But then when I started
looking at work as activism, both on the software side,
and on the sustainable agriculture and family farming
side, it felt like a mission. (Actually to the extent that
it's really easy to just overwork and not pay attention to
other stuff!)[36]

Ed Phillips's views of life are shaped by his conviction that we live
in a state of extreme abundance. From that point of view, it's difficult
to get too worried about jobs or income, since it's hard to imagine that
you would ever have any problem getting what you need. He grew up in
Washington D.C., hardly in the lap of luxury, but like most Americans,
he didn't suffer any privation either. His years in the free software movement (and business) lead him to conclude:

[Class is] a very problematic term... no one sees themselves as any class anymore. The whole class thing has sort
of dropped out... I see myself as a knowledge worker.[37]

This new category of "knowledge worker" has received a lot of attention since the mid-1990s. Knowledge work is not particularly new,
though. Programmers have been hard at work for decades, and long
before computers began to be widely implemented, middle managers
performed an analogous function, designing labor processes and over-
seeing the day-to-day work of production and clerical workers. Working with financial information dates back more than a century, and the
time-and-motion studies made famous by Frederick Taylor and Henry
Ford go back almost that far.

Beneath a lot of software programming lays an implicit rejection of
pointless work. Many skilled workers are glad to work hard but find no
appeal in artificially extending their work as a means of gaining financial
security. Plenty have better things to do than work! Independent contractors, motivated in part by a pursuit of "elegant design," are also motivated by a real urge to make the work easier, replicable, even automated,
goals which would simultaneously make their own future employment
redundant. Countless software improvements have been developed in
the last couple of decades to make complicated work easier.[38] Nowadays,
commercial WYSIWYG (what you see is what you get) software has made
print and web design accessible to relatively unskilled workers (the falling
wages associated with a great deal of routine design work reflect that). As
Ed Phillips put it,

I wouldn't want to be doing this same thing over and over
again...What would we do if it all actually worked and we
didn't have to spend tremendous amounts of time? Obviously in Free Software you're embracing the vicissitudes
and degradation of work, you're embracing deskilling in
a way, hoping it gets easier. So on the one hand, of course
we're increasing our skills and our knowledge and our
capabilities all the time, but we're also making it easier
to reuse software, so that it takes one day as opposed to
weeks to solve a problem, or to set up a network, or to
do these kinds of things. You want to be able to make it
reproducible; you want to work yourself out of a job. And
if you were really tied to the idea of making a living, then
it's going to make you nervous.[39]

Stefan Merten answers this by positing a social evolution that sur-
passes the self-contradictory limits of capitalist production:

... General Public License society will transcend the industrial model of production into a new form, which
[will] allow human potential to really flourish. In particular, machines [will be] used to set people free in the
sense that the machines [can] do the necessary things
while humans can be artists, engineers, ... whatever they
like. This way permanently rising productivity no longer results in the curse of unemployment but in the
benediction of freedom from necessity for mankind—a
world where the individual freedom of each single person is the precondition for the freedom of all.[40]

Until that happy day, the contradiction at the heart of the Net will
continue to fester. As wages fall and prestige for computer work dwindles
(along with a steady fall in employment as the commoditization of software finally slows down the inefficient drama of pointless "upgrades"), a
harsher future looms ahead for the former wunderkinds of the Information Age. Computer workers and the generations of obsolete software will
join the discarded skilled workers and the obsolete technologies that lit-
ter our recent past. The alternative, a general reorientation of our society
towards a good life for all, would simultaneously reclaim and rejuvenate
all the talents and accumulated knowledge that will otherwise end up
scrapped by a capitalism shaped by its usual harsh indifference.

NETWORKS OF COMMUNITIES

A powerful, urgent desire for community is the driving force behind so much of the communicative commons called the Internet. Thousands of programmers and designers have given millions of hours to build our new agora, the public commons of the so-called Information Age. As it has expanded and become more accessible, people enthusiastically jump in to the myriad corners of a rejuvenated commons to find like-minded folks with similar interests. The global reach available to anyone with a computer and a connection has brought forth a multitude of voices, songs, writings, images, and public creative expression.

A decade and a half has passed since the "take-off" of the Web. The full possibilities of peer-to-peer communication are only being tentatively explored; many people are trapped (temporarily) in the dominant channels of Internet commercialization. Nevertheless, it doesn't take much—not even any great skills—to move beyond the passive, consumerist model imposed by corporations trying to capitalize on the new commons.

The drive to connect has already produced countless new communities, based on mutual interests, talents, or behaviors. This was the dream of early pioneers in computer-mediated communications. Lee Felstenstein was one of the founders of the Community Memory project (he gained additional fame in the early 1980s as the designer of the first "portable" computer in a suitcase, the Osborne) and has this to say:

> The Community Memory Project had its origins in my quest for the right medium for the growth and realignment of communities. I had been through the 1960s in Berkeley, and had seen the episodic community creation in 1964 with the Free Speech Movement.[41]
>
> In the 1960s I thought that the cause of re-establishing functioning communities could be served by the newly established "underground press," and for a while I helped at the *Berkeley Barb*, one of the oldest such papers. But I saw the structure of that medium determine its economics and thereby its content, and by 1970 I knew that broadcast media were never going to serve the cause of decentralization of power within society.[42]

In pursuit of a media that would facilitate new power relations and revitalize communities, computerists came together in new communities themselves. The aforementioned Homebrew Computer Club is one example, as was the Community Memory Project (which existed in the Resource One warehouse in San Francisco before taking over a funky wooden warehouse in the then-forgotten west Berkeley, an area now massively gentrified). Pre-microcomputer programmers in the mid-70s "had a vision of computers as community-building devices" reports Eric S. Raymond in his history of hackers.[43] "To early ARPANET hackers... collaborative development and the sharing of source code... was more than tactic: it was something closer to a shared religion... developing into an almost Chardinist idealism about networked communities of minds."[44] The exodus from unfulfilling and/or shoddy work has continually brought together programmers and technicians in pursuit of non-market goals. Ed Phillips started out as a writer dedicated to sharing ideas and eventually became fascinated by the "writing" going on among free software developers, by the way that free software made technology "literary."

> What struck me was the community. There were all these people out there willing to share their ideas, and I found that just delightful. It was so much fun to play around with this stuff and people needed the help... They all bought in on the idea that sharing ideas was better than hoarding. Part of it was the way the scripting languages were designed. They're designed TO be open, they're designed FOR sharing.

> You could then base your work on their work. You end up contributing to it in some way, either through helping other people with documentation, or through making modifications to the software, and right away you're initiated into it and you're hooked and you start contributing... The real benefit of it is social.[45]

Typically, online communities are criticized for promoting disembodied and immaterial connections. Too often political campaigns that may once have mobilized a street action or something directly physical have instead turned into a cascade of emails and online petitions. But as the remarkable participation in the February 2003 global anti-war demonstrations revealed, the same electronic communities can network themselves to produce an unprecedented public demonstration.

Another interesting example comes from Payet's Local Harvest effort. Helping connect local agricultural producers with local buyers has many tangible benefits in the physical community as well as in altering political practices.

> Say if you're buying tomatoes from somebody who is growing them a couple of miles down from your house. If they were using some really bad practices, then you would find out and you would complain. If they were treating their employees terribly or they were using a

lot of pesticides and poisoning the creeks, local people would stop them. You can't really externalize those costs when you're externalizing them locally and your community is aware of it.[46]

Communities are formed on-line, in neighborhoods and regions, and among people with shared experiences at work or at play. After the global economic changes of the past decades, many working classes that shared workplaces or places to live disintegrated. Capital has reorganized production systems across the planet with just-in-time supply lines, disemploying entrenched, unionized workers in favor of transient, immigrant and temporary workforces wherever possible. The newly emerging communities on-line, facilitated by many of the net-based organizing efforts, represent another facet of an emerging recomposition of the working class. New sites and forms of resistance to capital accumulation are taking shape, and already beginning to make themselves felt in the anti-globalization and anti-war movements, technologically savvy immigration campaigns across the northern hemisphere, and with remarkable resilience in the unquenchable efforts of faceless digital rebels who refuse to succumb to the practices or priorities of business.

A SELF-ORGANIZING COMMONS

Decisions about which forms of fundamental research to pursue and which technologies to market are an expression of a social project... Technologies can be understood as expressions of social relations... Communication on the Internet will not lead automatically to a renewal of democracy by making everyone discover virtual communities and, through them, to found participatory grassroots democratic movements, leading directly and inevitably to a renewal of democracy in the west... such abilities were attributed to the Internet in its early days and are still in circulation. By attributing the power to bring about social change to media communication as an isolated factor, one is once again following the techno-determinist idea of utopia and fetishising technological communications media. Having said this, the Internet does have the potential to promote social progress, if it is made into a "project" as described above.

—*Armin Medosch*[47]

The digital commons is best understood as a conceptual counterpart to the earthly commons that has been largely enclosed by capital. As a contested arena of the General Intellect, the Net is a site of conflict between commons and private, democracy and dictatorship, freedom and slavery. Businesses committed to private property and commodity forms are opposed by legions of hackers and free software developers who are inspired by a range of motivations from personal fame to anti-capitalism.

One of the unforeseen consequences of the spread of the Internet has been its facilitation of collaborative research projects and the free dissemination of information. Nowadays there is more information online than ever about the state of the planet, healthy ecological practices, citizen-based campaigns, voluntary monitoring of waterways and industrial pollution, etc. Campaigns that directly combat capital's externalization of health and ecological "costs" emerge online and are adopted quickly far and wide following the open-source model. Alternative technologies, including some aspects of Free Software, are developed collaboratively across great distances through online networking (such as biofuels, organic agriculture, indymedia, grassroots advocacy for traditional medicines—the list goes on and on).

Efforts around the world are gradually producing a new commons, campaigning for basic rights to clean water, healthy food, open shorelines, affordable shelter, free communications, and transportation. Increasingly these efforts are linking up and finding ways to collaborate online, both to extend their immediate efforts, and to deepen political awareness and strengthen each other through solidarity. It seems a long way from a Bay Area hacker debugging software to the uprisings in South America, but both online self-representation and online journalism have helped connect those different activist poles.

Ed Phillips hopes the logic underpinning free software can percolate into other areas of social and intellectual life. Noting the connection between the explosion of network computing and the new prominence of free software, he warns:

> This connection may foretell new forms of community and free collaboration on scales previously unimagined. But it certainly won't happen by itself. It will take concerted efforts of many individual wills, and the questioning of many assumptions about the success and quality of the collaboratively open and the freely given. I don't think the network itself is what's going to lead to that.[48]

There are already over 30 million blogs, most starting in the past two years. Wikipedia has become the largest encyclopedia in the world and it continues to be collaboratively written and edited by tens of thousands of users. Social software sites such as MySpace and Friendster along with p2p file sharing systems like Bittorrent, Gnutella, and Soulseek have facilitated a whole new kind of public space where millions are engaged in every kind of interaction, from trivial to profound.

The Brazilian government funded a network of "puntos do cultura" where kids in urban areas got hands-on experience with digital media. Though the funding support only lasted a couple of years, it quickly produced an explosion of underground media in Brazil and an enthusiastic invasion of the net. The Sarai Center in New Delhi, India is another site of cultural and political innovation using and extending the web (in addition to publishing a fantastic annual book of essays).[49]

The temptation to take Free Software and Open Source as a metaphor for social organization is strong. In fact, social movements of the past decade increasingly eschew formal hierarchies and structures, preferring to work through informal, ad-hoc associations, usually based on consensus decision-making. This can best be understood as an ongoing process that builds on the largely invisible but undeniable progress made in self-managed group processes since the 1960s. However, the "open" metaphor is far from a successful political model. In most of the well-known and "successful" experiments with new social software, problems get solved in old-fashioned ways. For instance, Jimmy Wales founded Wikipedia and after five years remains a self-described "benevolent monarch" who steps in to banish recalcitrant wikipedians when the consensus-building norms don't resolve conflicts over what properly constitutes the problematic "neutral point of view." Indymedia open publishing platforms have largely had to erect barriers to pure openness when they have been deluged with fascist materials or other "news" outside of their acceptable political boundaries. Bruising battles over the limits of openness lay beneath most projects that grow beyond a limited circle of trusted associates. And this only describes projects that are primarily content-centered. It can be even worse in technology-development projects, which depend on wide collaboration but are usually dominated by a founder or "benevolent dictator" like Larry Wall's relationship with the Perl language, or Wales and Wikipedia.[50]

This begs the question of politics. Online there have been some fantastic beginnings and crucial experiments in collaboratively shaping our lives outside of traditional forms. But there is still a lot to figure out about how to make transparent the informal power behind open projects, how to democratically integrate our collaborative efforts into social norms that function openly and fairly, with accountability mechanisms we haven't yet discovered. And the dominant capitalist system is still standing in the way. Nations and corporations don't hesitate to destroy impediments to their control up to and including mass murder. But we also carry and reproduce dominant assumptions and norms about property and individual freedom that are powerful impediments to inventing a new life based on a common wealth.

The ongoing appropriation of the technosphere will have to go considerably further to fully realize its potential. Matteo Pasquinelli invokes an early 20th century Futurist tone in calling for us to embrace a bigger project:

> Don't hate the machine, be the machine. How can we turn the sharing of knowledge, tools and spaces into new radical revolutionary productive machines, beyond the inflated Free Software? This is the challenge that once upon the time was called reappropriation of the means of production.
>
> Will the global radical class manage to invent social machines that can challenge capital and function as planes of autonomy and autopoiesis? Radical machines that are able to face the techno-managerial intelligence and imperial meta-machines lined up all around us? The match "multitude vs. empire" becomes the match "radical machines vs. imperial techno-monsters." How do we start building these machines?[51]

Visionaries see such subversive machines emerging from the culture that invented Free Software. The German discussion list Oekonux hosts theoretical inquiries that describe the new society's seeds growing already in the interstices of this culture.

> In Oekonux there is a common sense that Free Software might be an early form of the new society embedded in the old society. (We call this new society "GPL society" to have a word for this new thing we're trying to explore.) We are describing a society beyond capitalism. The main difference is that this society is no longer based on exchange and exchange value and thus the term labor doesn't make much sense any longer. Instead the basis of this new society will be the individual self-unfolding ("Selbstenftaltung") combined with self-organization and global cooperation. Goods in this society are not sold but simply available and taken by those who need them. Of course such a society is difficult to imagine for people who grew up with only money on their mind.[52]

Brian Holmes takes up the war machine metaphor with a series of proposals for a "real democracy" growing out of the emergent commons in daily life. He argues that the current initiatives have to be "linked to a wider program for the transformation of what are the basic rules of social interchange... Such alternative forms, in all their diversity and intricacy, can also become war machines of a new and astonishing kind, in the aesthetic struggle to create the worlds in which we live."[53] He lays out three programmatic pillars: 1) a cultural and informational commons, 2) the egalitarian transformation of existing publicly funded cultural and scientific institutions, and 3) the re-invention on a new basis of the shredded safety net. "Only an ambition to change the rules of the economy, and, ultimately the existing form of the state, can supply the oppositional force that is needed in the early twenty-first century... [these proposals] are already underway [thanks to the so-called digital revolution] and do not depend on electoral victories for their realization... they point to an exodus from the present impasse."[54]

The ultimate fantasy for many people today is that a technology will automatically solve our problems. For political radicals it's all too easy to fall into this trap when it comes to the rise of Free-as-in-Libre and Open-Source Software (FLOSS). The gnarly drama of face-to-face discussion, political disagreement, and class, racial, and gender conflict cannot be escaped by creating elegant software, no matter how open it might be. As Jamie King wrote in *Mute* 27 in 2004, "What the idea of openness must tackle first and most critically is that a really open organization cannot be realized without a prior radicalization of the social-political field in which it operates. And that, of course, is to beg the oldest of questions."[55] What we see in the Free Software movement is not just a techno-fix so much as an evolving process of techno-creative collaboration. Rather than a linear process that establishes a technological foundation in which politics can become truly democratic, or a reverse linearity in which radical politics sets the stage for a new technosphere, we're in a confusing historic period characterized by a learn-as-we-go experimentalism. The radical political subjectivity that can make new use of an open technosphere emerges from the work that builds that apparatus, while that innovative work also reshapes the assumptions and expectations embedded in the broad cultural environment. The steps taken now might make possible a post-capitalist, self-directed, networked society, hundreds of thousands of local communities knit together in essential cooperation across regions, continents, and the globe.

CHAPTER 9:
BURNING MAN: A WORKING-CLASS, DO-IT-YOURSELF WORLD'S FAIR

After a while, the festival's emphasis on hedonism and overt displays of sexuality can seem like a hipster straitjacket and the overtones of New Age spirituality a gloss for a new type of vapid and self-congratulatory consumerism.... The essential point of Burning Man is not what it is now but what it suggests for the future, which is not just a new cultural form but the possibility of a new way of being, a kind of radical openness toward experience that maintains responsibility for community. Radical openness means no closure, perpetual process and transformation, and embracing paradox, contradiction, and uncomfortable states. Every instant becomes synchronistic, every contact a contact high.

—Daniel Pinchbeck[1]

East of Sacramento, California on the Interstate 80 freeway, I glance to my left as a pickup truck overtakes me. A blonde woman wearing devil's horns is flashing me an electrifying smile, gesturing and mouthing: Are you going to Burning Man? I smile back, nod, and give her the thumb's up. She pumps both arms triumphantly, and as they pull away, I'm left euphoric by the mysteriously powerful connection that passed from one metal box to another.

Hours later, having cleared the mighty Sierra Nevada not far removed from where starving Chinese coolies chiseled out the first transcontinental railroad tracks through howling blizzards, I passed the neon blandness of Reno's unmajestic skyline, gassed up, and proceeded into the desolation of the Great Basin. Leaving the interstate behind, I entered the world of rural Nevada, Indian tacos and trailers scattered among riparian oases, separated by countless miles of arid but spectacular landscape. The road is crowded with trailers, buses, mid-sized sedans, usually carrying bicycles on the back, clearly all heading north to the playa. One dirt road leaves to the right, and under some rare shade a couple is busy spray painting bicycles light blue against the tawny, dusty ground.

The mountain range that marks the end of the state highway at the towns of Empire and Gerlach looms ahead. Dust clouds appear to the east, kicked up by arrivals preceding me. No sooner do I see them than my throat cracks, the taste of dust on my tongue. Twenty minutes later I'm crawling in bumper to bumper traffic completely immersed in gusting dust-filled winds, awaiting an inspection that rivals airport security as "Rangers" try to ferret out scofflaws and stowaways. License plates hail from New York, Illinois, Oregon, British Columbia, Minnesota, all points between. Newly legalized Black Rock City radio is pumping tunes into the car, interspersed with occasional warnings that impossibly well-hidden stowaways will not elude the Rangers.

Signs line the incoming roadway. "Barter is just another word for commerce." "Don't Trade it, Pay it Forward." And dozens of others. After a brief search for the camp location, I park. The dust thickened on the car as I spent the next five days exclusively bicycling around Black Rock City.

Tuesday night: like a moth drawn to the light in the inky darkness of the desert, I pedal forward. A mad scientist has a keyboard hanging over his neck, attached to truck horns and bellows. As his fingers tickle the keys, flames shoot from tubes, pops and groans emerging from invisible holes and crevices. Three dozen cyclists surround the scene, smiling and pointing while in the background a drum and bass machine adds to the sound.

I take a ride in the 37-foot-high "Olivator," a vertical chair ascent for a calm view of the lasers and neon lights chasing each other across the nighttime playa. A dozen pyrocycles ride by, each towing a trailer with an oil derrick on it, spouting flame at the top. Later I am nearly run over by a motorized float full of people peering out of a TV screen, labeled "Sony Tripatron"... Two bikes tow a three-piece percussion ensemble, bass and trap drum set... At the camp called Bollywood an unbelievable rock 'n roll film from 1965 screens, *Gumnaam* or something like that... a blues band rocks the house at Hair of the Dog bar, a long-time installation at Black Rock City.

Another day, a dusty sun-soaked morning, early risers scurry about while others prepare to crash from the night's endless party. Cycling about, I encounter on the playa a copy of Bill Gates' *The Road Ahead*, spread open to a page on frictionless capitalism, awaiting the arrival of art cars to run over it. Returning to the Black Rock City streets, I'm accosted by a guy with a bullhorn next to a late model SUV. On it a camping chair says "soccer mom." He's yelling, "If you love Burning Man, come and pee on this Soccer Mom's SUV!"

One midweek evening we ride through gusting waves of dust to the "Man" to catch Reverend Billy and his Church of Stop-Shopping Revue; a big gospel chorus in gold lamé gowns swayed behind his syncopated sermonizing... it was funny and much more overtly political than the usual Burning Man fare. I particularly love their finale as they sing "We Ain't Sponsored, we ain't sponsored, we ain't sponsored..."

ONE-HOUR SCRUTINIZING

I went to Burning Man in 2003 as a self-designated "Official Scrutinizer," with a brief questionnaire offering passersby heavy or light scrutiny. "Heavy scrutiny" meant a 45-minute audio interview, "light scrutiny" meant quickly scribbled answers to a dozen multiple choice questions. My "performance" led to twenty-four quality interviews and countless fantastic conversations. I wanted to explore class consciousness among participants, to find out who they were, what they did the rest of the year, how they contextualized the experience, etc.

Those I encountered filled a range of occupations: health educator/ social worker, transportation planner, teacher, math professor (retired), testing and counseling of street kids, homeless youth study coordinator, welder/metal fabricator, software tester, human resources manager, environmental biochemist, teacher, freelance high tech research/marketing, handyman/auto mechanic, community development and technology consultant, computer repairman and apartment manager, teacher/ex-dot.com content provider, political organizer, immigration legal aide, veterinary assistant, house painter, builder, president marketing services/ open source software company, and business/technology consultant.

They covered a full age range, too: seven were 23–30 and another seven were 32–40. Five each were 41–50 and 51–63. Of the thirteen women and eleven men I spoke with, the vast majority believed there is a ruling class (20), while their own class identification was confused at best: 7 middle class; 5 working class; 7 both; 3 neither; 2 didn't know. Not surprisingly, nearly all of the respondents were white (though a smattering of people of color do attend). And due to my approach, the group was a self-selecting subset of the larger population, people drawn to the notion of "scrutiny," analysis, thinking, reflection. It is difficult to generalize about 29,000 people (the attendance at Burning Man has topped 40,000 in the years after 2003), and perhaps not worth trying. Also, many have abandoned Burning Man over the years for a variety of reasons. This inquiry is not an attempt to confront all the criticisms or objections to Burning Man.

In fact, I am not trying to defend the institution at all—for institution is what it has become. My own attempt to interact with the organizers of Burning Man led to a puzzling and ultimately absurd exchange with a self-designated media committee representative going by the moniker "Brother John." I thought to communicate my intentions to this committee as a courtesy. Much to my surprise my first email led to a response "rejecting" my "request," misunderstanding my own past attendance, and admonishing me to come to the festival to just experience it. According to Brother John, after I'd soaked it up for a year I could make a proposal the committee might "approve." I was shocked and wrote back my rejection of their authority. Brother John then indicated that he realized it was a relationship based on mutual agreement and they could not regulate me if I didn't accept it, but that the Burning Man Media Committee would expect me to submit to them anything I wrote PRIOR to publication! I stopped myself from responding that this policy violated all journalistic autonomy and was more akin to the Pentagon's approach to war coverage than the ostensible free community of Burning Man. I held my tongue and chose to ignore them from that time on.

Other complaints about the allocation of money to artists, the occasionally heavy-handed exercise of authority by drunken Black Rock City rangers, the airport security shakedown at the gates to catch stowaways, the ever-rising price of entry, etc., have been noted elsewhere. While I am aware of the many ways to criticize the failures of Burning Man, my own goal in attending, interviewing, and writing was different, as you'll see.

COMMERCE-FREE GIFT ECONOMY

If Burning Man is a cult, it is above all a cult of transformation.
                                                            —*Daniel Pinchbeck*[2]

… The campsite counters the isolation in which most of the people we met live year-round…
                                            —*Margaret Cerullo and Phyllis Ewen*[3]

Most people who come to Burning Man would never say—or even think—so, but clearly the vast majority are part of the sprawling American working class. When they're not at BM they have to go to work, mostly living from paycheck to paycheck and on credit. Once a year, for fun, they go on an expedition to the desert along with tens of thousands of others. And what do they do? They "set up" on the blank dusty slate of the white, flat playa. Then they live in a densely populated city and have a totally urban experience. But it's a familiar and strangely different city life. The lack of infrastructure beyond porta-potties and the semi-circular layout of Black Rock City leaves room for the harsh nature of the desert to impose itself. Commerce is formally excluded (with the notable exceptions of ice and the Center Camp café).

I asked my scrutinees how they felt about the commitment to a cash-free "gift economy." Most people were genuinely enthusiastic. Several emphasized that it was a major reason for their coming. "…I am so attracted to Burning Man because for close to a week I can exist without ever having to spend money, without ever having to worry about people asking for money—it's just eliminated." For a school teacher it is a "mental vacation, a sense of relief," while a female metal worker thought it "kind of hypocritical," mostly because of the espresso sales at Center Camp. One computer geek claimed "I would love to live in the gift economy 365 days a year!" Some of the lower wage participants, a handyman and a veterinary assistant, were adamant: "That's why I come here," and "I think life should be like this, it's the only way to live." A Berkeley apartment manager, who also fixes computers, described it as "a natural human impulse that is given free reign and encouraged here. It's just a normal thing that people want to do."

The commerce-free environment is "imperative. I wouldn't come here otherwise," said a street counselor, while a retired human resources staffer emphasized "it's the thing that inspired me and drew me to Burning Man… Doing something because you love to do it rather than because you have to do it is always refreshing and wonderful…" For one person the commerce-free environment was a means to break down class assumptions based on consumption patterns. "Here nobody cares how much money I make because I have all these other things to offer. Also the people who have a lot of money are able to see people who maybe have almost nothing—they scrimp and they save every single penny they have to come here—[while] it's just like another vacation for the wealthy." Not that everyone "buys" the story Burning Man tells itself: "I don't think it really is a commerce-free environment… it doesn't mean much to me to have this contrived, one-week gift economy. I see efforts to create alternatives, or to transform the world we live in, [get] co-opted and integrated by the dominant society. There is a gift economy that already exists, the living culture in people's daily lives, and Burning Man is a co-optation of it, selling it back to people. It's a product, like ethical consumerism in some ways…"

Thousands of "alternative" people go to the northern Nevada desert and build a miniature Las Vegas. Neon light and techno-music and amenities of urban night life are trucked along. A lot of people bring everything they want: the RV, the pavilion, the sinks, the astroturf, the refrigerators, and everything else. They lack for nothing and could almost be in the suburbs. Ironically, people come here to escape, but recreate a version of the world they left behind, down to the carpet on the floor and the wetbar in the corner.

> Family camping embodies many anticapitalist yearnings
> and a dream of a different life… It is a dream in which

there are no great inequalities and in which the market does not determine human relationships. Yet paradoxically, these preindustrial fantasies tie people more
tightly into the market. Mass production and mass marketing have made family camping possible for working-
class people. Families go further into debt in order to
make the investment in camping equipment. The experience of nature is mediated by commodities.
            —*Margaret Cerullo and Phyllis Ewen*[4]

Burning Man is a countercultural expression of the working class yearn-
ings described in the 1982 article above (read it again, replacing "family
camping" with "Burning Man"). The fabled nudity, wild art, rave music,
drugs, and sex are all manifestations of the specific subcultures that attend,
but underneath the spectacular behaviors are regular people. Once away
from the stifling conformity of "normal life" (especially work life), people
are free to experiment with costume, identity, and group behaviors in ways
that are difficult at home. For most attendees, Burning Man is a different
world subjectively.

Many attendees are strongly motivated by the chance to have a radically different relationship to their own work. Writing in the anthology
"After Burn," Katherine Chen interviewed a number of "burners" in
2000 to find out how they experienced the difference between the normal work lives and the volunteer work they do at Burning Man:

Volunteers like Leslie Bocksor, a software entrepreneur and consultant, described his volunteer experience as a refreshing oasis from the
constraints of the bottom line-obsessed paid work:

> [My volunteer work is] more rewarding because it doesn't
> have economics on top of it as a guiding principle...I
> have found that economics will change the nature of
> an interaction [in my nonvolunteer work], I might not
> be doing it if it was not economically feasible. Whereas
> with Burning Man, the guiding principle is more one of
> what's going to be best for the community and for myself
> and other members of the community.[5]

Another woman Chen spoke with was stuck all year in her word processing job, until she came to Burning Man:

> For Mandy Tilles, volunteer work helped alleviate her
> frustration with the constraints of her employment as a
> word processor in an engineering firm:

> "There is a definite line between who's the engineers
> and who's the admin help. It's this real old model, and
> it's quite oppressive and depressing to me. [In contrast,

when] I work with Burning Man I like putting on events because I get to show up, and people appreciate what I have to offer. I get to feel good about myself, and I get to go to these really fun events, and I get to see the fruit of my labor."[6]

One way to see Burning Man is as a Do-It-Yourself World's Fair. The much-touted freeing of imagination it embodies leads to entertaining and inspiring art projects from sculpture and installation to fire-breathing dragons and galleons with crowded bars inside. Moreover, the preponderant ethic of do-it-yourself art-making begins to permeate most interactions, deepening human connections in ways that are usually absent in daily lives. Art is alienated from everyday life by being commodified and separated, but Burning Man places art at the center of human activity. Burning Man slips an exciting notion into the back of its participants' minds: our greatest collective art project is living together. Every activity can be engaged artistically. One can find in anything a sense of aesthetic pleasure, communicative depth, and resonance with something true and passionate. The art of living becomes something tangible and reinforced by recurrent surprises of gift-giving and cooperation.

Burning Man is an enormous experiment in relearning to speak to each other directly, and reopening and using public spaces. It's a hands-on, throats-on, tongues-on experience. You learn to meet strangers with an open heart. Participants practice trust in a practical context removed from "normal life." Skill sharing, experimentation and appropriation of the techno-sphere for pleasure, edification and self-expression point to a deeper practical radicalization than what is usually attributed to Burning Man.

Like anything worth doing, Burning Man is fraught with contradictions. But within them are impulses and behaviors that connect to a wider social movement that exceeds the self-conceptions of its participants. Burning Man is a nascent attempt of the working class, not as a class per se, but as people who refuse to be mere workers, to recompose itself, and in so doing, to transcend class and the capitalist organization of life that stunt our humanity.

CLASS IN THE DUST

These are people without any well-integrated social place. Their lives are characterized by job instability, geographic mobility, divorce and remarriage, and distance from relatives... If "getting away from it all" represented an escape, it was an imperfect one... If it was an industrial nightmare they sought to escape, it was the products of industrial civilization that offered themselves to aid and abet their escape. If it was an escape from work and the clock they envisioned, they found the very meaning and experience of leisure defined and circumscribed by the images and rhythms and moral valuations of work.

—*Margaret Cerullo and Phyllis Ewen*[7]

When I asked my interviewees if they identify with the label "middle class," "working class," neither or both, I got wonderfully complex responses. A 63-year-old retired math professor explained, "I'm what they used to call déclassé. My parents were working class. I raised myself up to the middle class, and now … University professors—people with an upper middle class income and a sub-lower class mentality!" A 34-year-old social worker from Australia called himself "polyglot: I grew up in a string of mining towns and worked as a miner, but my parents were university educated and so was I in a country where that's rarer than here." The female metal worker put it bluntly: "I would say working class, definitely, I don't make enough money to be middle class." A mid-20s teacher, on his way from the east to the northwest, explained, "I work. I don't really think about [class] for me. I think about it for my parents. My mom was a nurse, my dad was a firefighter. We were middle America, right down the middle." A clown, who survives in San Francisco as a veterinary assistant, reinforced the resistance I encountered to questions about class. "I try not to think about it much. Like what class I belong to... probably working poor... It's only an issue when someone else makes it an issue." An NGO staffer in Berkeley in her late-30s characterized her own ambivalence and downward mobility thusly: "Absolutely I'm a middle class person. My parents were both lawyers. I was born into the middle class in Berkeley... But I am definitely the American working class. I live paycheck to paycheck. I don't own my home. I'm a wage slave…"

A 35-year-old Canadian making his first trip to Burning Man had one of the more unusual responses: "Neither. Because I cycle [between] jobs that pay ridiculously well [and those that don't]. For the least amount of work I've gotten paid the highest wage and for the hardest work I've gotten shit wages. I'm not middle class because I've been upper class and I've been lower class. I was the plant manager, so I had about 150 employees underneath me. Right now I'm working as an industrial cleaner at a ready-to-eat plant that makes sausages. I hose everything down with high pressure, high-temperature water, apply some chemicals that eat away at protein and then rinse it off and sanitize it. Then government inspectors inspect it. When people say 'what do you do?' I still say I'm a biochemist... [As a plant manager] I sat down and thought 'why am I always tired?' It's because I'm not doing what I want to do. Which led me to other questions: 'Well, what is it I DO want to do?' I don't know. 'Well, how do I find out what to do?' They don't teach ethics in school. They don't teach rational thinking processes in school. They don't teach you how to survive on your own. They teach you how to incorporate into the system, how to be a dependent."

After finding out how people labeled themselves I asked what the word 'class' means to them, and how people fall into one or another class. I've dispensed with identifying the individual speakers to show the range of opinions and how wide and vague the concept of class has become in our society.

> —I tend to think that there's only two classes: there's the people that have the levers of power and then there's the rest of us... I come here for the chaos and spontaneity to purposefully forget that manner of thinking.

> —Class means primarily the degree of economic self-determination that you're able to exercise.

> —I think if you know someone's class, you won't know anything about them... I think [class is] what gets us into trouble.

> —Class to me is a relationship, like capital is a relationship... it's usefulness as an analytic category has been somewhat deflated. At the same time that I think it is still a very real thing.

> —Smash it. It's ridiculous, it's horrible, it puts value on very few things and it's all run by the almighty dollar.

> —Class is a strata, it's a way of distinguishing groups so you know what boundaries to set for yourself... I think that class distinction is more important as you go further along and get higher up because you stand to lose more.

> —One definition is you are born into or enter as a result of your actions. Another is a sense of upbringing and education. Or your current circumstances. For example, my father is a taxi driver and I live in a neighbourhood surrounded by factories, sweat-shops, and prostitution. My last form of semi-regular income was as a labourer on construction sites, and I am regularly un/under-employed. Seemingly working class. However, I also went to a pretty prestigious high school, have a bachelors degree in fine arts, and currently work as a community service provider, pretty middle class.

—It means access to resources... it's also a way of recognizing excellence... There's some people that I really admire and look up to and I consider them to be "higher class" in a way.

—Class means being able to walk out of your wind-blown, sand-blown domicile without a shower in five days, looking fabulous! That is class... My idea of class has nothing to do with money. It has to do with education... blue collar is class. These people know their shit. But those who know, and those who can teach and those who can show and those who just are by example, that's class, heavy class.

—All class distinctions are subjective, there are no objective class classifications.

—I don't understand class distinctions personally. I don't need money to do a lot of things, so I feel wealthy.

—Well birth is a lot of it... I don't get the class thing, by the way. I think part of it is about self-imposed limitations, and that's really tragic.

—Largely birth. Birth, then education.

The prevailing amnesia and confusion is a product of the tangled history of the U.S. working class as told in Chapter 2. Exploring ideas about class among the people at Burning Man is to glimpse the outcome of a deeper and decades-long process of remolding consciousness in conformity with capitalist values. As cultural dissenters my scrutinees grasp for meaningful ways of framing their shared experiences, but by and large they reject class as a useful category. Instead, the more malleable and cozy notion of "community" takes center stage.

THE END OF COMMUNITY—LONG LIVE COMMUNITY!

Long working hours, the breakup of long-term personal associations, and, most important, the disappearance of women from neighborhoods during the day have accelerated the decline of civil society, the stuff of which the amenities of everyday life are made. In the 1980s and 1990s membership in voluntary organizations such as the Parent-Teachers' Association, veterans' groups, and social clubs declined but, perhaps more to the point, many of them lost activists, the people who kept the organizations together. Labor unions, whose membership erosion was as severe as it was disempowering, became

more dependent on full-time employees to conduct organizing, political action, and other affairs as rank-and-
file leaders disappeared into the recesses of the nonstop
workplace. The cumulative effect of this transformation
is the hollowing out of participation and democracy
where it really counts, at the grass roots.

—*Stanley Aronowitz*[8]

What we've lived through in the last 30 years is a radical decomposition of the working class. Of course two world wars wrought more
destruction and unraveled societies more completely, but the reorganization of life and work since the late 1970s has broken down communities
and ways of life that impeded profitability. Consequently, the world is now
much more transient. Everywhere people are in motion in the greatest
wave of human migration in history. Jobs have been exported, new people have arrived with different cultures, languages, memories, and expectations. In the few places that are relatively stable, the influx rapidly alters
labor markets, urban density, housing, transportation, pollution, and social tension. Even in the U.S., the chances of living at the same address for
more than five years is fairly small. Then there's the casualization of work,
the rise of temporary employment, contract labor, and the breakdown of
careers and permanent jobs. Nobody lasts at any given job longer than a
few years anymore. And there is no future at a given job. Unless you are
a nurse, doctor, or something like that, most people freelance or work at
several part-time jobs. That fragmentary existence lacks a real sense of
shared community, neighborhood, street life, or work life. The old ways
of being in community have broken down.

Burning Man inspires fierce loyalty among its adherents. Within the
sprawling Black Rock City limits thousands of people find their new "families," tribes, or communities in camps with elaborate infrastructure or a
simple cluster of tents around a shared "kitchen" space. Many attendees
find each other in the weeks and months prior to Burning Man by joining
in the planning process for complicated logistical efforts that underpin
theme camps and art projects. Returning year after year, Burning Man
camp groups often become ongoing "tribes" during the rest of the year,
sharing social lives outside of the once-a-year gathering. Others get established in a camp and begin to roam, exploring and often finding new
friends and communities that become life-long bonds. These relationships often have a passion and authenticity that is unlike the connections
one makes with coworkers or neighbors in everyday life.

Burning Man promises its participants a reclaimed, revitalized,
reborn sense of community. Upon arrival everyone is greeted with a
hearty "welcome home" even if they've never been there before. I asked

my scrutinees what the word "community" means:

—The opposite of feeling isolated and unsupported... a feeling of being able to lean on your neighbor.

—An investment looking for a payback.

—Where you can lean on and know your neighbors, you help each other out... You're easy to control when you're just one person with no strong community backing.

—Something that has its real and its ideal sides. The ideal is a lot of sharing and thoughtfulness and planning to make sure everyone's ok. And the real one is knowing that that's the best way to take it, but not always having the courage to do that.

—The common ground constantly has to be renegotiated or re-evaluated... community here is interesting because of its temporariness... You can't ever step outside how our societal relations are influenced by capitalism but you can certainly try, and I think Burning Man is a possibility.

—An environment, doing things and being... It's a platform for playing with ideas about everyday life.

—All the parts dependent on each other, all working together, living and non-living.

—Shared purpose, shared values. Another type is based on geography, and is based on default... The most profound meaning is a sense of identity.

—Involvement, equality and respect, safety, love.

—Oh God. Such an overused word in the Bay Area, such a code word... drop the community in any speech and it shows that you're a good person and that you value human interaction. It's become the 'motherhood and apple pie' of the left... Community ideally is a group of people together whether by choice or circumstance, who feel a shared interest, a shared destiny, a shared responsibility... it's so temporary and so tenuous [at Burning Man] and you can just leave if you want, which is not what real community is about. A real community, you can't just pick up and go, it would matter if you left.

The normal impulse in life is to cooperate and to do things together. The market and the capitalist economy seek to break that. You are tacitly pressured to hold back so you can then sell to somebody, instead of sharing your skills and energy. Burning Man is a chance to experience unmediated cooperation. The deeper truth of living is somehow briefly tasted here as an extreme experience, but it's actually quite normal. People seek community, to connect with each other in authentic ways, regardless of the contradictions inherent in the expensive Burning Man experience. BM provides a context to create trust, which leads people to envision other kinds of living and to share efforts to bring it about.

It is also a community based on freely chosen work, the often arduous effort to build a camp or art installation, and provides a tangible experience of self-managed, cooperative effort. Unlike the fragmented specialization of the capitalist division of labor, the community work at Burning Man calls on everyone's creativity and resourcefulness to contribute to the general well-being. There are no financial incentives shaping people's work at Burning Man, but a friendly competition to make memorable, useful and playful contributions to collective projects. For many people such an experience of work sharply contrasts to the repetitive drudgery that fills their work lives the rest of the year. At Burning Man, too, everyone is encouraged to improvise and make do, inspiring a culture of technological and artistic experimentation, again in contrast to the reliance on experts and pre-established formulas that tend to regulate daily work experience with technology.

MAKING TECHNOLOGY OURS

At Burning Man they take responsibility for the infrastructure and that they're able to pull together this working city and pull it apart that quickly—it shows that if we do have a crisis, that those kinds of people are going to be the ones who say, "hey we can actually take responsibility for our water, for our power, for our coming together in these groups and survive." We're actually in this situation of tremendous abundance. This idea of scarcity is an artifact of industrialism… We have excess, not scarcity.[9]   —*Ed Phillips*

One of the constituent elements of the emerging culture visible at Burning Man is a classically working class predisposition for tinkering, playing, innovating, and doing things that are useful. And doing it with a real sense of rugged individualist independence: "I can fix that. I don't need anybody to tell me how to do that, I can do it myself." In spite of the individualist ethic, it's always a collective process, handing down knowledge and techniques. Technology, gadgets, electronics—this is how a lot of Americans do art, albeit often unconsciously. At Burning Man people share machinery and electric light and urbanization in a heavily technological event. As one of the teachers I interviewed put it, "Everything here is technology, all these bikes, the flames, the domes, the pyramids, that's all technology." But people have very different ideas about technology, often independent of their own engagement with it.

An avid bicyclist, who got involved repairing bikes at her first Burning Man described herself as a technophobe. "When I hear 'technology' and 'tinkerer,' I don't relate that to fixing bikes for some reason." Our biochemist, who is as high-tech as a person can be, explained, "Back in the 1950s they said all this technology was going to save time. Well it didn't. I've got less time than I would have even 20 years ago."

A former software engineer hilariously characterized herself this way: "I'm pretty low-tech here, although I have a titanium computer, a color printer, a laminating machine, and two 80 gig firewire drives and all the equipment. This is my low-tech year... I work, weld, and grind and I'm fabulously happy around tools... I don't know what I'm doing, it's great. I am not a trained mechanic. I am not a person who knows any of the crap that I'm doing. I love not having the idea behind me that says 'no you can't use this tool for that.' I don't know what you use this tool for, fuck it, this is what I'm doin' with it!"

A social worker who does research on the street observed the same creative involvement: "One of the things I really like at BM is that you see this endless 'we're gonna take something and we're gonna do something different with it, because nothing's available that let's us do this thing.' It's one of the true joys and delights of being here."

His colleague was repelled by the heavy dependence on fossil fuels at Burning Man: "...the whole idea of art cars that burn gasoline seems ridiculous. And these flamethrowers are all burning petroleum-based products. But on the other hand gasoline is also used in a lot of different, interesting, creative, and beautiful ways... Obviously we couldn't be out here in this godforsaken place without technology."

The ability to appropriate the technosphere, make it part of you, make it do what you want, is an essential aspect of self-liberation. Gaining confidence by doing little things can lead to challenging and reshaping bigger things. The crucial part is how the material experience shapes one's imagination. Burning Man reclaims technological know-how, withdraws it from market relations and reapplies it to activities and projects whose purpose is pleasure rather than profit. But more importantly, the same logic and practice of technological reappropriation potentially undergirds another life—a post-capitalist life. Radical change on a global scale depends on our cleverness and our skills—and our ability to use technologies in ways that enhance our humanity, our freedom, and are consistent with interdependence and ecological sanity.

LIBERATED WORK VS. USELESS TOIL

The historical emergence of a huge social surplus in industrially advanced capitalist societies, [permitted] a considerable fraction of the population to live outside the wage-labor system, at least for a substantial period of their adult lives. Many are marginals, hippies, freelance artists and writers, and graduate students who never enter the professional or academic workforces except as temporary, part-time workers. Rather than seeking normal, full-time employment in bureaucratic, commercial, or industrial workplaces they prefer to take jobs as office temps or find niches that do not require them to keep their nose to the grindstone, to show up to the job at an appointed hour, or to work for fifty weeks out of the year....   —*Stanley Aronowitz*[10]

Burning Man grew out of a subculture of people who recognized that a life worth living takes place outside of wage-labor, in addition to or instead of paid work. Its growth demonstrates a hunger for social experiences outside of the "normal" economic constraints of earning, buying, and selling, as a way to deepen and extend human life. For many, it's also an opportunity to do good work, unmediated by the twisted goals of economic life.

The female metal worker captured a typical approach to survival: "I go through phases, I work for a while, and then it'll get to the point where I can take some time off... My life just goes on an as-needed basis. When I can afford time then I take time, when I can't afford time then I make the money so I can afford time later."

The ex-dotcommer would like to survive as a cartoonist, but expressed a dark realism, typical of many in her generation: "I'm not sure if I can get money doing what really lights me up. So I would rather do something menial with my hands, or work in a café or something, to free up my creative energy to work on my own projects."

The veterinary assistant/clown straddles the split life: "Money is something I need to survive, and work is something I need to do to have money to survive, and I have a job that I don't hate. That's not what I am, that's part of what I am, but I'm a lot more complex than that."

An NGO staffer who emailed his questionnaire from Vancouver emphasized his different subjective experience when "working" at Burning Man. "There's a considerably higher level of fun with these engagements—not only because of the type of work, but also because the knowledge of the end result, the work's temporality and the personal connections that I have with the work."

The apartment manager who also fixes computers admitted, "The experience of Burning Man makes my ache greater in my life... I go home, and I'm in planned time and I'm running on clocks, and I don't know how to stop that cycle... I understand what the people who make the rules are telling me I should do with this green paper, but I just don't know how to translate it into something that is fun and satisfying. By contrast, when you get ready for the Burn you work your tailbone off. And because you're creating something different and new and you're challenging yourself, even though it's work, it has this bonus attached. You're doing something that's going to promote your survival, it's going to help other people, it's going to be something really unique."

The handyman/auto mechanic clearly wants out of normal economic life: "I personally hate working for money. If I could work and not have to take money, it would be great. I love what I do. If I could somehow pull it off and not have to accept money, I'd do it in a heartbeat."

Burning Man has a powerful effect on the imagination. It is not "real" liberation, but a temporary faux "escape" from the economy (that costs you hundreds of dollars). Nonetheless, it's a real experiment, and a direct manifestation of yearning. People yearn to escape the limits of economic life, to be more than just "workers." There aren't many chances to experience a crowd of like-minded people, sharing a collective euphoria produced by artistic and technological self-activity. At Burning Man there is a taste of such a post-economic life, even if the sour aroma of the cash nexus is barely hidden beneath the playa.

CHAPTER 10
A VASTLY BETTER WORLD AWAITS

As Colin Ward notes, quoting Paul Goodman: "A free society cannot be the substitution of a 'new order' for the old order; it is the extension of spheres of free action until they make up most of social life."[1]

The realities of radical struggle in the postmodern condition show that cosmopolitical liberation under a single sign is a modernist fantasy. Total liberation does not exist, it never has existed, and it never will exist; to seek it is to give in to a Utopian urge to free the entire world once and for all, to achieve the transparent society.

—Richard J.F. Day[2]

When I look around, now and in the past for which we have good information, I see recurrent manifestations of the future being crafted in the present; I see people not only extricating themselves from subsumption but in the times and spaces liberated, crafting newness, new ways of being, new ways of relating, new moments of new worlds. The problem for capital, and I think it recognizes this quite clearly, is how to either crush or re-internalize such exteriority, to prevent it from growing, becoming more powerful and more and more obviously visible alternatives to its way of organizing life.

—Harry Cleaver[3]

Nowtopians work in the invisible corners of daily life. Their projects, experiments, initiatives, and movements have solid roots stretching back to the mid-20th century, now spanning several generations of effort to transform society. Grass-roots, bottom-up, consultative, cooperative, innovative, consensus-favoring, open-minded, tolerant—all these qualities are common to many of Nowtopia's inventors, and are distinctively uncommon in capitalist society. But it would be folly to only note the positive, liberatory, and hopeful qualities that underpin the Nowtopians. Irrational religiosity, self-righteous moralism, subcultural exclusivity, class and race unconsciousness, misanthropy, Malthusianism… well, lists are easy to make.

In describing the emergent Nowtopia, hiding all around us in plain view, I don't claim any certainty, historically or politically, that these specific efforts will survive. I hope, also, that my discussion of the contradictions each field faces makes clear that any of them can succumb to the pernicious logic of markets and money, and many of them certainly will (clearly biofuels and open source software are well along to being dominated by large corporations; the Burning Man festival is a multimillion dollar operation, etc.). After all, Nowtopians are just folks who are a bit out front, moving ahead without institutional support to invent a more humane and ecologically sane world. Most Nowtopians have evolved skills with public discussion, group processes, and shared decision-making. Still, all the foibles, contradictions, vices, and confusions that beset anyone living in this mad world affect Nowtopians too.

Nowtopia situates these behaviors in terms of the self-emancipation of the working class. I realize that few people think in such terms, but the point of this book is to place the efforts I describe in the social and historical context of early 21st century capitalism. The familiar understandings of labor, unions, even revolution, as derived from 20th century ideologies, are a dead-end when it comes to the demands of social transformation in this era. By describing people who are making practical transformations, and creating new communities in the practice of these activities, I see an emerging type of working-class self-activity, and hopefully, self-consciousness. This is not to say that the simple accretion of more and more of these activities will by themselves make a new world. At some point political power, the control of the state (with its military and police), and the primary economic institutions of society, becomes an unavoidable challenge to radical social change.

These emergent fractions of a 21st century working class are not a vanguard; I am not suggesting Nowtopians are *the* new working class, nor that they alone can change the world. The "old-fashioned" industrial working class is larger right now, globally, than it has ever been. No meaningful transformation of life can happen without the engagement of many, if not most, of those global proletarians. But the old accommodations with state capitalism and social democracy that 20th century working class politics settled for, are closed. Global climate change, war, crashing biodiversity, waste and industrial pollution, mass starvation, and epidemic disease are just the top of a long list of pressing reasons to radically change how we live on earth. Our work together is shaped and driven by invisible hands and uncontrollable forces when it should be directed by us. Getting from the disparate experiments in work and technology, and early stages of new social communities that we see in *Nowtopia*, to the big political challenges ahead, is an open and unknowable process of politics-to-come. But to get there will require overcoming some familiar problems that we already know, sometimes too well.

THE CO-OPTATION TRAP

One of the most difficult problems for cultural inventors is, ironically, *success*. The initial passion to start something new and to bring it into existence is one of life's great pleasures. All one's talents and knowledge is focused on the creative birthing of something unprecedented, very much a "baby" for its new "parents." In the same way that nurturing a new child reveals surprising reservoirs of untapped energy, new projects attract volunteers who work harder than they've ever worked at a waged job, learning as they go, improvising, inventing, adjusting, and sticking with it until the goal is reached. Long hours of intense concentration and hard work are also their own rewards.

Once a stable state is reached, the surrounding society's demands slowly reassert themselves. Raw materials, rent, energy, water, telecommunications, transport, all tend to cost money in capitalist society, and cannot always be scavenged or gleaned. Soon enough, the new effort faces the age-old pressure to conform, if for no other reason than to generate revenue to pay bills. If the passionate individuals who started the effort find themselves facing economic hardship due to the income they gave up while creating the project, they may want a salary instead of returning to (or continuing) their paid work.

Inevitably, the surrounding society of business begins to pull, to co-opt, to seduce these new initiatives. Sooner or later the monetary pressure becomes a defining aspect of the ongoing project, and at that point the choices narrow. Is there a benefactor (sugar daddy? local monarch?)? Is there a revenue stream available from the activity or production of the project (can it "pay for itself")? Is there a business model that can attract investors? Are there grants available from foundations or local government?

The outcome for those who succumb to the imperative to become a business is usually a degradation of the *quality of work*. The urgency to make money forces even the most conscientious to cut corners, to hurry up production, to force down costs and prices up. Moreover, responding to the "demands of the market" is a proven way to lose the *coherent use* of technology for human and ecological well-being, and with it, the elevation of human values and lived experience ("community") *over* market rationality and profitability. Instead of finding new ways to reduce work, to slow down the pace of life, to enhance local ecology for its own sake, competitive pressure drives effort towards gaining monetary advantage.

This is not a new phenomenon by any means. For example, publishers, writers, and artists painstakingly invented an alternative underground 'zine subculture in the 1970s and 1980s, only to see their work subsumed by more commercial efforts. Steven Duncombe points out in his sharp history of the 'zine movement that, "[death by commercialization] is the history of bohemia since the 19th century."[4] Artists and writers push boundaries, break new ground, resettle abandoned urban neighborhoods, found new theaters, galleries, and museums. After a time the avant garde becomes mundane, the sketchy neighborhoods gentrified, the cultural facilities financial black holes. When radical projects survive to become institutionalized as businesses (for- or non-profit), narratives are preserved and hopefully resources are available for their successors, and for the less "successful" in their time and community. Alternative institutions are simultaneously a potential rich resource and an ossified obstacle to new rebellious energy. Space, equipment, expertise, and experience can jump-start new initiatives by relieving them of the need to reinvent the wheel. But the resources held in alternative institutions are not always easily shared, sometimes due to incompatible motives or visions, or because the "rich" organization feels quite poor, that it cannot yet share its relative wealth without fear of its own collapse. From the outside looking in, the organization can look like any other self-interested business. Nevertheless, the experience that accumulates in the alternative institution over time can be a fertile ground for new initiatives that might break out of this pernicious circle.

Theoreticians like the Italian Marxist Antonio Gramsci and the British historian Eric Hobsbawn shared an interest in cultural politics not as an end in itself, but as an arena of ferment from which new efforts could erupt. Political expression, stuck in a subcultural niche, is a necessary but insufficient condition for social change. Similarly, Nowtopian initiatives are essential precursors to a broader political movement, though none of them is a guarantee that such a movement will happen (nor even that they themselves will be a part of it!). The most vital resource embodied in successful alternative institutions is open access to alternative histories (including histories of those institutions), which can be shared into the future. But not if the culture does not value history.

WE'RE *HISTORY*

Widespread historical amnesia is a defining feature of life in the United States. Our culture has converted an honorable recognition—"you're history"—into an insult. In light of the cumulative wisdom that naturally gathers in the memories of "class warriors," an amnesiac gap is very helpful to a capitalism that continually renovates the appearances of life (while ensuring that the underlying dynamics remain untouched). Some activist circles challenge this directly by producing alternative histories,[5] as breaking news and as critical investigation of the past. Alternative media like underground zines, micro-power radio, and small press publishing has been augmented by the Internet and its incredibly broad and (so far) durable platform. These marginal media combine with the advantages of the Net to become an increasingly important repository of collective memory otherwise suppressed.

The decomposition of the broad working class over the past decades has broken many of the transmission belts of class memory. Urban redevelopment and suburbanization have contributed equally to a profound dispersal of previous human networks, scattering former neighbors and co-workers in every direction. The slow, arduous effort to reconnect across generations, distances, income, race, and gender requires patience and nurturance. Neither quality comes easily to impatient young radicals attracted to direct action and do-it-yourself politics.

Some people in DIY subcultures, impatient for change and inclined towards action, reinforce the ahistoricism of our culture. George McKay analyzed the youthful DIY scene in the United Kingdom during the 1990s. He reminds us that ahistoricism corresponds to a lack of attention to the future or to long-term strategic thinking.

> ...A clear potential downside of youth can be its rejection of both expertise and history, of radical history which is often hard enough to narrate or recover anyway, without the next generation of activists—the very people that history is of most use to—contributing to its erasure by their focus on youth and the self.
>
> —*George McKay*[6]

The ongoing exaltation of youth by a consumer culture in thrall to the new can be unconsciously reproduced by young radicals. The first stirrings of radical rejection and revolt are usually accompanied by an impatient urgency. Taking time to examine historical precedents in order to better understand political dynamics and more carefully focus energies requires perspective and respect for those who came before. Determination to invent the new forms capable of shattering the old deadening world is a common quality of young rebels since at least the 19th century Romantics. Contemporary radicals anxious to halt the gears of planetary destruction are often driven by an understandable and admirable urgency. The ponderous wheels of history still roll at their own lurching pace, though, and it serves critical opposition to pay it attention.

THE PRIVILEGE TRAP

As the sectarian politics of the late sixties and seventies, and the identity politics of the eighties, have sadly proved, celebrating otherness may be useful as self-therapy, but it is relatively useless as political strategy.

—*Steven Duncombe*[7]

That which is oppressed and resists is not only a who but a what. It is not only particular groups of people who are oppressed (women, indigenous, peasants, factory workers, and so on), but also (and perhaps especially) particular aspects of the personality of all of us: our self-confidence, our sexuality, our playfulness, our creativity.

—*John Holloway*[8]

*E*veryone has many reasons to contest this world, and radical politics must start from that recognition. Given the general speedup and intensification of work, the breakdown of communities and families, we might imagine a general revolt brewing among people subjected to these dynamics. But political action has not yet emerged to protest these social processes. A great shift did occur in political organizing after the 1960s, which moved the focus from broad critiques of power, wealth, and economic injustice to focus on race, gender, and sexual preference. Plenty of grassroots efforts have continued to contest the condition of public schools, local environmental justice, food safety, etc., but the sense of a wide political opposition has largely crumbled.

This saga has been analyzed a lot, but what has been overlooked is the way the concept of "privilege" has come to dominate so much thinking among politically active people. Born from the numerous divisions fracturing society along race and gender lines, as well as the extreme stratification of wealth and poverty, the discourse on "privilege" has been an attempt to come to grips with the differences among people in political movements and to challenge the power imbalances that map those differences.

We can trace its origins to the important emergence of anti-racist organizing, especially among white activists. This was urgently needed to address the reproduction of racist and sexist behaviors in left movements from the anti-Vietnam War effort to the burgeoning environmental movements. It started out as a reasonable and important repudiation of a common-enough white and/or middle class sense of entitlement, which manifested in ignorance of people who didn't already have the same social rights or economic comforts as the white and/or middle class. The critique of privilege, usually white or male, was meant to reveal the embedded structural power that some populations hold over others. Like class analysis, such sweeping analyses tend to gloss over specific experiences that contradict the larger argument. (Obviously there are plenty of men, and plenty of white people, who do not have any real power in their lives; the relative advantage of being male or white in a predominantly racist and patriarchal society doesn't always translate into specific experiences—or advantages—for particular individuals.) By equating the uneven distribution of systemic social power with individual experiences a lot of potential political alliances have been undercut. In other words, some activists who foreground this critique have had a frustrating tendency to reject the participation of white people and/or men simply because of their status, independent of the specific conditions of their lives, their ideas, or their behaviors.

The discourse around privilege in everyday terms shifted from targeting an *oblivious state of mind,* to targeting a *measurable standard of living* and/or a *discernable set of rights.* Confusion about who is "privileged" and who qualifies as a legitimate political subject was sowed by this shift. Many white radicals feel pressure to be self-critical as the test of their own political legitimacy, which has served to further confuse where political agency can legitimately arise.

I have heard many stories among white activists, especially males, who have felt shut up not for their ideas but for their *status.* Some argue that this is just, representing an historic turning of the tables, but the moments where this table-turning is empowering are far outnumbered by those where it leads to a numbing paralysis imposed by a cloud of guilt and recrimination. Permaculture activist and anti-globalization Green Bloc organizer Erik Ohlsen tells his story:

> I've been programmed as an activist [so that] when I hear "class," privilege and race come to mind... I've never been hungry or poor... I come from a middle-class family and I'm trying to be working-class...At times people get down on activists who are "privileged white males"... I got shut up because I'm a white male... There are a lot of us who come from these suburban middle-class families who have become conscious to all these issues and want to make a difference... I value the conversation about classism and racism in the activist communities—it's important to challenge people's programmed ideologies and programmed cultural behaviors, but not to say I'm better and you're worse... It's just about acknowledging it, and then saying "let's work together to make this better."[9]

Emphasizing "privilege" implicitly concedes scarcity as the norm. Once the political meaning of "privilege" shifts from an oblivious state of mind to material comfort or basic rights, the rightful expectation of generalized well-being is flipped over. Instead of insisting on one's missing social and economic rights, the political energy focuses instead on attacking other people who *appear* to enjoy them already. This unconsciously reinforces a zero-sum dynamic; if some people gain others must lose. But isn't one goal of social transformation to raise everyone to a basic standard of comfort and equality?

Instead of exploring our shared predicament and looking for commonalities, the emphasis on "privilege" tends to focus on identifying impediments to social change in ongoing racism first and foremost. The overwhelming stratification of wealth is profoundly unfair, too. But by holding responsible vast numbers of people who depend on their wages and salaries and are relatively powerless (albeit not presently poor), radicals reinforce divisions among people who will need to unite.

> A politics of affinity... is not about abandoning identification as such; it is about abandoning the fantasy that *fixed, stable* identities are possible and desirable, that one identity is better than another, that superior identities deserve more of the good and less of the bad that a social order has to offer... In the social factory *everyone* becomes a worker, which deprivileges the point of material production; but at the same time, everyone becomes a *worker*, which reimposes an expanded, but still delimited, conception of the working class as the identity behind all identifications.
>
> —*Richard J.F. Day*[10]

For many politically active people, the attack on racism and inequality took the form of self-examination and too often, endless self-criticism that left people demoralized and demobilized, and highly mistrustful of each other. At its worst extremes the grassroots campaign to uproot oppression in daily life led to a neo-Maoist focus on identity and heredity as the defining qualities of any individual, rather than actual behavior or thinking. Once progressives shifted their rhetoric to attacking "white privilege," the prospects for thinking cooperatively about political alliances were seriously diminished, because if you weren't inclined to make white racism the lead issue, you were branded, either directly or implicitly, racist.

Because of this confusion, leftists can overlook or even oppose worthy currents of subversion when they erupt from educated, or affluent, or even just white people. The preconception that oppositional political subjectivity "belongs" to "real workers" or the "truly oppressed" is based on political assumptions rooted in 20th century paradigms. The contemporary discourse on "privilege" has had the perverse effect of devaluing whole segments of political opposition ("It's just a bunch of middle-class white people"). It has also tended to reinforce a pernicious tendency to hierarchy in this society by continuing to rank people by status.

In Atlanta, Rachel Spiewak is a cofounder of the Sopo Bicycle Cooperative and promoter of Critical Mass rides in that car-centric southern city. In May 2006 she attended a Bicycle Organization Organization Project (BOOP) conference in Milwaukee where she sat through an "anti-oppression" training (which she found offensive) conducted by colleagues from the all-white Boulder, Colorado area.

> In Atlanta we know that skin color does not dictate consciousness... I don't care about awareness or attitude. I care about what people are doing. Are people treating each other with respect? Are people treating each other like we all have the same amount of worth? Are people making environmentally responsible choices? Do all people have access to doing these things? The change I want to see in the world is in the "doing."
>
> The golden rule is not about who or what you are, and it's not about consciousness. It's about what you DO. If we lay the groundwork for being able to DO these things, i.e. we reorient material culture, then we will see shifts in social culture. There will be more opportunities to build community and observe the full humanity of each other, despite socialization that dictates who counts less as a person and why. The ideological shift will follow, quietly and slowly, and we'll take it for granted.
>
> —*Rachel Spiewak*[11]

Spiewak's comments show how the overemphasis on racial politics and politics of privilege can confine political activity to the level of the *individual* and focus on *perfecting personal behavior* rather than actively doing work that attacks the capitalist system or even systemic discrimination. The ongoing legacies of black slavery, Indian genocide, and a century of imperial wars against "chinks, gooks, japs, niggers, injuns, hadji's," etc., haunt radical politics as much as they haunt American society in general. Finding a way forward without negating this barbaric past and its continuing influence in the present, is a task that continues to elude radicals. The identity politics and anti-racist organizing developed over the past decades have been important but they have not solved the problem. These movements have been and still are useful to bring attention to the oblivious or semi-conscious discrimination enacted within radical alternative movements, but it is all too easy for the emphasis on so-called "privilege" to seriously hamper a clear appraisal of the enormous similarities faced by people at many different locations of this stratified and hierarchical society. As Richard Day puts it, "If the multitudes are ever to come together in any way, this will be the result of a long process of building solidarity and dealing with differences and structured oppressions that plague movements for radical alternatives as much as they do the political mainstream…"[12]

One task that this book has set for itself is to break down the idea of the "middle class," especially the notion that people so designated have a life radically different than those who supposedly fall below the threshold. So-called "middle class" life is not "privileged." Granted, the material well-being of most people defined as middle class is far better than a huge majority of the world population. But material comfort should be considered a universal human right, rather than a privilege, and anyway, "material comfort" must be carefully and democratically rethought in light of our increased biological and ecological awareness.

Similarly, it is problematic to refer to the freedom to act, or a sense of personal agency, or unfettered access to public spaces as examples of "white privilege," as some do. These qualities are aspects of a normal daily life that should be taken for granted by everyone. That they aren't is a reprehensible remnant of the racist roots of our society, but the path forward is not to attack or suspend them as undue privileges, but to extend them to all without qualification. Our rhetoric should reflect our commitment to extending rights and freedoms to everyone, not to attacking the population that *seems* to enjoy rights and freedoms relatively unhindered. (The perception that white people or men have the ability to live freely is itself highly exaggerated, in my opinion, since this society only gives a tiny minority anything approaching real freedom.) Nowtopians are engaged in practical projects that depend on new relationships around leadership, skill-sharing, and power dynamics within groups, practices that are probably more useful to combat racial and gender inequality than dogmatic doctrines of privilege.

In the new communities of Nowtopians we consistently encounter a range of people from affluent to poor, often—but not always—in multiracial constellations. It is common to find that some of the people making the new world today are white and sometimes well-paid. If radical political organizing continues to use a blanket rule of "identity" over behavior, it will reinforce the existing divisions that already keep people fighting each other more than fighting the system. In embracing a new politics of work, outside of wage-labor, Nowtopians lay the foundation for new alliances across the old boundaries, on the basis of practical aspirations and activities.

THE TECHNOLOGY TRAP

> If language originated in gestures, and if gesture and toolmaking (the simplest form of technology) evolved together, this would imply that technology is an essential part of human nature, inseparable from the evolution of language and consciousness. It would mean that, from the very dawn of our species, human nature and technology have been inseparably linked.
>
> —*Fritjof Capra*[13]

The subcultures described in this book all have creative, productive, appropriative relationships with the technosphere. Among chopper bike clubs and Burning Man artists we find a joy in making new artistic uses of discards; waste veggie oil engine tinkerers are determined to radically alter our relationship with fuel; community gardeners and permaculturists are engaged in redesigning urban spaces, reinventing a new self-sufficiency amidst the hyper-dependent structures of modern cities; free software coders are building an evolving infrastructure for an emergent collective self-management while countless numbers of people contribute their creative works to the online world. All these efforts, and many more not listed here, manifest deeply creative possibilities that arise in the reappropriation of modern technology.

These Nowtopian initiatives provisionally shape the "free" technosphere of a post-capitalist world. As the connections between these efforts become clearer, a broader political movement can ask the deeper questions that socially should determine the assumptions and practices of science and technology. Which machines, which technologies should we use in which ways to achieve which results? How much work is needed? What are the ecological consequences of a given style of work, a specific type of technology? Such simple questions reflect an extremely advanced relationship with technology and any answers are by nature *advanced*, not primitive, regardless of the specific technological choices made.

Technology revolts grounded in ecological and social activism go back several decades. Many people have taken part in efforts to clean or save a local waterway or beach or forest. Volunteers monitor rivers and lakes, challenge groundwater contamination, combat industry's toxic releases, and so on. Thousands of people joined various anti-nuclear organizations

during the late 1970s and early 1980s and many became life-long proponents of solar and wind power as rational alternatives to nuclear and fossil
fuel energy. Millions of women have grappled with a male-biased, often
ineffective medical system. They've been joined by plenty of men who
have also come to mistrust western medicine. Alternative technologies
have proliferated in the past decades in response to dissatisfaction with
the results of corporate and government-controlled development.

Under capitalism most technological decisions are left to private investors. Major infrastructural investments are usually left to the government, which spends public money to benefit private interests. Whether a
technology is "regulated" by the state or not, few people ever get consult-
ed about the direction it should take. Similarly, the priorities for scientific
research are never submitted to popular scrutiny. Science- and technol-
ogy-based political efforts almost always have to fight rear-guard battles to
stop the advance of anti-social technologies (e.g., nuclear power, GMO
agriculture, or designer babies).

U.S. culture is particularly enamored of new technology, succumb-
ing with alarming predictability to the far-fetched claims of one huckster
or propagandist after another. (The best example of this has to be the
nearly $1 trillion spent publicly on the ridiculous and impossible anti-
ballistic missile system known as "Star Wars.") People generally seem to
think that some new invention will solve any problem that might arise.
Constant renovation of common household objects has helped shape a
society obsessed with the New (and Improved!). A whiz-bang techno-fix
is always just around the corner. Steady promotional drumbeats playing
at all times on all channels highlight fixes, innovations, and new conve-
niences while never offering an integrated examination of the overarching relationships among things and people, devices and users, apparatus and "apparatee"... As Ralph Waldo Emerson put it so hauntingly in
the 19th century, "Things are in the saddle, and ride mankind."[14]

Conversely, anti-technology ideology has crippled a small but influential subculture of radicals in North America since the 1980s. John Zerzan
and David Watson writing in the anarchist magazine *Fifth Estate*, and more
recently Derrick Jensen have taken the early stirrings of critical engagement with technology into a dead-end. They are among the best known
radical voices associated with "neo-primitivism" or "anti-civilization" anarchism, promoting a fetishized notion of anti-technology that mirrors
the techno-fix mentality of consumerism. Rejecting human intention
and creative fluidity, the neo-primitivist line argues against any engagement with technology (a category that is always left undefined—does it
include shovels? thumbtacks? books? radios? computers? nuclear bombs?
language?). Anti-technologists believe that machines can only be used in

one way (the destructive way) and so leave no room for human ingenuity, invention, or play. A kind of cargo cult mentality insists that all aspects of the technosphere are demonstrably more powerful over the human condition than the political and social arrangements that define the uses to which technologies are put. Striking an "original sin" tone, Zerzan in particular has insisted that radicalism requires nothing less than a total rejection of "technology" and "civilization." Mirroring Bush-like Manichaeism, the anti-technology zealots claim that if you are not against *all* technology, you are *in favor* of *all* technology and thereby all the worst aspects of barbaric civilization.

This way of thinking has played extremely well to young anarchists who want to be the "most radical." Strident denunciations and subcultural expulsions historically echo the sectarian cul-de-sac honed by the Situationists in the 1960s and hardened further by their U.S. and British followers in the 1970s, who insisted that any effort by any group was inherently sold-out and co-opted by the logic of capital, closing down any possibility of revolution.[15] Harry Cleaver answered this problem in an online discussion in 2003:

> To imagine the capitalist machine like an internal combustion engine that inevitably harnesses the explosions within for its own purposes—thus no "outside"—is to assume no possibility of revolution, no possibility of total rupture. I think such a metaphor is not only depressing but fails to capture our daily experience of resistance and rebellion that though it may only be temporary and limited and even recuperated, is constantly renewed and in its renewal, in its recreation of an "outside," is the real material basis for any realistic notion of actually getting beyond the capital-labor relation once and for all.
>
> —*Harry Cleaver*[16]

Interestingly, the anti-technology ideologues were inspired by the same anthropological research that influenced a generation of permaculturists. Anthropologist Marshall Sahlins discovered in pre-agricultural societies a human life in which needs were met with only a couple of hours' effort per day. His work has been extended by permaculture-influenced thinkers who have reframed the analysis of so-called "primitive peoples" to show that they had dense, complicated, and ecologically "efficient" lifestyles in their respective environments. Frequently these people altered the terrain to suit their needs in ways that "moderns" find difficult to recognize. The exciting implications of these insights, developed further by permaculturists, inform the deep aspirations of the emerging culture. They show it is indeed possible for humans to live

differently, to create a world where onerous work is eliminated wherever possible, and reduced to a minimum where not; a human life beau-
tifully integrated with local ecology to provide an abundance of healthy
food for the entire food web, using the least energy and effort as can be
designed most elegantly into the system.

Ted White has been deeply involved in both the outlaw bicycling
subculture and the small-scale organic farming movement. He captures
the voluntary simplicity embraced by many:

> I think fancy technologies are a kind of dead end—or
> a bottomless pit, maybe is a better way of putting it. My
> hope and dream is that the world peak in oil produc-
> tion will have such a strong impact on the world that
> most technologies will simplify or just go away… I think
> it will challenge us to be better people with better pri-
> orities—and we can still have fun making this transi-
> tion—we already are—that's the kind of attitude that
> bike riding and gardening have instilled in me.[17]

Previously, utopian dreams didn't rely on simplifying technologies
to cope with shortages and limits. In 1963, writer James Boggs pictured
a looming "workless society," in which it would be technologically possible… "to simply walk out on the streets and get milk and honey."[18] The
once prevalent dreams of generalized abundance, what Murray Bookchin
dubbed "post-scarcity anarchism," made possible by widespread automation and increased leisure time, have been negated by three decades of
ruthless capitalist rationalization. Today, most people work longer and
harder than people did thirty years ago to maintain the *same living standard.* The easy life of abundance has also been derailed by the reality of
technological "advance," which, because the advances are never properly
evaluated, are labeled as "progress." Technological time-bombs—chemical, radioactive, and biological—are ticking in labs, factories, and fields
across the world. Meanwhile, workers in traditional factory or factory-like
occupations, strive to conserve their status, income, and social rights that
are associated with that employment rather than challenge the employers' technological foundations and imperatives.

Boggs thought the strongest push for liberation from scarcity and
stupidity would come not from factory workers, busy defending their
jobs, but from the outsiders whom society had marginalized. "The workless society," he concluded, "can only be brought about by the actions
and forces outside the work process."[19] Truly, in order to develop the society in which work is radically transformed and reimagined as a shared
effort to make life wonderful, the logic of capital must be left behind
entirely. The new renaissance of ecological technology that will under-

pin a radically redesigned life demands an unprecedented *unleashing* of creative and inventive energies across the cultures of the world.

TAKING LEAVE, TOGETHER

> Paolo Virno defines exodus as "an engaged withdrawal, a 'founding leave-taking' that consists in a mass defection from the State"... if anyone achieves escape velocity, they will eventually be brought back to earth, and so had best be concerned from the outset about where they will land, lest they unwittingly reproduce or be re-integrated by the system of states and corporations. This self-conscious leave-taking, or exodus, is central to what the autonomists call "the constituent power of the multitude."
> —*Richard J.F. Day*[20]

> Only those who are free from slavery can dare imagine what being really free would be... It is a luxury that we should be able to afford: the luxury of imagining a future that would actively bring together everything we are capable of.
> —*Michael Hardt and Toni Negri*[21]

> Anti-politics cannot therefore just be a question of positively doing "our own thing," because "our own thing" is inevitably negative, oppositional. Nor, however, can it just be negative: actions that are purely negative may be cathartic, but they do nothing to overcome the separation on which capitalist rule is based. To overcome that separation, actions must point-beyond in some way: strikes that do not just withdraw labor but point to alternative ways of doing (by providing free transport, a different kind of health care); university protests that do not just close down the university but suggest a different experience of study; occupations of buildings that turn those buildings into social centers for a different sort of political action; revolutionary struggles that do not just try to defeat the government but to transform the experience of social life.
> —*John Holloway*[22]

Class consciousness, the goal of leftist organizing and defined as the prerequisite of social revolt, is historically rare. Some historians impute class consciousness back in time onto successful upheavals, when the actual participants may have conceived of their activities in quite dif-

ferent terms. Questions of class and shared subjective states of mind are
endless fodder for historical and psychological debate. Shared identities
and awareness emerge unpredictably and inconsistently, even when so
much of our lives are relatively similar. Against a potential conscious com-
mon-ground, capitalism manufactures and reinforces hierarchies and
differences which compellingly reproduce themselves in even the most
unlikely corners of life.[23]

But the lack of a formal "class consciousness" does not mean that
new collective identities based on shared life experiences are not taking
shape. These days new formations usually embrace the vague, all-purpose
label "community" to describe themselves. Communities find themselves
in all areas and at all levels of daily life. Some are global in scope while
many face the unmet needs found in their local situations. Community is
made when gathering to confront the WTO or the G8, when taking over
a vacant lot for a garden, or coming together to investigate a city's history on bicycle. Dovetailing with insurgent movements in the global south
confronting issues of basic survival, one notion of community represents
the front-line defense against transnational capitalism and the atomization it seeks to impose on individual lives. Communities become weapons
of collective resistance and action in places like South Africa or India or
Bolivia, when people band together to reconnect electricity or water that
have been disconnected for lack of payment.

For the past three decades, capitalism has sought to impose a system
that forces everyone to "pay for themselves," whether through the privatized commodification of basics like water and power or through the rising fees of public goods like transport, communications, etc. Work has
been imposed on anyone deemed "dependent" on the social safety nets
constructed during the 20th century (which are now largely shredded).
Paradoxically the wage relationship has become increasingly precarious
at the same time that money has become ever more central to defining
one's life chances.

The outcome of today's contest for history is anything but clear. It
is yet undecided which paths we will follow and which we will turn away
from. The formation of shared subjectivities, whether in terms of class,
gender, ethnicity, or community, is fraught with contradiction and confusion. What seems true is that few people are reducible to any particular
categorical identity. Instead, most people are a bundle of sensibilities, influences, and beliefs that crisscross sociological and political categories.
Hybrid identities and precarious economic lives make a common awareness elusive. But as Brian Holmes asks, "can we use a more-or-less natural
resistance to the contemporary forms of exploitation as a starting-point
in the attempt to make a world out of our new understandings of what

might be worth doing together in society? We need new and persuasive explanations for what is worth doing together, and why certain activities should be granted the resources for further development, without always invoking the current excuse: 'Because they make money.'"[24]

New communities are already finding each other in activities, even hard work, that responds to needs other than money. Nowtopians define new communities based on needs whose provision is increasingly privatized or subject to rising costs within the system, but which they address directly, outside of market relations. Franco Barchiesi addresses the rise of this new sensibility:

> The theme of needs becomes decisive in the definition of the community as a radical project of decommodification based on insurgent everyday practices… Assuming communities as spaces of needs where antagonist political projects are nurtured ultimately allows social movements to differentiate themselves from "essentialist" understandings of community as based on inherent, pre-existing, a-historical facts (territory, ethnicity, language, etc.).
>
> —*Franco Barchiesi*[25]

The brutal wars initiated by the United States after 9/11 represent the early death throes of a mortally wounded empire. The once-flexible and dynamic U.S. has proven to be the ultimate dinosaur in the new networked, open source, cooperative, and collaborative world in formation. Heroic, inspired resistance to U.S. militarism has further unveiled the weakness, insanity, and lack of imagination that sits in the driver's seat of the "most powerful" state in history.

The widening arc of innovative and subversive initiatives over the past fifteen years has already diminished the ability of any global behemoth to impose its will. A "many-headed hydra" of direct action, direct democracy, and a deep commitment to ecological restoration and health contest the smooth functioning of global capitalism at every turn. World Social Forums have brought together tens of thousands of global activists from locales across the North and South in unprecedented discussion and debate. Direct connection among thinkers and activists across an impossibly broad range of initiatives circulates knowledge and tactics on the Internet with inspiring speed. Complicated dances of new communities with the increasingly hollow forms received from the 20th century will continue to play out for some years yet. Regardless of the persistence of recuperative forces and dynamics, these moments of "non-subordinate" behavior are an essential foundation for deep social changes. Among the diverse and uncategorizable multitudes, a shared sensibility is beginning to emerge. Physicist Fritjof Capra describes its roots and scope:

> The resistance against patriarchy, the domination and control of nature, unlimited economic growth and material consumption, originated in the powerful social movements that swept the industrial world in the 1960s. Eventually, an alternative vision emerged from these movements, based on the respect of human dignity; the ethics of sustainability; and an ecological view of the world. This new vision forms the core of the worldwide coalition of grassroots movements.
>
> —*Fritjof Capra*[26]

Nowtopia, like Utopia, is a "no place," but unlike Utopia, it is also an "everywhere." It is appealing to imagine a harmonious and peaceful transition to a sensible, humane, and comfortable life for everyone. Nowtopian efforts are always, consciously or not, working in that direction. An unfolding potential can and does erupt in the most surprising places, seemingly simple and limited but also embodying deeper aspirations for a more profound transformation. Our shared fate is bound up in our ability to consciously redirect our collaborative energies to a world of our own design. The experimental and tentative efforts that I've dubbed Nowtopia are stepping stones to a thorough-going reinvention of life. A politically savvy Nowtopia has yet to appear, but the foundations, already under construction for several decades, are solidifying and strengthening at least as fast as the planet is descending into chaos. Our tasks become more urgent the longer we delay the larger transformation that our local efforts promise and demand.

How wonderful can life be? Shouldn't we be trying to find out?

NOTES

NOTES TO PAGES 9–16

1   Michael Hardt and Antonio Negri, *Empire* (Cambridge, MA: Harvard University Press, 2000), 204.

2   Karl Marx, *A Contribution to the Critique of Political Economy*, Preface (Moscow: Progress Publishers, 1977).

3   Joanna Kadi locates the origins of class identity in "education, values, culture, income, dwelling, lifestyle, manners, friends, ancestry, language, expectations, desires, sense of entitlement, religion, neighborhood, amount of privacy." Joanna Kadi, *Thinking Class: Sketches from a Cultural Worker* (Cambridge, MA: South End Press, 1996), 53. This list is so encompassing that it would be impossible to argue against it. Of course all these things go in to the stew that is personal identity, and personal identity is inevitably a product of class society. But in the face of such myriad influences, it's not very illuminating to explain class with this list.

4   A longer version of my personal employment history up to the early 1980s is in *Processed World #17*, "The Making of a Bad Attitude," reprinted in *Bad Attitude: The Processed World Anthology* (London: Verso, 1990), 94.

5   Karl Polanyi, *The Great Transformation* (Boston: Beacon Press, 2001).

6   On this subject, see also: Harry Cleaver, *Reading Capital Politically* (Oakland: AK Press, 2000); Nick Dyer-Witheford, *Cyber-Marx: Cycles and Circuits of Struggle in High Technology Capitalism* (Champaign-Urbana: University of Illinois Press, 1990); Michael Hardt and Antonio Negri, *Multitude: War and Democracy in the Age of Empire* (New York: Penguin, 2004); Paolo Virno, *A Grammar of the Multitude* (New York: Semiotext(e)/Foreign Agents, 2004). Dozens of websites provide texts, ongoing discussions, and extensive links to related sources. An excellent starting point is Nate Holdren's blog "What In the Hell…" at whatinthehell.blogsome.com. Some venerable websites worth perusing are www.generation-online.org, www.metamute.org, www.rekombinant.org, each publishing a wide variety of materials often well outside the realm of self-defined autonomist Marxism. Other important journals can be tracked online: *Multitudes* (http://multitudes.samizdat.net/spip.php?rubrique816), *The Commonor* (www.thecommonor.org.uk), *Midnight Notes* (www.midnightnotes.org).

7   A thorough treatment of this tendency is presented in Steve Wright, *Storming Heaven: Class Composition and Struggle in Italian Autonomist Marxism* (London: Pluto Press, 2002).

8   See discussion at www.riff-raff.se/en/6/callcenters_en.php (accessed January 10, 2008).

9   Hardt and Negri, *Multitude*, 308.

NOTES TO PAGES 17–38

1   "The richest 1% of people in the world receive as much as the bottom 57%, or in other words less than 50 million of the richest people receive as much as the 2.7 billion poorest." from World Bank economist Branko Milanovic, 1999, cited in Doug Henwood, *After the New Economy* (New York: New Press, 2003), 132.

2   Ibid.

3   Adam Curtis's 4-hour, 4-part BBC documentary, *The Century of the Self*, does an excellent job of tracing the rise of consumerist personalities and politics across

the 20th century.

4   Beverly J. Silver, *Forces of Labor: Workers' Movements and Globalization Since 1870* (Cambridge, UK: Cambridge University Press, 2003), 19–20.

5   See Noel Ignatiev, *How the Irish Became White* (New York: Routledge, 1996) for one very good account of this historic process.

6   The black newspaper *The Elevator* (1865–1898) railed vituperatively against the competition—Chinese and European immigrants—in 1865: "We have enough, and more, of them here now, eating our substance, polluting the atmosphere with their filth, and the mind with their licentiousness." *The Elevator* also advised avoiding the mistakes of the eastern states which erred by inviting "the discontented and vicious of all Europe to their shores." Cited in Douglas Daniels, *Pioneer Urbanites: A Social and Cultural History of Black San Francisco* (Berkeley: University of California Press, 1990).

7   There are many good books for more information on this admittedly abbreviated labor history. Here are a few: Jeremy Brecher, *Strike!* (Cambridge, MA: South End Press, 1998); Root & Branch Collective, *Root & Branch: The Rise of the Workers Movements* (Greenwich, CT: Fawcett Crest, 1975); Martin Glaberman, *Wartime Strikes* (Detroit: Bewick Editions, 1980); Harvey O'Connor, *Revolution in Seattle* (Seattle: Left Bank Books, 1981); Sidney Lens, *The Labor Wars* (New York: Anchor Doubleday, 1974); Richard O. Boyer and Herbert M. Morais, *Labor's Untold Story* (New York: United Electrical Workers Union, 1955); Samuel Yellen, *American Labor Struggles, 1877–1934* (New York: Monad Press, 1974, originally published 1936); Alexander Saxton, *The Indispensable Enemy: Labor and the Anti-Chinese Movement in California* (Berkeley: University of California Press, 1971); Ira Cross, *The History of the Labor Movement in California* (Berkeley: University of California Press, 1935); David F. Selvin, *A Terrible Anger: The 1934 Waterfront and General Strikes in San Francisco* (Detroit: Wayne State University Press, 1996).

8   Guy Debord, originally published in 1967 as *La société du spectacle;* English edition translated by Donald Nicholson-Smith (New York: Zone Books, 1994). See also Guy Debord, *Comments on the Society of the Spectacle,* trans. Malcolm Imrie (London: Verso, 1990).

9   Robert Putnam's best-selling *Bowling Alone* (New York: Simon & Schuster, 2000) exhaustively explores the factors contributing to the demise of American community. While ultimately inconclusive, his work attributes a large portion of the breakdown to several factors: changes in work, suburban sprawl, television, and generational change, with a fair amount of overlap among these causes.

10 Toyotaism is fleshed out thoroughly in Pietro Basso, *Modern Times, Ancient Hours* (London: Verso, 2003). Basso describes how "Toyotaism" led to the colonization of every spare moment in a minute, an hour, a day at work, so that where once a production worker might have had as much as 20% of a given minute or hour as "dead-time" waiting for the next task to be ready, management techniques have squeezed that margin down to the point where 57 seconds of each minute the worker is busy, with the ultimate target of having workers work 60 of every 60 seconds.

11 I was a co-founder of *Processed World,* much of which can be seen online at www.processedworld.com.

12 Jeff Schmidt, *Disciplined Minds: A Critical Look at Salaried Professionals and the Soul-Battering System that Shapes Their Lives.* (New York: Rowman & Littlefield, 2000), 204.

13 Ibid., 40

14 Ibid., 208

15 Barbara Epstein, *Political Protest and Cultural Revolution: Nonviolent Direct Action in the 1970s and 1980s* (Berkeley: University of California Press, 1991), a good

overview of this era.

16 This project started in the 1980s independently as a twice-annual newsletter and has since gained partial funding from the Federal Environmental Protection Agency, while still retaining its independence. The newsletter can be reached via its editor at ellieely@earthlink.net, or at the EPA website, www.epa.gov/owow/monitoring/volunteer/vm_index.html (accessed April 2, 2007).

17 *Our Bodies, Ourselves* remains the bible of this movement, and now has a well-developed companion website at www.ourbodiesourselves.org (accessed April 2, 2007).

18 This is not to deny the value of modern allopathic approaches for a range of conditions.

19 Maurizio Lazzarato, "General Intellect: Towards an Inquiry into Immaterial Labour," www.geocities.com/immateriallabour/lazzarato-immaterial-labour.html (accessed January 10, 2008).

20 The best articulated version of this argument is in Michael Albert's work on Participatory Economics, online at zmag.org, and in his books, *Looking Forward* (Cambridge, MA: South End Press, 1991) and *Moving Forward* (Oakland, CA: AK Press, 2000).

21 John and Barbara Ehrenreich, "The Professional Managerial Class," in *Between Labor and Capital* (Cambridge, MA: South End Press, 1979).

22 Barbara Ehrenreich, *Fear of Falling: The Inner Life of the Middle Class* (New York: HarperPerenniel, 1989).

23 Barbara Ehrenreich, *Bait and Switch: The (Futile) Pursuit of the American Dream* (New York: Metropolitan Books, 2005).

24 Barbara Ehrenreich, *Nickel and Dimed: On (Not) Getting By in America* (New York: Metropolitan Books, 2001).

25 Beverly J. Silver, *Forces of Labor: Workers' Movements and Globalization Since 1870* (Cambridge, UK: Cambridge University Press, 2003), 34.

26 Madeleine Bunting, *Willing Slaves: How the Overwork Culture is Ruling Our Lives* (London: HarperCollins, 2004), 7

27 Ibid., 10

28 Barbara Ehrenreich, *Nickel and Dimed*.

NOTES TO PAGES 39–54

1 Lyric from *Broke*, a comedy with music by Merle "Ian Shoales" Kessler, performed at The Marsh in San Francisco, November 2003.

2 André Gorz, *Reclaiming Work: Beyond the Wage-Based Society* (Malden, MA: Polity Press in association with Blackwell Publishers Ltd., 1999; originally published as *Misères du present: richesse du possible* by Editions Galilée 1997), 53.

3 For a full analysis of the price of oil in combating working class militancy, first in the so-called First World, then turning the attack to the oil-producing workers themselves later, see Midnight Notes Collective, *Midnight Oil: Work, Energy, War, 1973–1992* (New York: Autonomedia, 1992).

4 For example, the Gross Domestic Product "grows" when a person gets into a car accident, leading to the consumption of emergency services, follow-up medical services, a new car or repair to the old one, etc. GDP measures the movement of monetary value, regardless of whether or not it is a negative expenditure, worthless, or actually making life worse (think military production). Many alternative systems to measure the quality of life have been designed (the Genuine Progress Indicator being one, www.rprogress.org/projects/gpi/), but none have yet supplanted the pernicious GDP.

5 From the internet discussion list called aut-op-sy, June 19, 2003: <aut-op-sy@lists.

village.virginia.edu> Re: AUT: class composition links (on Holloway etc) by H. Cleaver.

6   Harry Cleaver, "Marxian Categories and the Crisis of Capital," in *Revolutionary Writing: Common Sense Essays in Post-Political Politics*, ed. Werner Bonefield (New York: Autonomedia, 2003), 43.

7   John Holloway, *Change the World Without Taking Power* (London: Pluto Press, 2002), 142–45.

8   Tiziana Terranova, *Network Culture: Politics for the Information Age* (London: Pluto Press, 2004), 30–31.

9   From the internet discussion list called aut-op-sy, July 6, 2003 <aut-op-sy@lists. village.virginia.edu>.

10 Author's interview with Ben Gillock in San Francisco, CA, June 2, 2003.

11 Kyle Bravo, *Making Stuff & Doing Things: A Collection of DIY Guides to Doing Just About Anything.* (Portland, OR: Microcosm Publishing, 2005).

12 Stephen Duncombe, *Notes from Underground: Zines* (London: Verso, 1997), 185.

13 Even punk zines can be traced back to the 1930s and the emergence of science fiction clubs. To further promote and explore their ideas about the new genre and their thoughts on the future more broadly, club members launched what they called "fanzines." This discussion is amplified in Stephen Duncombe's excellent book *Notes from Underground: Zines.*

14 Matte Resist, "Do It Yourself or Don't Do It Yourself," *Resist* 42 (2001).

15 V. Vale, ed.,*Search & Destroy #1-6: The Complete Reprint* (San Francisco: Re/search Publications, 1996).

16 Duncombe, *Notes from Underground: Zines,* 40–41.

17 Ibid., 192.

18 George McKay, *DIY Culture: Party and Protest in Nineties Britain* (London: Verso, 1998), 19.

19 Fred Turner, *From Counterculture to Cyberculture: Stewart Brand, the Whole Earth Network, and the Rise of Digital Utopianism* (Chicago: University of Chicago Press, 2006).

20 The Exploratorium is an apparent alternative museum, but one that is firmly rooted in Cold War militarism, having been founded by Frank Oppenheimer, an atom bomb designer. It was the first popular science museum that urged visitors to have hands-on, self-directed learning experiences.

21 Author's interview with Nick Bertoni, Feb. 25, 2006 at Tinker's Workshop in Berkeley, CA.

22 Ibid.

23 Richard J.F. Day, *Gramsci Is Dead: Anarchist Currents in the Newest Social Movements* (London: Pluto Press/Between The Lines, 2005), 19.

24 Author's interview with Nick Bertoni , Feb. 25, 2006.

25 Day, *Gramsci Is Dead,* 128.

NOTES TO PAGES 55–79

1   Dyer-Witheford, *Cyber-Marx,* 237.

2   Ibid., 233

3   David Holmgren, *Permaculture: Principles and Pathways Beyond Sustainability* (Hepburn, Australia: Holmgren Design Services, 2002), 13–14.

4   Karl Marx, *Grundrisse* (New York: Penguin, 1993), 705.

5   Marx, *Grundrisse,* 700, 706.

6   Paolo Virno, "General Intellect," www.generation-online.org/p/fpvirno10.htm (accessed January 10, 2008).

7   Pamela H. Smith, *The Body of the Artisan* (Chicago: University of Chicago Press, 2004).

8   Author's interview with Erik Ohlsen in Sebastopol, California, January 16, 2006.

9   Peter Bane, "Finding a New Way Forward," *The Permaculture Activist* 51 (February 2004): 2.

10 Ibid.

11 They are: 1. Observe and interact / 2. Catch and store energy / 3. Obtain a yield / 4. Apply self-regulation and accept feedback / 5. Use and value renewable resources and services / 6. Produce no waste / 7. Design from patterns to details / 8. Integrate rather than segregate / 9. Use small and slow solutions / 10. Use and value diversity / 11. Use edges and value the marginal / 12. Creatively use and respond to change. Holmgren, *Permaculture*.

12 Toby Hemenway, "Top Feeders, Bottom Feeders... but No Middle Class" *The Permaculture Activist* 38 (February 1998): 6.

13 David Holmgren, "Permaculture and the Third Wave of Environmental Solutions," *The Permaculture Activist* 50 (May 2003): 6.

14 Holmgren, *Permaculture*.

15 Holmgren, "Permaculture and the Third Wave," 5.

16 John Wages, "The Permacultural Eye," *The Permaculture Activist*, 57 (August. 2005): 4.

17 Bart Anderson, "Mysteries of the Soil Food Web," *The Permaculture Activist* 61 (August 2006): 11.

18 Holmgren, *Permaculture*, 37.

19 Edward Hyams, *Soil and Civilization* (New York: Harper & Row, 1976; orig. pub. London, England: Thames and Hudson, 1952), 17.

20 Holmgren, *Permaculture*, 20.

21 Holmgren, *Permaculture*, 2–3.

22 Holmgren, *Permaculture*, 218.

23 Wes Jackson, "Toward an Ignorance-based Worldview," *The Permaculture Activist* 57 (Autumn 2005): 28–30.

24 Thomas S. Kuhn, *The Structure of Scientific Revolutions*, 3rd edition (Chicago: University of Chicago Press, 1996).

25 Toby Hemenway, "Beyond Wilderness: Seeing the Garden in the Jungle," *The Permaculture Activist* 51 (February 2004): 20–21.

26 Peter Bane, "Keystones and Cops," *The Permaculture Activist* 50 (May 2003): 21.

27 Craig Holdredge and Steve Talbott, "The Question Science Won't Ask," *Orion* (July/August 2006): 29.

28 Ibid.

29 Robert Frenay, *Pulse: The Coming Age of Systems and Machines Inspired by Living Things* (New York: Farrar, Straus and Giroux: 2006).

30 Jeremy Narby, *Intelligence in Nature: An Inquiry into Knowledge* (New York: Jeremy Tarcher/Penguin Group, 2005).

31 Dozens of thinkers have pushed the boundaries of our assumptions in this area, notably Fritjof Capra and Bruno Latour.

32 Frenay, 326.

33 Ibid., 395.

34 Fritjof Capra, *The Hidden Connections: A Science for Sustainable Living* (New York: Random House, 2002), 36–37.

35 Michael Pollan, The *Omnivore's Dilemma*. (New York: Penguin, 2006), 145, citing the quote from an essay by Wendell Berry in the 1971 *Last Whole Earth Catalogue* that influenced the new urban gardening movement.

36 Pollan, *The Omnivore's Dilemma*, 142–144.

37 Holmgren, *Permaculture*, 2.

38 Clifford D. Connor, *A People's History of Science: Miners, Midwives and "Low Mechanicks"* (New York: Nation Books, 2005), 276.
39 Steven Shapin, *The Scientific Revolution* (Chicago: University of Chicago Press, 1996), 95.
40 Shapin, ibid., 33.
41 Smith, Pamela H., *The Body of the Artisan*, 239.
42 Shapin, *The Scientific Revolution*, 123–24.
43 Ibid., 150–151.
44 Quoted in *Proteus: A Nineteenth Century Vision*, a documentary film by David Lebrun, 2004.
45 That differences in temperature, pressure, and density tend to even out in a physical system which is isolated from the outside world; in other words, energy tends to dissipate.
46 Holmgren, *Permaculture*, 71.
47 Darrell Frey, "What Profits?$?$?: Trials of a Self-Funded Researcher," *The Permaculture Activist* 38 (February 1998): 19.
48 Hemenway, "Beyond Wilderness," 20–21 (see note 28).
49 Ohlsen interview, 2006.
50 Mark Leger in email correspondence with author, 2006.
51 Ohlsen interview, 2006.
52 Holmgren, *Permaculture*, 43.
53 Ohlsen interview 2006.
54 Ibid.
55 Heather Humus, "Food Not Laws: A grassroots educational project," in *Urban Wilds: Gardeners' Stories of the Struggle for the Land and Justice*, 2nd edition, ed. Cleo Woelfe-Erskine. (Oakland, CA: water/under/ground publications, 2002), 19–21.
56 Ibid.

NOTES TO PAGES 81–107

1   Peter Lamborn Wilson and Bill Weinberg, *Avant Gardening: Ecological Struggle in The City and The World* (New York: Autonomedia, 1999), 25.
2   H. Patricia Hynes, *A Patch of Eden: America's Inner-City Gardeners* (White River, VT: Chelsea Green, 1996) 156.
3   Ibid., citing Jennifer Bennett, *Lilies of the Hearth: The Historical Relationship Between Women and Plants* (Camden East, Ontario: Camden House, 1991).
4   Read more about this in Sylvia Federici, *Caliban and the Witch* (New York: Autonomedia, 2004).
5   Hynes, *A Patch of Eden*, xi.
6   Laura J. Lawson, *City Bountiful: A Century of Community Gardening in America*. (Berkeley: University of California Press, 2005), 171, citing Introductory letter from M.L. Wilson to the secretary of agriculture, July 16, 1945. Attached to a report, *Progress Reports of State Directors of Cooperative Extension Work on the Victory Garden and Home Food Production Programs, June 15, 1945*, mimeograph.
7   Patricia Yollin, "A Little Bit of Eden in Bayview," *San Francisco Chronicle*, September 15, 2004, A1.
8   Bronx United Gardeners, "Bronx United Gardeners: We're Here to Stay" in *Urban Wilds*, 54.
9   Hynes, *A Patch of Eden*, 103.
10 Michael Pollan, *The Omnivore's Dilemma*, 142–144.
11 When then-Governor Ronald Reagan sent in National Guard troops to retake the lot a massive riot ensued; about four miles away, I sat in my sixth grade classroom when a diluted cloud of tear gas came wafting in.

12 Pollan, *The Omnivore's Dilemma.*
13 Pam Peirce, *Golden Gate Gardening* (Davis, CA: agAccess, 1993).
14 Author's interview with Pam Peirce, January 10, 2006, at the Horticulture Dept., City College of San Francisco.
15 See Jesse Drew, "Call Any Vegetable," in *Reclaiming San Francisco: History, Culture, Politics*, eds. James Brook, Chris Carlsson, and Nancy J. Peters (San Francisco: City Lights, 1998).
16 Peirce, author's interview.
17 Hynes, *A Patch of Eden*, 216.
18 Ibid.
19 Ibid., 228.
20 Ibid., 93.
21 A thorough treatment of the structural racism in federal programs going back 150 years is in Meizhu Lui, Bárbara J. Robles, Betsy Leondar-Wright, Rose M. Brewer, and Rebecca Adamson, *The Color of Wealth: The Story Behind the U.S. Racial Wealth Divide* (New York: New Press, 2006), 96–98.
22 Author interviews with Mark Leger, by email in 2003 and in person 2006.
23 Susan Derby, "Salad Days: In West Oakland, Urban Gardeners Are Turning Vacant Lots into Produce Markets," *Terrain* (Summer 2003).
24 Leger, author's interviews.
25 City Slicker Farms Annual Report, 2006. (City Slicker Farms, 737 Henry St., Oakland, CA).
26 Author's interview with Nan Eastep, October 2004 at City Slicker Farms, Oakland, California.
27 Susan Derby, "Salad Days."
28 Woelfe-Erskine, *Urban Wilds.*
29 Cleo Woelfe-Erskine, "Farming in the Motor City," in ibid., 42.
30 Sarah Ferguson, "A Brief History of Greening on the Lower East Side," in *Avant Gardening*, 86.
31 Sarah Ferguson, "The Death of Little Puerto Rico," in *Avant Gardening*, 78.
32 John Wright, "Clearcutting the East Village," in *Avant Gardening*, 128–130.
33 *New York Times*, Feb. 16, 2000.
34 Ferguson, "The Death of Little Puerto Rico," 69.
35 "Thank You Karl Linn," in The American Community Gardening Association's *The Community Gardener* 4, Nos. 2–3 (May 2005). Linn quit his landscaping business to spend years promoting community gardening in Philadelphia, New York, and Washington, before coming to Berkeley for his last twenty-five years. He had a broad perspective on ecological and social issues and was widely recognized for his huge contributions to rethinking urban sustainability. He spent several years as a board member of the San Francisco League of Urban Gardeners.
36 Leger, author's interview.
37 Peirce, author's interview.
38 Leger, author's interview.
39 Eastep, author's interview.
40 Peirce, author's interview.
41 Mark Leger and I co-edited *Bad Attitude: The Processed World Anthology* (London: Verso, 1999).
42 Leger, author's interview.
43 Eastep, author's interview.
44 Hynes, *A Patch of Eden*, ix.
45 Leger, author's interview.
46 Eastep, author's interview.
47 "There is nothing romantic about being dispossessed of land while you feed the

majority of the world. According to UN statistics, women hold title to one percent of the world's land while they produce more than 50 percent of the world's food. In sub-Saharan Africa women produce more than 80 percent of the food, and in Asia between 50 and 60 percent… women's contribution through gardening to the world's food supply is chronically underestimated." Hynes, *A Patch of Eden,* 155–156.

48 Lawson, *City Bountiful,* 119.
49 Hynes, *A Patch of Eden,* 109.
50 Peirce, author's interview.
51 Eastep, author's interview.
52 Margarida Correia, "Harvest in the City: New York Gardeners Bring Fresh, Healthy Food to the Less-Affluent," *Earth Island Journal* 20, No. 3 (Autumn 2005).
53 Andrea del Moral, "Community Supported Agriculture: Interviews with Three Urban Farmers," in *Urban Wilds,* 43.
54 Cleo Woelfe-Erskine, "Urban Farms," in *Urban Wilds,* 33.
55 Justin Valone, "Urban Farm Renewal: sowing the seeds of resistance in San Francisco" indymedia.org Aug. 19, 2005.
56 Lawson, *City Bountiful,* 301.
57 Author's interview with Jeffrey Miller, December 7, 2005, San Francisco, CA.
58 Lawson, *City Bountiful,* 256.
59 Hynes, *A Patch of Eden,* 109.
60 Wilson and Weinberg, *Avant Gardening,* 33.
61 Grange Halls were the meeting places for the radical populists and farmers in the Midwest during the 19th and early 20th centuries.
62 Leger, author's interview.
63 Art Armstrong, "Observations of a Virgin Gardener," *Victory!* 1, (Fall 2001), newsletter of Action Communiterre, Montreal, Canada, 8.
64 *Grist.org,* Feb. 13, 2006.

NOTES TO PAGE 115–156

Interviews conducted for this chapter

Martin Luegers, 34, CRUD, Chopper Riding Urban Dwellers, Industrial Designer.
Ted White, Bikumentarist, 41, filmmaker, gardener.
Jessie Basbaum, 25, Bike Kitchen SF, private investigator.
Catherine Hartzell, 24, Bike Kitchen, SF, Immunology lab researcher.
Robin Havens, 31, *Rip It Up!,* bike mechanic, bike repair teacher, public school teacher.
Eric Welp and Jimmy, Chain Reaction, Washington, DC bikeshop at Shaw Ecovillage.
Ben Guzman, 30, Bike Kitchen, Los Angeles, film editor.
Bill di Paola, 30s, Times Up! NYC, political organizer.
Jay Broemmel, 30s, Heavy Pedal/Cyclecide Bike Rodeo, SF, metal fabricator.
Megulon-5, 31, C.H.U.N.K. 666, Portland OR, computer programmer.
Jarico, Cyclecide, San Francisco.
Rachel Spiewak, Sopo Bicycle Cooperative, Atlanta, GA.

Bike co-ops (not comprehensive)

Bicas (Tucson, AZ), Bike Kitchen (SF), Bike Kitchen (LA), Chain Reaction (DC), Center for Appropriate Transportation/Eugene Bicycle Works (Eugene, OR), Recycle-A-Bicycle (NYC), Pedal Revolution (SF), BikeHut (SF), Bicycle Community Project (SF), North Portland Bicycle Workers (Portland, OR), Re-Cyclery Bicycle Collective (Ashville, NC) Community Resource Center, Bike Church @ Neighborhood Bike Works (Philadelphia PA), Santropol Roulet (Montreal), La Voie Libre/

Right To Move (Montreal), Third Ward Community Bike Center (Houston), The Hub Bike Co-op, (Minneapolis), Oberlin Bike Co-op (Oberlin, OH), Bike Church (Santa Cruz), Ciclofficina (Rome: Exsnia, Macchia Rosa; Milan: BULK), Plan B (New Orleans), Blackstone Bicycle Works (Chicago), Ohio City Bicycle Co-op (Ohio City), Recycle Ithaca's Bicycles (Ithaca, NY), Sopo Bicycle Cooperative (Atlanta, GA).

For a regularly updated listing of DIY bike shops across the Americas that grew out of an annual conference called "BikeBike!" write to The Bicycle Organization Organization Project, P.O. Box 1811, Tucson, AZ 85702, or check the web at: www. bikecollectives.org.

Zines in my collection

Sin on Wheels, Cognition, Bike Pride, C.H.U.N.K. 666, Voice of Da, Giddy Up!, Resist, Mudflap, The Illiterate Digest, Rip it Up!, Chainbreaker, bike.not, Operation: Courier, Moving Target, the derailleur, V.jer.

Bike Clubs (not comprehensive)

Cars-R-Coffins, SCUL, Choppercabras, Bike Rodeo (SF), Rat Patrol (Chicago), Chunk 666 (Portland, OR), Hard Times Bike Club (Minneapolis), Heavy Pedal Cyclecide (SF), Pedal Camp At Burning Man, Klunkerleaguenow, Bikerodnkustom, Dead Baby Bike Club (Seattle), Zoo Bombers (Portland, OR), Chopper Riding Urban Dwellers (CRUD) (SF)

1   Robin Havens, author's interview, Dec. 20, 2003.
2   Megulon-5, author's interview, Feb. 5, 2003.
3   For one of many analyses see James Kunstler, *The Long Emergency: Surviving the Converging Catastrophes of the Twenty-First Century* (New York: Grove/Atlantic, 2005).
4   David Buchbinder, "Rise of 'mutant bike' culture," *Christian Science Monitor,* Oct. 24, 2003.
5   John Forester, *Effective Cycling* (Cambridge, MA: MIT Press, 1992)
6   Megulon-5, author's interview.
7   Robin Havens, author's interview.
8   Jessie Basbaum, author's interview, Sept. 24, 2004.
9   Ted White, email interview with author, June, 2004.
10 www.geocities.com/ratpatrolhq/Manifesto1.html.
11 Megulon-5, author's interview.
12 *C.H.U.N.K. 666,* (April 1997).
13 Martin Leugers, author's interview, March 22, 2004.
14 In 2006, the Bike Kitchen moved to Mission and 9th Streets near San Francisco's Civic Center.
15 Jessie Basbaum and Catherine Hartzell, author's interview, Sept. 24, 2004.
16 Ben Guzman, author's interview, Dec. 7, 2003.
17 Robin Havens, author's interview.
18 Eric Welp, Chain Reaction, Washington DC, interview conducted by Jasmine Chehrazi, Dec. 23, 2004.
19 Ted White. author's interview.
20 www.bikesnotbombs.org/eab.htm.
21 Robin Havens, author's interview.
22 Rachel Spiewak, author's interview by email, June 25, 2006.
23 Robin Havens, author's interview.
24 Christy Thornton, *Sin on Wheels* 1 (2001).
25 Cited by Laura Fraser in *Shaping San Francisco.* www.shapingsf.org.

26 *Journal of the American Medical Assocation*, 1896; 27:491, cited in *Sin on Wheels* 1.
27 *Sin on Wheels* 1.
28 "Hey Baby... Can I get a ride?" *Chainbreaker* 1 (n.d.).
29 *Sin on Wheels* 1.
30 "Mercury on the Rebound..." *Voice of Da* 3 (Winter 1996).
31 Malatesta, "Stay on 2 Wheels," *Mercury Rising* 2 (November, 1991).
32 Mercury Rising Collective, "Get The Message: Mercury Rising has Risen!" Interview by Chris Carlsson. *Processed World* 29 (Summer 1992).
33 Bob McGlynn, "Road Warriors and Road Worriers," *Processed World* 15 (Winter 1985).
34 Pelona in "Get the Message."
35 *Operation: Courier* (2002).
36 "Bike Messenger Strike in NYC?" *Processed World* 20 (Fall 1987).
37 See Chris Carlsson, ed., *Critical Mass: Bicycling's Defiant Celebration* (Oakland, CA: AK Press, 2002)
38 David Ronfeldt and John Arquilla characterize Critical Mass as "an unusually loose netwar design" in their book *Networks and Netwars: The Future of Terror, Crime, and Militancy.* (Santa Monica, CA: Rand Institute, 2001).
39 Maggie Bowman, "Bicycle Cherry Throws Down at the Warriors Ride," *Sin on Wheels* 1 (2001).
40 *www.bikesummer.org.*
41 Eric Welp, Chehrazi interview.
42 Ibid.
43 Robin Havens, author's interview.
44 Ben Guzman, author's interview.
45 Jessie Basbaum, author's interview.
46 Bill DiPaola, author's interview.
47 Jessie Basbaum, author's interview.
48 Megulon-5, author's interview.
49 Ben Guzman, author's interview.
50 Eric Welp, Chehrazi interview.
51 Jessie Basbaum, author's interview.
52 Ibid.
53 Megulon-5, author's interview.
54 Ben Guzman, author's interview.
55 Bill DiPaola, author's interview, July 23, 2003
56 Ben Guzman, author's interview.
57 Megulon-5, author's interview.
58 Martin Leugers, author's interview.
59 Jimmy, Chain Reaction, Washington DC, interview conducted by Jasmine Chehrazi, Dec. 23, 2004.
60 Rachel Spiewak, author's interview.

NOTES TO PAGES 157–184

1 Claudia Eyzaguirre, author interview in San Francisco, CA, June 8, 2004.
2 Lyle Estill, *Biodiesel Power: The Passion, the People, and the Politics of the Next Renewable Fuel.* (Gabriola Island, BC: New Society, 2005), 254.
3 Claudia Eyzaguirre, "My Vegetarian Car," *San Francisco Bay Guardian*, January. 1, 2003.
4 energy.biofuels.coop/2006/02/06/breaking-camp.
5 Lyle Estill, "The Biodiesel Watershed," *New Statesman* (May 15, 2006), www.new-

statesman.com/200605150069.

6   Rudolf Diesel (1858–1913) invented the diesel engine in 1893. "Diesel original-
    ly thought that the diesel engine, (readily adaptable in size and utilizing locally
    available fuels) would enable independent craftsmen and artisans to endure
    the powered competition of large industries that then virtually monopolized
    the predominant power source—the oversized, expensive, fuel-wasting steam
    engine. During 1885 Diesel set up his first shop-laboratory in Paris and began
    his 13-year ordeal of creating his distinctive engine... Diesel expected that his
    engine would be powered by vegetable oils (including hemp) and seed oils. At
    the 1900 World's Fair, Diesel ran his engines on peanut oil." www.hempcar.org/
    diesel.shtml (accessed July 22, 2007).

7   A full chapter on the brief history of biodiesel is in Greg Pahl, *Biodiesel: Growing
    a New Energy Economy* (White River, VT: Chelsea Green Publishing, 2004).

8   *Fat of the Land* © 1995 written, edited and produced by Nicole Cousino and
    Sarah Lewison.

9   Joshua Tickell, *From the Fryer to the Fuel Tank: The Complete Guide to Using Vegetable
    Oil as an Alternative Fuel*, 3rd edition (New Orleans: Joshua Tickell Publications,
    2003).

10 Lyle Estill, *Biodiesel Power*, 49, 94.

11 Johanna Seltz, "The Vegetarian Bus," *Boston Globe*, January 26, 2006.

12 Donita Sparks, www.firedoglake.com/2006/07/21/the-spin-im-in-angels-with-
    attitude.

13 Jonathan Youtt, author interview in San Francisco, CA, June 17, 2004.

14 Bianca Sopoci-Belknap, author interview in San Francisco, CA, June 2, 2003.

15 Ben Gillock, author interview in San Francisco, CA, June 2, 2003.

16 Claudia Eyzaguirre, author interview.

17 See Chapter 8, "Virtual Spine of the Commons," for more on free software.

18 energy.biofuels.coop/2006/02/04/more-than-fuel.

19 Ben Gillock, author interview.

20 Joshua Bearman, "For French Fries or Fuel," *LA Weekly*, May 14, 2004. www.alter-
    net.org/print.html?StoryID=18706.

21 Claudia Eyzaguirre, author interview.

22 Lyle Estill, "The Biodiesel Watershed."

23 John Vidal, "Biofuels Warping the Food System," *The Guardian*, July 5, 2007.
    environment.guardian.co.uk/energy/story/0,,2118875,00.html.

24 energy.biofuels.coop/2006/06/09/sustainable-biodiesel.

25 Ibid., Rebekah, comment 1669.

26 Ben Gillock, author interview.

27 Lyle Estill, *Biodiesel Power*, 39 and 124.

28 Bianca Sopoci-Belknap, author interview.

29 Sara Hope Smith, author interview in Berkeley, CA, May, 2004.

30 Ibid.

31 Bianca Sopoci-Belknap and Ben Gillock. author interview.

32 Lyle Estill, *Biodiesel Power*, 45.

33 Bianca Sopoci-Belknap and Ben Gillock,. author interview.

34 Matthew Hirsch, "Fat to Fuel," *San Francisco Bay Guardian*, December 7, 2005.

35 Lyle Estill, *Biodiesel Power*, 80.

36 Lyle Estill, "The Biodiesel Watershed."

37 Darrin Burgess, "Gas from Trash," *Yes! magazine*, Fall 2004.

38 energy.biofuels.coop/2006/02/04/more-than-fuel.

39 energy.biofuels.coop/2006/02/04/more-than-fuel.

40 Sara Hope Smith, author interview.

41 Claudia Eyzaguirre, author interview.

42 Ibid.

43 Ben Gillock, author interview.
44 Ibid.
45 Claudia Eyzaguirre, author interview.
46 Jared Blumenfeld, quoted in Matthew Hirsch, "Fat to Fuel."
47 Claudia Eyzaguirre, author interview.
48 Sara Hope Smith, author interview.
49 Jonathan Youtt, author interview.
50 Ben Gillock, author interview.
51 Sara Hope Smith, author interview.
52 Joshua Bearman, "For French Fries or Fuel."
53 energy.biofuels.coop/2006/02/04/more-than-fuel.
54 Sara Hope Smith, author interview.
55 BP recently struck a deal with the University of California, Berkeley, investing
    $500 million in a new transgenic biofuel research facility.
56 "Stirring in the Corn Fields," *The Economist*, May 14, 2005.
57 Matthew Hirsch, "Fat to Fuel."
58 allthingsbiodiesel.blogspot.com/2006/01/looking-behind-looking-ahead.html.
59 Lyle Estill, *Biodiesel Power*, 201.
60 Claudia Eyzaguirre, author interview.
61 Lyle Estill, *Biodiesel Power*, 142.
62 energy.biofuels.coop/2006/02/04/more-than-fuel.
63 Sara Hope Smith, author interview.
64 Donita Sparks, www.firedoglake.com/2006/07/21/the-spin-im-in-angels-with-
    attitude.
65 Lyle Estill, *Biodiesel Power*, 96.
66 Sara Hope Smith, author interview. (Smith resigned from the Berkeley Biofuel
    Oasis and moved away in late 2006).
67 See Chapter 4: Contesting the Evolution of Science.
68 Sara Hope Smith, author interview.
69 www.commonvision.org/index.php?id=46.

NOTES TO PAGE 185–212

1 Will Doherty, author's interview at the offices of the Electronic Freedom Foundation, February 24, 2004.
2 Karl Marx, "The Fragment on Machines," in *The Grundrisse*, 693.
3 Maurizio Lazzarato. "General Intellect: Towards an Inquiry into Immaterial Labour." www.geocities.com/immateriallabour/lazzarato-immaterial-labour.html.
4 Eric S Raymond, "Origins and History of Unix, 1969–1995, www.catb.org/~esr/
   writings/taoup/html/ch02s01.html (accessed July 11, 2007).
5 Ibid.
6 Joyce Slaton, "Remembering Community Memory—The Berkeley Beginnings
   of Online Community," SF Gate (www.sfgate.com/cgi-bin/article.cgi?f=/g/
   a/2001/12/13/commmem.DTL&hw=Remembering+Community+Memory&s
   n=007&sc=669), Dec. 13, 2001.
7 I worked for their spin-off, Pacific Software, during that early software boom
   in 1980–81, watching as the company grew from three to 22 employees before
   crashing back to five after losing out to what became Oracle and Informix. Most
   of the work I did was to compile and mail marketing packets for the relational
   database program or prepare nondisclosure agreements for engineers from potential corporate buyers for the innovative packet-switching software Community Memory had developed. The irony of Community Memory is that while they
   were committed to a unique vision of a totally free open-ended public computer

network, they simultaneously "bought in" to the proprietary software model, only to lose out in the marketplace to larger businesses. The dotcom boom-and-bust of 1997–2001 was easy to see coming with the memory of that earlier period still fresh.

8   *Processed World* grew out the early experience of the automated office. It began in the San Francisco financial district in 1981 and came to be known as "the magazine with a bad attitude," in part due to its steady coverage of the day-to-day work experiences of the white-collar working class and temp workers during that important transitional period, a coverage that returned repeatedly to *attitude* as the crucial linchpin of employment as opposed to skill or experience. For more, see www.processedworld.com.

9   Julian Stallabrass. "Digital Commons," *New Left Review* 15 (May-June 2002).

10 Ibid.

11 The irony runs deeper still because the GPL ultimately submits to a larger logic of property rights that narrows the purpose of Free Software to its consumption, ignoring its production. "The focus on freedom in Free-as-in-Libre Open Source Software (FLOSS) does not concern, and even denies production and labour. It is this denial that blocks us from increasing our power in the face of the spectacle." Martin Hardie, "Change of the Century: Free Software and the Positive Possibility," *Mute* 2, No. 1 (2005): *Underneath the Knowledge Commons.*

12 www.catb.org/~esr/writings/cathedral-bazaar/ (accessed July 11, 2007).

13 Matteo Pasquinelli, "Cultural Labour and Immaterial Machines," in *Curating Immateriality, DATA Browser 03*, ed. Joasia Krysa (New York: Autonomedia, 2006), 270.

14 Simon Worthington, "Patently Obvious," *Mute* 2, No. 1 (2005): *Underneath the Knowledge Commons*, 18.

15 Richard Barbrook, "The Hi-Tech Gift Economy," www.firstmonday.org/issues/issue3_12/barbrook/index.html, rev. ed. 2005.

16 Stefan Merten, "Free Software and the GPL Society," interview by Joanne Richardson in *subsol*, published in Joanne Richardson, ed., *An@rchitexts: Voices from the Global Digital Resistance* (New York: Autonomedia, 2003).

17 Tiziana Terranova, *Network Culture*, 94.

18 Geoff Cox, Joasia Krysa, and Anya Lewin, eds., *Economizing Culture: On the (Digital) Culture Industry, DATA Browser 01,* (New York: Autonomedia, 2004).

19 Trebor Scholz, "The Truth About Networks" from www.fiberculture.org.

20 John Robb's Global Guerrillas blog is an excellent source on this topic (*www.globalguerrillas.blogspot.com*). The Iraqi insurgency has ensnared the U.S. for years now, and more recently Hezbollah turned the tables on the Israeli's supposedly invincible war machine.

21 Will Doherty, author's interview.

22 Guillermo Payet, author's interview, May 28, 2004, Santa Cruz, CA.

23 Ed Phillips, author's interview, Dec. 5, 2005, San Francisco, CA.

24 Guillermo Payet, author's interview.

25 The term "cognitariat" was coined by Francisco Berardi "Bifo" in "The Factory of Unhappiness," cited in Matt Fuller's interview with Bifo, "Cognitariat and Semiokapital," in *An@rchitexts.*

26 Will Doherty, author's interview.

27 Eric S. Raymond is a hacker who maintains the fetchmail project (an e-mail software). He was one of the first to analyze the reasons for the success of Free Software and its social organization.

28 Unless otherwise specified, the citations of Linus Torvalds are taken from an interview done by Rishabh Aiyer Ghosh, *Qu'est-ce qui motive les développeurs de logiciels libres?, First Monday* 3, No. 3 (March 1998).

29 Pekka Himanen, *L'ethique hacker et l'esprit de l'ère de l'information* (Paris: Exils, 2001).
30 Matthias Studer, "Gift and Free Software" *The Commoner* 9 (Spring/Summer 2004), www.thecommoner.org.
31 Brian Holmes, "The Flexible Personality: For a New Cultural Critique," in *Economising Culture*, 33–35.
32 Will Doherty, author's interview.
33 Ibid.
34 Ibid.
35 Guillermo Payet, author's interview.
36 Ibid.
37 Ed Phillips, author's interview.
38 A contrary view was offered by Giovanni Marruzzelli in an email correspondence. He quotes Perl-founder Larry Wall's description of the three virtues of a programmer: impatience, laziness, and hubris. "In some ways, programmers often tend to make simple work more complicated. If you don't like complicated things, you would not try to be a programmer."
39 Ed Phillips, author's interview.
40 Geert Lovink, "Oekonux: Interview with Stefan Merten," April 2001, www.nettime.org.
41 Lee Felsenstein, as told to Bernard Aboba, "How Community Memory Came to Be, Part 1," *Internaut* 1, 1994, http://oldeee.see.ed.ac.uk/online/internaut/internaut-01/comm.html.
42 Lee Felsenstein, on the origins of Community Memory, www.Transaction.net.
43 Eric S.Raymond, "Origins and History of the Hackers, 1961–1995,", www.catb.org/~esr/writings/taoup/html/hackershtml. (Accessed, July 11, 2007).
44 Ibid.
45 Ed Phillips, author's interview.
46 Guillermo Payet, author's interview.
47 Armin Medosch, "Society in Ad-hoc Mode," in *Economising Culture*, 139–44.
48 Ed Phillips, author's interview.
49 The annual readers are published by The Sarai Programme, Centre for the Study of Developing Societies, 29 Raipur Road, Delhi 110054, India (and available in the U.S. through Autonomedia in Brooklyn). www.sarai.net.
50 See the ChangeLog interview with Larry Wall at lwn.net/2001/featuers/Larry-Wall.
51 Matteo Pasquinelli, "Radical Machines Against the Techno-Empire. From Utopia to Network," www.rekombinant.org/article.php?sid=2257.
52 Lovink, "Oekonux: Interview with Stefan Merten."
53 Brian Holmes. "Three Proposal for a Real Democracy, Information-Sharing to a Different Tune," www.geocities.com/immateriallabour/holmes-three-proposals.html.
54 Ibid.
55 Jamie King, "The Packet Gang," *Mute 27* (Dec. 2004). info.interactivist.net/article.pl?sid=04/01/30/1158224.

NOTES TO PAGE 213–234

1 Daniel Pinchbeck, "Heat of the Moment: The Art and Culture of Burning Man," *Artforum* (Nov., 2003).
2 Ibid.
3 Margaret Cerullo and Phyllis Ewen, "'Having a Good Time': The American Family Goes Camping," *Radical America* 16, Nos. 1–2 (Spring, 1982).

4   Ibid.
5   Katherine Chen, "Incendiary Incentives: How the Burning Man Organization
    Motivates and Manages Volunteers" in *After Burn: Reflections on Burning Man,*
    eds. Lee Gilmore and Mark Van Proyen (Albuquerque, NM: University of New
    Mexico Press, 2005), 114.
6   Ibid.
7   Cerullo and Ewen, "Having a Good Time."
8   Stanley Aronowitz, *How Class Works: Power and Social Movements* (New Haven, CT:
    Yale University Press, 2003), 220.
9   Ed Phillips, author interview.
10 Aronowitz, *How Class Works,* 59.

NOTES TO PAGES 235–253

1   Day, *Gramsci Is Dead,* 217.
2   Ibid., 154.
3   Harry Cleaver, Email on public "aut-op-sy" discussion list, June 22, 2003: <Re:
    AUT: class composition (response to Chris on inside and outside)>.
4   Duncombe, *Notes from Underground: Zines,* 15.
5   *Shaping San Francisco* is one such project that I've been involved with: *www.shap-
    ingsf.org.*
6   McKay, *DIY Culture,* 14.
7   Duncombe, *Notes from Underground: Zines,* 185.
8   Holloway, *Change the World Without Taking Power,* 157.
9   Erik Ohlsen, author's interview, January 16, 2006, Sebastopol, California.
10 Day, *Gramsci Is Dead,* 145,185.
11 Rachel Spiewak, author's interview by email, June 2006.
12 Day, *Gramsci Is Dead,* 155.
13 Capra, *The Hidden Connections,* 58.
14 "Ode, Inscribed to William H. Channing," www.emersoncentral.com/poems/
    ode_inscribed_to_william_h_channing.htm.
15 Ken Knabb's *Situationist International Anthology* remains the best single English-
    language source for the history and writings of this important group. Much of it
    is online at www.bopsecrets.org.
16 Harry Cleaver, email on public "aut-op-sy" discussion list, July 6, 2003: <Re: AUT:
    class composition (response to Chris)>.
17 Ted White, author's interview by email, 2003.
18 James Boggs, *The American Revolution,* 1963, cited in Steve Wright *Storming Heav-
    en,* 85.
19 Ibid.
20 Day, *Gramsci Is Dead,* 148.
21 Hardt and Negri, *Multitude.*
22 Holloway, *Change the World Without Taking Power,* 213.
23 As Sylvia Federici cogently points out when writing about the origins of capi-
    talism, "…[it] has been above all an accumulation of differences, inequalities,
    hierarchies, divisions, which have alienated workers from each other and even
    from themselves." Federici, *Caliban and The Witch,* 115.
24 Brian Holmes, "The Spaces of A Cultural Question," an email interview con-
    ducted by Marion von Osten, 2004, www.republicart.net.
25 Franco Barchiesi, "Communities between Commons and Commodities: Subjec-
    tivity and Needs in the Definition of New Social Movements," *The Commoner* 6
    (Winter 2003). www.thecommoner.org.uk.
26 Capra, *The Hidden Connections,* 219.

SELECTED BIBLIOGRAPHY

Adilkno, Foundation for Advancement of Illegal Knowledge Staff. *Cracking the Movement: Squatting Beyond the Media.* New York: Autonomedia, 1994.

Albert, Michael. *Looking Forward.* Cambridge, MA: South End Press, 1991.

—— *Moving Forward.* Oakland. CA: AK Press, 2000.

Aronowitz, Stanley. *False Promises.* New York: McGraw Hill, 1973.

—— *How Class Works: Power and Social Movement.* New Haven, CT: Yale University Press, 2004.

Barbrook, Richard. *The Class of the New.* London: Mute, 2006.

—— *Imaginary Futures: From Thinking Machines to the Global Village.* London: Pluto Press, 2007.

Basso, Pietro. *Modern Times. Ancient Hours: Working Lives in the Twenty-First Century.* London: Verso, 2003.

Bonefield, Werner. editor. *Revolutionary Writing: Common Sense Essays in Post-Political Politics.* New York: Autonomedia, 2003.

Boyer, Richard O. and Herbert M. Morais. *Labor's Untold Story.* New York: United Electrical Workers Union, 1955.

Bravo, Kyle. ed. *Making Stuff and Doing Things.* Portland, OR: Microcosm, 2005.

Brecher, Jeremy. *Strike!.* Cambridge, MA: South End Press, 1998.

Brook, James, Chris Carlsson, and Nancy J. Peters, eds. *Reclaiming San Francisco: History. Culture. Politics.* San Francisco: City Lights Books, 1998.

Bunting, Madeleine. *Willing Slaves: How the Overwork Culture is Ruling Our Lives.* London: HarperPerennial, 2005.

Capra, Fritjof. *The Hidden Connections: A Science for Sustainable Living.* New York: Anchor, 2004.

Carlsson, Chris. *Critical Mass: Bicycling's Defiant Celebration.* Edinburgh. Oakland, CA: AK Press, 2002.

—— *Bad Attitude: the Processed World Anthology.* London: Verso, 1990.

Casid, Jill H. *Sowing Empire: Landscape and Colonization.* Ann Arbor: University of Minnesota Press, 2005.

Castells, Manuel. *The Rise of the Network Society.* Oxford: Blackwell Publishing, 2000.

Cleaver, Harry. *Reading Capital Politically.* Oakland, CA: AK Press, 2000.

Conner, Clifford D. *A People's History of Science: Miners. Midwives. and "Low Mechaniks."* New York: Nation Books, 2005.

Cox, Geoff and Joasia Krysa, eds. *Engineering Culture, Data Browser 02.* New York: Autonomedia, 2005.

Cox. Geoff, Joasia Krysa, and Anya Lewin, eds. *Economising Culture, Data Browser 01.* New York: Autonomedia, 2005.

Cronon, William. ed. *Uncommon Ground: Rethinking the Human Place in Nature.* New York: W. W. Norton & Company, 1996.

Cross, Ira. *The History of the Labor Movement in California.* Berkeley: University of California Press, 1935.

Croteau, David. *Politics and the Class Divide: Working People and the Middle-Class Left. Labor and Social Change).* Philadelphia: Temple University Press, 1995.

Dagget, Dan. *Gardeners of Eden: Rediscovering Our Importance to Nature.* Santa Barbara, CA: Thatcher Charitable Trust, 2005.

Daniels, Douglas. *Pioneer Urbanites.* Berkeley: University of California Press, 1990.

Day, Richard J. F. *Gramsci Is Dead: Anarchist Currents in the Newest Social Movements.* London: Pluto Press, 2005.

Debord, Guy. *La société du spectacle;* originally published in 1967. English edition translated by Donald Nicholson-Smith. New York: Zone Books, 1994.

—— *Comments on the Society of the Spectacle.* translated by Malcolm Imrie London: Verso, 1990.

Duncombe, Stephen. *Notes from Underground: Zines and the Politics of Alternative Culture* (Haymarket Series). London: Verso, 1997.
—— *Dream: Re-imagining Progressive Politics in an Age of Fantasy.* New Press, 2007.
Dyer-Witheford, Nick. *Cyber-Marx: Cycles and Circuits of Struggle in High Technology Capitalism.* Chicago: University of Illinois Press, 1999.
Ehrenreich, Barbara. *Bait and Switch: The. Futile) Pursuit of the American Dream.* New York: Henry Holt, 2006.
—— *Nickel and Dimed: On (Not) Getting By in America.* New York: Henry Holt, 2002.
Epstein, Barbara. *Political Protest and Cultural Revolution: Nonviolent Direct Action in the 1970s and 1980s.* Berkeley: University of California Press, 1991.
Estill, Lyle. *Biodiesel Power: The Passion. the People. and the Politics of the Next Renewable Fuel.* Gabriola, BC: New Society Publishers, 2005.
Federici, Sylvia. *Caliban and the Witch.* New York: Autonomedia, 2005.
Frenay, Robert. *Pulse: The Coming Age of Systems and Machines Inspired by Living Things.* New York: Farrar. Straus and Giroux, 2006.
Gilmore, Lee and Mark Van Proyen. eds. *AfterBurn: Reflections on Burning Man.* Albuquerque, NM: University of New Mexico Press, 2005.
Glaberman, Martin. *Wartime Strikes.* Detroit MI: Bewick Editions, 1980.
Gorz, Andre. *Reclaiming Work: Beyond the Wage-Based Society.* Malden, MA: Polity Press, 2000.
—— *Farewell to the Working Class.* London: Pluto Press, 2001.
Hardt, Michael and Antonio Negri. *Multitude: War and Democracy in the Age of Empire.* New York: Penguin, 2005.
—— *Empire.* Cambridge, MA: Harvard University Press, 2000.
Hawken, Paul. *Natural Capitalism: Creating the Next Industrial Revolution.* New York: Back Bay Books, 2000.
—— *Blessed Unrest: How the Largest Movement in the World Came into Being and Why No One Saw It Coming.* New York: Viking, 2007.
Henwood, Doug. *After the New Economy: The Binge and the Hangover That Won't Go Away.* New York: New Press, 2005.
Holloway, John. *Change the World Without Taking Power: The Meaning of Revolution Today.* London: Pluto Press, 2005.
Holmgren, David. *Permaculture: Principles and Pathways Beyond Sustainability.* Hepburn, Australia: Holmgren Design Services, 2002.
Huws, Ursula. *The Making of a Cybertariat.* New York: Monthly Review, 2003.
Hyms, Edward. *Soil and Civilization (The Past in the Present).* London: Thames and Hudson, 1952.
Hynes, H. Patricia. *A Patch of Eden: America's Inner-City Gardeners.* White River, VT: Chelsea Green Publishing Company, 1996.
Jacoby, Russell. *Picture Imperfect: Utopian Thought for an Anti-Utopian Age.* New York: Columbia University Press, 2005.
Kadi, Joanna. *Thinking Class: Sketches from a Cultural Worker.* Cambridge, MA: South End Press, 1996.
Kingston, Paul. *The Classless Society. Studies in Social Inequality).* Palo Alto, CA: Stanford University Press, 2000.
Krysa, Joasia. ed. *Curating Immateriality, Data Browser 03.* New York: Autonomedia, 2006.
Kunstler, James. *The Long Emergency: Surviving the Converging Catastrophes of the Twenty-First Century.* New York: Grove/Atlantic, 2005.
Latour, Bruno. *Politics of Nature: How to Bring the Sciences into Democracy.* Cambridge, MA: Harvard University Press, 2004.
—— *Pandora's Hope: Essays on the Reality of Science Studies.* Cambridge, MA: Harvard University Press, 1999.

———We Have Never Been Modern. Cambridge, MA: Harvard University Press, 2007.

Lawson, Laura. City Bountiful: A Century of Community Gardening in America. Berkeley: University of California Press, 2005.

Lens, Sidney. The Labor Wars. New York: Anchor Doubleday, 1974.

Leondar-Wright, Betsy. Class Matters: Cross-Class Alliance Building for Middle-Class Activists. Gabriola, BC: New Society Publishers, 2005.

Lovink, Geert. Dark Fiber: Tracking Critical Internet Culture (Electronic Culture: History. Theory. and Practice). Cambridge, MA: MIT Press, 2003.

Lui, Meizhu. and Bárbara J. Robles. Betsy Leondar-Wright. Rose M. Brewer. and Rebecca Adamson. The Color of Wealth. New York: The New Press, 2006.

Markoff, John. What the Dormouse Said: How the 60s Counterculture Shaped the Personal Computer. New York: Viking, 2005.

Marx, Karl. Capital—A Critique of Political Economy: Volume 1—The Process of Capitalist Production. New York: International Publishers, 1982.

McDonough, William. Cradle to Cradle: Remaking the Way We Make Things. New York: North Point Press, 2002.

McKay, George. editor. DIY Culture: Party and Protest in Nineties Britain. London: Verso, 1998.

Midnight Notes Collective. Midnight Oil: Work. Energy. War. 1973–1992. New York. NY: Autonomedia, 1992.

Narby, Jeremy. Intelligence in Nature. New York: Tarcher, 2006.

Nettime, ReadMe! ASCII Culture and the Revenge of Knowledge. New York: Autonomedia, 1999.

Notes from Nowhere, eds. We Are Everywhere: The Irresistible Rise of Global Anti-Capitalism. London: Verso, 2003.

O'Connor, Harvey. Revolution in Seattle. Seattle: Left Bank Books, 1981.

Pahl, Greg. Biodiesel: Growing A New Energy Economy. Chelsea Green, 2005.

Peirce, Pam. Golden Gate Gardening. Davis, CA: agAccess, 1993.

Petrini, Carlo. Slow Food Revolution: A New Culture for Eating and Living. New York: Rizzoli, 2006.

Pinderhughes, Raquel. Alternative Urban Futures: Planning for Sustainable Development in Cities throughout the World. New York: Rowman & Littlefield, 2004.

Polanyi, Karl. The Great Transformation. Boston: Beacon Press, 2001.

Pollan, Michael. The Omnivore's Dilemma. New York: Penguin Press, 2006.

Putnam, Robert D. Bowling Alone: The Collapse and Revival of American Community. New York: Simon & Schuster, 2001.

Richardson, Joanne, ed. Anarchitexts. New York: Autonomedia, 2004.

Rodgers, Christy, ed. What If? A Journal of Radical Possibilities. Vol 2 (2002).

Ronfeldt, David and John Arquilla. Networks and Netwars: The Future of Terror. Crime and Militancy. Santa Monica, CA: Rand Institute, 2001.

Root & Branch Collective. Root & Branch: The Rise of the Workers Movements. Greenwich, CT: Fawcett Crest, 1975.

Ross, Andrew. No-Collar: The Humane Workplace and Its Hidden Costs. Philadelphia: Temple University Press, 2004.

Saxton, Alexander. The Indispensable Enemy: Labor and the Anti-Chinese Movement in California. Berkeley, CA: University of California Press, 1971.

Schell, Jonathan. The Unconquerable World: Power. Nonviolence. and the Will of the People. New York: Metropolitan Books, 2003.

Schmidt, Jeff. Disciplined Minds: A Critical Look at Salaried Professionals and the Soul-Battering System that Shapes Their Lives. New York: Rowman & Littlefield, 2000.

Selvin, David F. A Terrible Anger: The 1934 Waterfront and General Strikes in San Francisco. Detroit: Wayne State University Press, 1996.

Shapin, Steven. The Scientific Revolution. Chicago: University Of Chicago Press, 1998.

Silver, Beverly J. *Forces of Labor: Workers' Movements and Globalization Since 1870* (Cambridge Studies in Comparative Politics). Cambridge, UK: Cambridge University Press, 2003.

Smith, Michael. *Art of Natural Building.* Gabriola, BC: New Society Publishers, 2002.

Smith, Pamela H. *The Body of the Artisan: Art and Experience in the Scientific Revolution.* Chicago: University Of Chicago Press, 2006.

Steffen, Alex. *Worldchanging: A User's Guide for the 21st Century.* New York: Harry N. Abrams, 2006.

Tea, Michelle, ed. *Without a Net: The Female Experience of Growing Up Working Class (Live Girls).* Emeryville, CA: Seal Press, 2004.

Terranova, Tiziana. *Network Culture: Politics for the Information Age.* London: Pluto Press, 2004.

Theriault, Reg. *The Unmaking of the American Working Class.* New York: New Press, 2003.

Tickell, Joshua. *From the Fryer to the Fuel Tank: The Complete Guide to Using Vegetable Oil as an Alternative Fuel.* New Orleans: Tickell Energy Consultants, 2000.

Turner, Fred. *From Counterculture to Cyberculture: Stewart Brand. the Whole Earth Network. and the Rise of Digital Utopianism.* Chicago: University of Chicago Press, 2006.

Vale, V. *Search & Destroy #1–6: The Complete Reprint.* San Francisco: V/Search Publications, 1996.

Virno, Paolo. *A Grammar of the Multitude.* New York: Semio-text(e), 2004.

Walker, Pat. editor. *Between Labor and Capital.* Cambridge, MA: South End Press, 1979.

Whorton, James C. *Nature Cures: The History of Alternative Medicine in America.* Oxford: Oxford University Press. USA, 2004.

Wilson, Peter Lamborn and Bill Weinberg. eds. *Avant Gardening: Ecological Struggle in the City and the World.* New York: Autonomedia, 1999.

Woelfle-Erskine, Cleo, ed. *Urban Wilds: Gardeners' Stories of the Struggle for Land and Justice.* Oakland: water/under/ground publications, 2002.

Woelfle-Erskine, Cleo, July Oskar Cole, and Laura Allen, eds. *Dam Nation: Dispatches from the Water Underground.* New York: Soft Skull Press, 2007.

Wright, Erik Olin, ed. *Approaches to Class Analysis.* Cambridge, UK: Cambridge University Press, 2005.

Wright, Steve. *Storming Heaven: Class Composition and Struggle in Italian Autonomist Marxism.* London: Pluto Press, 2002.

Yellen, Samuel. *American Labor Struggles 1877–1934.* New York: Monad Press, 1974. originally published 1936.

Zweig, Michael, ed. *What's Class Got to Do With It?: American Society in the Twenty-First Century.* Ithaca, NY: ILR Press, 2004.

INDEX

ABOUT THE AUTHOR

Chris Carlsson, director of the multimedia history project *Shaping San Francisco*, is a writer, publisher, editor, and community organizer. For the last twenty-five years his activities have focused on the underlying themes of horizontal communications, organic communities, and public space. He was one of the founders, editors, and frequent contributors to the ground-breaking San Francisco magazine *Processed World*. He also helped launch the monthly bike-ins known as Critical Mass that have spread to five continents and over 300 cities. He has edited four books, *Bad Attitude: The Processed World Anthology* (Verso: 1990, co-edited with Mark Leger), *Reclaiming San Francisco: History, Politics, Culture* (City Lights: 1998, co-edited with James Brook and Nancy J. Peters), *Critical Mass: Bicycling's Defiant Celebration* (AK Press: 2002), *The Political Edge* (City Lights Foundation: 2004). He published his first novel, *After The Deluge*, in 2004 (Full Enjoyment Books), a story of post-economic San Francisco in the year 2157. Carlsson makes his living as a book designer, editor, and typesetter, though he fantasizes about someday making enough to survive as a writer! He is a member of Media Workers Union Local 100 in San Francisco. He is also recent board president of CounterPULSE, a San Francisco-based arts organization, where he has been producing a series of public talks since January 2006, and conducting award-winning bicycle history tours for over a decade.

FRIENDS OF AK PRESS

Help sustain our vital project!

AK Press is a worker-run collective that publishes and distributes radical books, audio/visual media, and other materials. We're small: a dozen individuals who work long hours for short money, because we believe in what we do. We're anarchists, which is reflected both in the books we publish and in the way we organize our business: without bosses.

AK Press publishes the finest books, CDs, and DVDs from the anarchist and radical traditions—currently about 18 to 20 per year. Joining the Friends of AK Press is a way that you can directly help us to keep the wheels rolling and these important projects coming.

As ever, money is tight as we do not rely on outside funding. We need your help to make and keep these crucial materials available. Friends pay a minimum (of course we have no objection to larger sums!) of $25 per month ($30 for those outside the US), for a minimum three month period. Money received goes directly into our publishing funds. In return, Friends automatically receive (for the duration of their membership), as they appear, one FREE copy of EVERY new AK Press title. Secondly, they are also entitled to a 10% discount on EVERYTHING featured in the AK Press distribution catalog—or on our website—on ANY and EVERY order. We also have a program where individuals or groups can sponsor a whole book.

PLEASE CONTACT US FOR MORE DETAILS:

AK Press
674-A 23rd Street
Oakland, CA 94612
friendsofak@akpress.org
www.akpress.org

AK Press
PO Box 12766
Edinburgh, Scotland EH8 9YE
ak@akedin.demon.co.uk
www.akuk.com

Join the ongoing discussion of social transformation embodied in *Nowtopia*. Find links to folks in your area, offer your opinions and ideas, and share comradely criticism with like-minded (and totally different) people!

www.nowtopia.org
www.nowtopia.net